Nixon, Kissinger, and U.S. Foreign Policy Making

Nixon, Kissinger, and U.S. Foreign Policy Making examines for the first time the important role of crisis management in the making of U.S. foreign policy during the Nixon-Kissinger years. The book offers a critical account of the manner in which the president and his national security advisor – notorious for their tight grip on the machinery of U.S. foreign policy – dominated the structures and processes of foreign policy making. By drawing on a wealth of previously classified documents, Asaf Siniver reveals the story of the Washington Special Actions Group (WSAG), which managed foreign policy crises in the Nixon administration. In this thoroughly researched account of the performance of Nixon, Kissinger, and the WSAG in four international crises, Siniver provides a fresh analysis of the important relationship among structures, processes, and personalities in the making of U.S. foreign policy during international crises.

Dr. Asaf Siniver is Lecturer of International Relations at the Department of Political Science and International Studies, University of Birmingham, United Kingdom.

Nixon, Kissinger, and U.S. Foreign Policy Making

The Machinery of Crisis

ASAF SINIVER

University of Birmingham

CAMBRIDGE UNIVERSITY PRESS
Cambridge, New York, Melbourne, Madrid, Cape Town, Singapore, São Paulo, Delhi

Cambridge University Press
32 Avenue of the Americas, New York, NY 10013-2473, USA

www.cambridge.org
Information on this title: www.cambridge.org/9780521897624

First published 2008

Printed in the United States of America

A catalog record for this publication is available from the British Library.

Library of Congress Cataloging in Publication Data

Siniver, Asaf, 1976–
Nixon, Kissinger, and U.S. foreign policy making : the machinery of crisis /
Asaf Siniver.
　　p.　cm.
Includes bibliographical references and index.
ISBN 978-0-521-89762-4 (hardback : alk. paper)
1. United States – Foreign relations – 1969–1974.　2. United States – Foreign
relations – 1969–1974 – Decision making.　3. Nixon, Richard M. (Richard Milhous),
1913–1994.　4. Kissinger, Henry, 1923–　5. Crisis management in government –
United States – Case studies.　6. United States – Foreign relations – Case studies.
I. Title.
E855.S56　2008
327.73009′047 – dc22　　　　2008027147

ISBN　978-0-521-89762-4 hardback

Contents

List of Figures   *page* vii

Acknowledgments   ix

Abbreviations   xi

Dramatis Personae   xiii

    Introduction   1

1. Structures, Processes, and Personalities in U.S.
    Foreign Policy   12

2. The Making of U.S. Foreign Policy During the
    Nixon-Kissinger Years   40

3. The Incursion into Cambodia, Spring 1970   71

4. The Jordanian Crisis, September 1970   115

5. The India-Pakistan War, December 1971   148

6. The Yom Kippur War, October 1973   185

    Conclusion   224

Bibliography   233

Index   249

List of Figures

2.1. The Nixon Administration's NSC Structure   *page 59*

See figure section following page 114.

1. First meeting of the National Security Council
2. President Nixon and advisors at the Pentagon
3. President Nixon with CIA Director Richard Helms
4. President Nixon with Defense Secretary Melvin Laird
5. National Security Decision Memorandum 8
6. National Security Decision Memorandum 19
7. King Hussein of Jordan is greeted by President Nixon and Secretary of State William Rogers
8. President Nixon announcing his decision to send U.S. troops into Cambodia
9. President Nixon bowling at the White House
10. President Nixon meeting with President Yayah Kahn of Pakistan
11. The Joint Chiefs of Staff
12. Swearing-in ceremony of George H. W. Bush as U.S. Ambassador to the United Nations
13. President Nixon with Prime Minister Indira Gandhi
14. President Nixon, Henry Kissinger, and Israeli Prime Minister Golda Meir in the Oval Office

15. President Nixon facing the media at the end of the Yom
    Kippur War
16. President Nixon, Henry Kissinger, Gerald Ford, and
    Alexander Haig in the White House

Acknowledgments

This book started as a doctoral dissertation at the University of Nottingham, and I am in debt to many individuals and institutions that assisted me along the way. I am grateful to the School of Politics and International Relations at the University of Nottingham, Universitas 21, the British Academy, the ORS Awards Scheme, the Royal Historical Society, and the Lyndon Baines Johnson Presidential Library for their valuable financial support. This book relies heavily on primary research conducted in American and British archives, and I am grateful for all the help I received from the dedicated staff at the Nixon Presidential Material Project in College Park; the Lyndon Baines Johnson Presidential Library in Austin; the Miller Center of Public Affairs at the University of Virginia, Charlottesville; and the National Archives in London.

I wish to extend particular thanks to Helmut Sonnenfeldt and William Quandt, members of Henry Kissinger's National Security Council staff, who were very generous with their input and time. Special thanks go to Neville Wylie and Matthew Jones from the School of Politics and International Relations at the University of Nottingham for providing valuable comments at various stages of my research, and to my colleagues Mette Jolly, Elizabeth Monaghan, and David Kiwuwa for making life in room A1 slightly more bearable during our doctoral years. I am also grateful to the anonymous reviewers who suggested numerous helpful changes to the manuscript. Ken Karpinski's copyediting was meticulous, and the staff at Cambridge University

Press, especially Emily Spangler and Eric Crahan, provided consistently excellent editorial advice and support. My greatest debt of gratitude goes to Richard Aldrich – a teacher, a mentor, and an unrelenting source of inspiration. As my doctoral supervisor, Richard has taught me numerous valuable lessons about academia, and thanks to him I keep on writing even when I have nothing to say. Finally, and most important, I wish to thank my family for their continuous support and understanding over the years. Too many weekends and evenings in the past three years were spent with Richard Nixon and Henry Kissinger and not as nearly enough were spent with my two daughters, Talia and Evie, who were born while I was working on this book. I thank my parents for their continued support and pride in me, even when there was very little of which to be proud. Above all, this book could not have been possible without the unyielding support of my wife, Alison, who stood by me throughout the various stages of my academic career and had even read and commented on the manuscript numerous times – surely a sign of true love. This book is better for all these people; its mistakes and shortcomings are solely mine.

Abbreviations

ARVN	Army of the Republic of Vietnam
CIA	Central Intelligence Agency
COSVN	Central Office of South Vietnam
DCI	Director, Central Intelligence
FCO	Foreign and Commonwealth Office
FPA	Foreign Policy Analysis
FRUS	Foreign Relations of the United States
GVN	Government of Vietnam
HAK	Henry A. Kissinger
HAKOF	Henry A. Kissinger Office Files
JCS	Joint Chiefs of Staff
MAC	Military Aircraft Command
MACV	Military Assistance Command, Vietnam
MF	Meeting Files
MMF	Minutes of Meeting Files
NA	National Archives, London
NATO	North Atlantic Treaty Organisation
NPMP	Nixon Presidential Materials Project
NSC	National Security Council
NSCF	National Security Council Files
NSCIF	National Security Council Institutional Files
NSDM	National Security Decision Memorandum
NSSM	National Security Study Memorandum
NVA	North Vietnamese Army

PFLP	Popular Front for the Liberation of Palestine
PPPS	Public Papers of Presidents of the United States
RVNAF	South Vietnamese Air Force
SALT	Strategic Arms Limitation Talks
SEATO	South East Asia Treaty Organisation
SRG	Senior Review Group
UN	United Nations
USG	United States Government
VC	Vietcong
WHCF	White House Central Files
WSAG	Washington Special Actions Group

Dramatis Personae

Abrams, General Creighton   Commander, U.S. forces in Vietnam, 1968–1972

Agnew, Spiro Vice President of the United States, 1969–1973

Assad, Hafez President of Syria, 1971–2000

Blood, Archer K. U.S. Consul General in Dacca, 1970–1971

Brezhnev, Leonid General Secretary of the Communist Party of the Soviet Union, 1964–1982

Brown, Dean U.S. Ambassador to Jordan, 1970–1973

Bush, George H. W. U.S. Ambassador to the United Nations, 1971–1973

Colby, William Director, Central Intelligence, 1973–1976

Cushman, Robert Deputy Director, CIA, 1969–1971

Dinitz, Simcha Israeli Ambassador to the United States, 1973–1979

Dobrynin, Anatoly Soviet Ambassador to the United States, 1962–1988

Ehrlichman, John D. Assistant to the President for Domestic Affairs, 1969–1973

Farland, Joseph U.S. Ambassador to Pakistan, 1969–1972

Freeman, John British Ambassador to the United States, 1969–1971

Gandhi, Indira Prime Minister of India, 1966–1977

Green, Marshall Assistant Secretary of State for East Asian and Pacific Affairs, 1970

Gromyko, Andrei Soviet Foreign Minister, 1957–1985

Haig, Alexander M. Senior Military Assistant to the President for National Security Affairs, 1969–1970; Deputy Assistant to the President for National Security Affairs, 1970–1973; White House Chief of Staff, 1973–1974

Haldeman, H. R. 'Bob' White House Chief of Staff, 1969–1973

Halperin, Morton H. Senior staff member, NSC, 1969

Helms, Richard Director, Central Intelligence, 1966–1973

Hussein bin Talal King of Jordan, 1952–1999

Johnson, U. Alexis Under Secretary of State for Political Affairs, 1969–1973

Karamessines, Thomas Deputy Director of Plans, CIA, 1967–1973

Keating, Kenneth U.S. Ambassador to India, 1969–1972

Kennedy, Colonel Richard T. Director, Staff Planning and Coordination, NSC; Deputy Assistant to the President for NSC Planning, 1969–1975

Kissinger, Henry A. Assistant to the President for National Security Affairs, 1969–1975; Secretary of State, 1973–1977

Laird, Melvin R. Secretary of Defense, 1969–1973

Lake, Tony Staff member, NSC, 1969–1970

Lon Nol, General Cambodia's Prime Minister, Commander in Chief and Head of State, 1970–1975

Lord, Winston Staff member, NSC, 1969–1970; Special Assistant to the Assistant to the President for National Security Affairs, 1970–1973

Lynn, Larry Staff member, NSC, 1969–1970

Meir, Golda Prime Minister of Israel, 1969–1974

Mitchell, John U.S. Attorney General, 1969–1972

Moorer, Admiral Thomas H. Chairman, Joint Chiefs of Staff, 1970–1974

Morris, Roger Staff member, NSC, 1969–1970

Nixon, Richard M. President of the United States, 1969–1974

Nutter, Warren G. Assistant Secretary of Defense for International Security Affairs, 1969–1973

Packard, David Deputy Secretary of Defense, 1969–1971

Quandt, William B. Staff member, NSC, 1972–1974

Rabin, Yitzhak Israeli Ambassador to the United States, 1968–1973

Rahman, Sheikh Mujibur Leader of the Awami League; Prime Minister of Bangladesh, 1972–1975

Rodman, Peter Staff member, NSC, 1969–1977

Rogers, William P. Secretary of State, 1969–1973

Sadat, Mohamed Anwar President of Egypt, 1970–1981

Saunders, Harold Staff member, NSC, 1969–1974

Schlesinger, James Secretary of Defense, 1973–1974

Scowcroft, Brent Deputy Assistant to the President for National Security Affairs, 1973–1975

Sihanouk, Prince Norodom Ruler of Cambodia, 1953–1970; head of government in exile, 1970–1975

Sisco, Joseph Assistant Secretary of State for Near Eastern and South Asian Affairs, 1969–1974; Under Secretary of State for Political Affairs, 1974–1976

Sonnenfeldt, Helmut Senior staff member, NSC, 1969–1974

Watts, William Staff member, NSC, 1969–1970

Westmoreland, General C. William U.S. Army Chief of Staff, 1968–1972

Wheeler, General Earle G. Chairman, Joint Chiefs of Staff, 1964–1970

Yahya Khan, General Agha Mohammad President, Minister of Defence, and Minister of Foreign Affairs of Pakistan, 1969–1971

Zumwalt, Admiral Elmo R., Jr. Chief of Naval Operations, 1970–1974

Nixon, Kissinger, and U.S. Foreign Policy Making

Introduction

> The statesman is therefore like one of the heroes in classical drama who has a vision of the future but who cannot transmit it directly to his fellow-men and who cannot validate its 'truth'... It is for this reason that statesmen often share the fate of prophets, that they are without honor in their own country, that they always have a difficult task in legitimizing their programmes domestically, and their greatness is usually apparent only in retrospect when their intuition has become experience.[1]
>
> Henry Kissinger, 1964

Henry Kissinger made this observation five years before being appointed Assistant to the President for National Security Affairs to President Richard Nixon, and nine years before becoming U.S. Secretary of State and arguably one of the most powerful men in world politics. One cannot help but admire his prophetic vision, as these words would eventually come to symbolise the legacy of U.S. foreign policy under the partnership of Richard Nixon and Henry Kissinger.

This book explores the making of American foreign policy during the Nixon years. More specifically, it is concerned with the mechanism of crisis decision-making during four major foreign policy crises between 1969 and 1974. To date, questions about the organisation of the foreign policy machinery and its impact on the making of foreign

---

[1] H. Kissinger, *A World Restored* (New York: Grosset & Dunlap, 1964), 329.

policy have been overshadowed by more descriptive accounts of the main achievements of the Nixon administration in foreign affairs. This is regrettable since broad lessons about the linkage between structure and process in foreign policy on the one hand, and the importance of leadership and personality on the other, can be learnt from the experience of the Nixon and Kissinger years – lessons which are particularly pertinent to foreign policy making during international crises.

The book reflects some four years of work supported by various research grants and fellowships, which enabled me to be among the first to examine the newly released collections of the National Security Council Institutional Files series at the National Archives in College Park, Maryland. Hitherto, the range of original material concerning the making of foreign policy during the Nixon years has been limited. The picture has now changed. We are no longer dependent on journalists' and participants' accounts. The recently released National Security Council (NSC) series (along with other collections) offers original, high-quality material that has never been seen before. These new findings form the founding stones of this book, as they allow us, for the first time, to construct a more comprehensive narrative of the making of the Nixon administration's foreign policy during international crises. Furthermore, the declassification of a vast amount of governmental records from that period at the National Archives in London has enabled me to examine the making of U.S. foreign policy from a multi-archival perspective.

The objectives of this book are two-fold: first, to examine how President Nixon reshaped the machinery of U.S. foreign policy upon entering the White House, with particular emphasis given to the reorganisation of the NSC; and second, to analyse the impact this restructuring had on the process of decision-making during international crises, which was designed to 'routinize' procedures and create a more familiar environment for policy makers. Stated differently, this book seeks to explain how the introduction of hierarchical, formalistic structures to the machinery of U.S. foreign policy affected the process of decision-making during international crises.

Importantly, this analysis assigns a central role to the cognitive make-up of the president and his national security advisor (NSA), Henry Kissinger. In the making of U.S. foreign policy, personality is often indistinguishable from institutional structures and behaviours, and therefore any analysis of the achievements and failures in Nixon's foreign policy must be examined on both levels.

At the heart of this book is a study of the Washington Special Actions Group (WSAG) and its performance in international crises during the Nixon presidency. The WSAG (pronounced Wa-Sag) was an interdepartmental group within the NSC, tasked with anticipating, monitoring, and managing international crises and providing the president with the relevant information and advice. By examining the workings of the WSAG, this book will attempt to offer fresh analysis about the linkage between structure and process in U.S. foreign policy crisis decision-making.

The performance of the WSAG is analysed during four international crises: the incursion into Cambodia in the spring of 1970, the Jordanian Crisis of September 1970, the India-Pakistan War in December 1971, and the Yom Kippur War in October 1973. These four cases were not selected randomly. Primarily, the selection was driven by the availability of archival records. The population of potential case studies for this book is not unlimited. The research objectives require sufficient material evidence on the process of crisis decision-making to generate tangible generalisations. Other potential case studies, such as the Chile coup in 1973 and the Cyprus crisis of 1974, were rejected because they were not supported at the time of research by the kind of fresh, high-quality archival sources that the crises selected here can offer. Furthermore, all four crises are traditionally ranked highest in terms of threat to U.S. national security during the Nixon administration, especially with reference to the potential threat of war with the Soviet Union.[2] Moreover, crisis decision-making during the Nixon administration is examined here because it provides a range of well-documented cases for comparison. By contrast, fresh primary evidence on crisis decision-making of subsequent U.S. administrations is relatively scant. At the same time, already a large number of studies look at crisis decision-making during previous administrations, such as the 1962 Cuban Missile Crisis, the Berlin crises of 1948 and 1961, Suez, and Dien Bien Phu. Lastly, the four crises also offer diversity. Although

---

[2] G. M. Herek, I. L. Janis, and P. Huth, 'Decision Making during International Crises: Is Quality of Process Related to Outcome?,' *Journal of Conflict Resolution*, 31:2 (June 1987), 203–226.

the period under investigation in this book is relatively short, the crises are discrete in their geographic locations, their trajectories as individual crises, and indeed their management. Each of the four crises provides a different perspective on how the structure of decision-making constrained, or conditioned, the process of decision-making.

The invasion of Cambodia by U.S. ground forces in the spring of 1970, following an increase in Vietcong attacks from Cambodian sanctuaries, led to the expansion of the war in Vietnam into neutral territory. The domestic unrest in the United States which followed the invasion not only led to the withdrawal of the American troops within two months but also paved the way for the historic legislation of the War Powers Act, designed to restrict presidential power to deploy forces abroad without prior congressional approval. The management of the Jordanian Crisis in September 1970 was conducted under different circumstances altogether. This episode consisted of three distinct phases of crisis management as events in the Middle East unfolded. First, initial crisis assessments followed the hijacking of several western aircraft en route to Jordan by a Palestinian guerrilla group. Second, within a week, the process was complicated further as civil war ensued in Jordan between the moderate, pro-western regime of King Hussein and Palestinian guerrillas, backed by Syria and Iraq. The third phase of the crisis followed the invasion of Jordan by Syrian forces, an event which nearly triggered a direct confrontation between the two superpowers. The war between India and Pakistan at the end of 1971 provides perhaps the most telling account of the role of the Nixon-Kissinger partnership in setting the agenda and the process of foreign policy in the face of a dissenting bureaucracy. Known as 'The Tilt' because of Nixon and Kissinger's decision to support Pakistan despite the advice of the bureaucracy, this case also provides an interesting insight into the role of bureaucratic politics and cognition in the making of foreign policy decisions. The fourth Arab-Israeli war in October 1973 is unique because the process of decision-making was invariably constrained by the adverse domestic effects of the Watergate affair. Furthermore, it ultimately changed the balance of power between Nixon and Kissinger, thus cementing the emergence of Kissinger as the key actor in the U.S. foreign policy.

When examining these four crises as a continuous process of crisis decision-making, a rather telling pattern emerges. Notwithstanding the obvious idiosyncrasies of each crisis, one would expect to see a common behaviour of decision-making, as the major variables – Nixon, Kissinger, the WSAG, and ultimately the NSC structure – remained constant. Furthermore, one would also expect to see an element of policy learning from previous crises – at least tentatively, the management of the India-Pakistan war, for example, ought to have been smoother and more efficient than that of the incursion into Cambodia.

However, this is not the case. Interestingly, the most consistent pattern of crisis decision-making during the Nixon administration is its inconsistency. Each crisis is characterised by a unique process of decision-making, almost regardless of the very clear, formalistic structure put in place by Nixon and Kissinger during the first year of the administration. While the president and his chief foreign policy advisor had a lucid concept of foreign policy and how to interpret its implementation into the organisational process, ironically, in some crises, it was exactly this rigid structure which frustrated the WSAG and prevented it from performing adequately.

Methodology: The Case-Study Approach

Case-study methods offer an invaluable contribution to the development of scientific knowledge. Their ability to cross-compare relatively detailed descriptions of events stands in contrast to some methodological shortcomings which can be associated with quantitative research.[3]

Any discussion regarding the research design of comparative methods must first answer the fundamental question, 'What makes these cases comparable?'[4] This question has bearing on the research design and, more specifically, the selection of cases. Despite the methodological and practical challenges that case-study research is often confronted with, it is by no means impossible to design, conduct, and analyse case

[3] H. Eckstein, 'Case Study and Theory in Political Science,' in F. I. Greenstein and N. W. Polsby (eds.), *Handbook of Political Science* (Reading, MA: Addison-Wesley, 1975), 79–138; A. L. George, 'Case Studies and Theory Development: The Method of Structured, Focused Comparison,' in P. Lauren (ed.), *Diplomacy: New Approaches in History, Theory, and Practice* (New York: Free Press, 1979) 43–68.

[4] Eckstein, 'Case Study and Theory in Political Science'; A. Lijphart, 'The Comparable Cases Strategy in Comparative Research,' *Comparative Political Studies*, 8 (July 1975), 158–177; G. Peters, *Comparative Politics, Theory, and Method* (New York: New York University Press, 1998).

studies effectively. As with other fields of social inquiry, the researcher should capitalise on the benefits of the approach but at the same time be aware of its limitations – most notably the fact that it is often unfeasible to apply quantitative, large-N methods to the study of foreign policy. Thus, the nature of the field and the relatively limited number of events and processes make the application of small-N comparative studies highly desirable. This book largely builds on Alexander George's method of 'structured, focused comparison.'[5] This approach views the treatment of a case as a process; the approach is 'focused' because it selectively examines the information relevant to the study according to the researcher's purpose; it is 'structured' because the comparison is controlled, and the same set of questions is asked of each case. The first phase in the process is designing the research (identifying the problem; specifying the requirements for case selection); the researcher then moves to examining the case studies according to the research design; and then develops the theoretical implications of the comparisons of the case studies.[6] While this method has been criticised for its lack of scientific rigour,[7] its advantages lie in its particular applicability to studies of politics and foreign policy in which processes and problems are limited in number, which render statistical, large-N research designs inappropriate.[8] George's method also offers the historical depth and patterns of generalisation which are often not accounted for by quantitative and deductive approaches.[9]

This book employs the case-study method to explain the impact of structural settings on the process of decision-making during international crises in the Nixon administration by examining six components of crisis decision-making. Despite the apparent uniqueness of each crisis and the variations in contexts of time, geography, and content, by raising similar questions about each of these cases within the context of the WSAG apparatus, some valuable causal inferences on the linkage

[5] George, 'Case Studies and Theory Development.'

[6] Ibid., 54–59.

[7] C. Achen and D. Snidal, 'Rational Deterrence Theory and Comparative Case Studies,' *World Politics*, 41:2 (January 1989), 143–169.

[8] P. J. Haney, *Organizing for Foreign Policy Crises: Presidents, Advisers, and the Management of Decision Making* (Ann Arbor: University of Michigan Press, 2002), 28.

[9] T. V. Paul, *Asymmetric Conflicts: War Initiation by Weaker Powers* (Cambridge: Cambridge University Press, 1994), 35–36.

between structure and process can be drawn. To determine the nature of the relationship between structural settings and the decision-making process, the following six areas are examined in each of the cases with reference to the performance of the WSAG:

1. How were objectives surveyed?
2. How were alternative courses of action evaluated?
3. How was information searched for?
4. How was new/contradictory information integrated into the process?
5. How were potential benefits/costs evaluated?
6. How were implementation and monitoring mechanisms developed?

These questions pertain to distinct phases of a 'rational' decision-making process.[10] Over the years, several studies have suggested that the ideal decision-making process must include certain components; some have attempted to establish a causal inference between 'high-quality' process, or good performance of these tasks, and positive outcome of the crisis.[11] However, while these studies raise important questions about the linkage between process and outcome, often methodological problems of case selection and limited sources outdo whatever positive contributions these studies have to offer. To illustrate, in their examination of crisis decision-making during the India-Pakistan War, Herek et al. rely on a single source to codify the performance of the Nixon administration, compared with seven sources used to examine the performance of the Truman administration during the

[10] See G. Allison's Model I, in *Essence of Decision: Explaining the Cuban Missile Crisis* (Boston: Little, Brown, 1971).
[11] Herek, Janis, and Huth, 'Decision Making During International Crises'; M. Shafer and S. Crichlow, 'The Process-Outcome Connection in Foreign Policy Decision-Making: A Quantitative Study Building on Groupthink,' *International Studies Quarterly*, 46:1 (March 2002), 45–68. See also I. L. Janis, *Groupthink: Psychological Studies of Policy Decisions and Fiascoes* (Boston: Houghton Mifflin, 1982, 2nd ed.); A. L. George, *Presidential Decisionmaking in Foreign Policy: The Effective Use of Information and Advice* (Boulder, CO: Westview Press, 1980); J. G. Stein and R. Tanter, *Rational Decision Making: Israels Security Choices, 1967* (Columbus: Ohio State University Press, 1980); P. J. Haney, 'Decision-Making during International Crises: A Reexamination,' *International Interactions*, 19:3 (1994), 177–191; Haney, *Organizing for Foreign Policy Crises*.

initial stages of the Korean War.[12] Moreover, the assignment of 'positive,' 'negative,' and 'neutral' marks to crisis management performance does little to further our understanding of the *making* of foreign policy. The reader is then left with more questions than answers about why and how decisions were made. A case in point is Haney's analysis of the Nixon administration's crisis management of the Jordanian Crisis and the Yom Kippur War. The following excerpt from Haney's study exemplifies the flaws in this approach: 'I have given "neutral" codings to the group's performance of Task 3 (information search) and Task 4 (information assimilation). Quandt and Dowty agree that the search for information (Task 3) in the crisis was adequate but not exhaustive (i.e., "neutral").'[13]

The objective of this book is not, therefore, to assign normative values to these tasks but rather to establish how they were followed and executed in the formalistic, hierarchical framework instituted by Nixon and Kissinger. What can we then learn about the impact of structures on the decision-making process? Can we formulate some broader lessons about the linkage between structure and process in U.S. foreign policy making? How do the cognitive schemes of policy makers alter the causal relationship between structures and processes of policy making? The evidence presented in this book suggests that structures and processes of foreign policy making are important regardless of whether the president heeds the advice of the bureaucracy or operates against it. It is often argued that the NSC system during the Nixon years 'did not matter' because, ultimately, Nixon and Kissinger made decisions regardless of the institutional input. This book challenges this common misperception on three accounts. First, the NSC system *did* matter because it ultimately provided the president with the required information and advice. That Nixon then decided to act against the advice did not make it wrong or unimportant, as the purpose of institutional (the foreign policy bureaucracy) or group (the WSAG forum) advice is exactly that – to recommend a particular course of action – not to force it upon the president. In other words, decisions were made by

[12] Herek, Janis, and Huth, 'Decision Making During International Crises,' 209–210.
[13] P. Haney, 'The Nixon Administration and Middle East Crises: Theory and Evidence of Presidential Management of Foreign Policy Decision Making,' *Political Research Quarterly*, 47:4 (December 1994), 950.

Nixon (and Kissinger) not in an institutional vacuity but based on the input of the bureaucracy and, more specifically, the WSAG. Second, not only did the NSC system fulfil its general operational function, but its unique structures and procedures mattered as well, because they matched (and, indeed, were the product of) the individual policy-making style of the president and his chief foreign policy advisor. It would be erroneous to assume that had Nixon and Kissinger operated with Lyndon Johnson's lax and confused NSC system, the processes of decision-making would have still been the same because Nixon and Kissinger ultimately determined the outcome. However, this counter-factual reasoning fails to acknowledge that institutional structures and processes are not designed to determine outcomes, only to *help* the president to make an informed decision. Had Nixon and Kissinger relied on President Johnson's flimsy NSC apparatus, they would have certainly not received the same high-quality input which the more hier-archical and organised system provided them later on, thus leading to a skewed process of decision-making from the beginning.

Finally, and building on the first two points, institutional structures and procedures matter because when the president follows the theoret-ical design of the system and uses it to its full potential, the outcome is evidently more favorable in terms of national interests. That the United States found itself in a thorny position (domestically and internation-ally) during and following the Cambodian and Indo-Pakistani episodes cannot be separated from the poor attention Nixon and Kissinger had given to the institutional input during the management of the two crises. Conversely, America's position and leverage in the Middle East improved significantly in the aftermath of the Jordanian Crisis and the Yom Kippur War – to a large degree due to the smooth and effective process of decision-making during the two crises (the Jordanian Crisis in particular). In both cases, the president (and more so Kissinger dur-ing the Yom Kippur War, following Nixon's preoccupation with the Watergate affair) paid close attention to institutional contributions. The NSC system is important because when used properly by the pres-ident, it has the potential to deliver outcomes of higher quality than if otherwise ignored or bypassed. In this analysis, the all-important factor which links the system (its structures and processes of decision-making), on the one hand, and the outcome, on the other hand, is the president. More specifically, we are interested in the psychological make-up and cognitive schemes of the leader and his most influential advisor, as they ultimately conditioned the institutional characteristics of the decision-making process. As will be discussed later, the unique cognitive structures of Nixon and Kissinger can explain not only the theoretical design of the NSC system but also very often the difference between success and failure in managing foreign policy crises.

Chapter Outline

Chapter 1 presents a theoretical framework for the study of U.S. presidents and their foreign policy systems beyond the immediate experience of the Nixon administration. It is grounded in the literature of foreign policy analysis (FPA) which will explore the main themes of U.S. foreign policy making that will be discussed in succeeding chapters. The second chapter examines the radical restructuring of the NSC system during the Nixon-Kissinger years, including the shift from a cabinet-oriented system to a staff system. There is also here a well-informed account of the role of the national security advisor and of the Nixon-Kissinger relationship. The chapter also explains the emergence of the WSAG as the key body in charge of anticipating, monitoring, and managing international crises and providing the president with the relevant information and advice. Chapters 3 through 6 evaluate the performance of the WSAG according to the six categories set out earlier, by examining four cases of international crisis decision-making during the Nixon administration. The book concludes with an overview of Nixon and Kissinger's failure to produce an effective system of crisis management, explicable due to the inevitable gap between their abstract paradigm of foreign policy systems and the realities of policy making. The conclusion also provides pertinent and well-drawn observations about the functioning of the NSC system and ends with a discussion of the idiosyncrasies of the foreign policy system under Nixon, with a forward-projection to the experiences of succeeding administrations.

A Note on Sources

A significant amount of data was collected from the recently declassified series of the National Security Council Institutional Files at the

Nixon Presidential Material Project at the National Archives, College Park, Maryland. Additional archival research was conducted at the Lyndon Baines Johnson Presidential Library in Austin, Texas; The Miller Center for Public Affairs in Charlottesville, Virginia; and the National Archives in London, United Kingdom. So far, little is known of the WSAG, and the declassification of thousands of secret documents in the form of minutes of meetings, memoranda, working papers, and briefing books will help to shed light on the workings of an important component of the machinery of U.S. foreign policy during the Nixon years. Historical accounts and memoirs of participants, as well as interviews, audiovisual material, and other primary and secondary sources, have also been used, such as the *Foreign Relations of the United States (FRUS)* series and the *Public Papers of the Presidents of the United States (PPPUS)*, as well as the National Security Archive website. In cases of discrepancy between the historical accounts and the archival records, the latter version was adopted.

I

Structures, Processes, and Personalities in U.S. Foreign Policy

> The vast bulk of 'liberals' in the U.S. Foreign Service / State Department establishment believe that the allegedly thin margin of Mr. Nixon's victory will make it impossible for the new Nixon team to impose any deep or meaningful change either upon the internal system which has nurtured them or upon the outward working of the system in terms of U.S. foreign policy operations.[1]
>
> Bryce Harlow (Nixon's aide), 11 November 1968

The complex nature of the foreign policy machinery during the Nixon years calls for the use of more than a single theoretical framework for the dual purpose of advancing knowledge and theory testing. Indeed, Henry Kissinger himself acknowledged that '[in] the world in which we find ourselves now... it is necessary for us to conduct a more complicated foreign policy without the simple categories of a more fortunate historical past.'[2]

While this book does not purport to use the case studies to validate or refute alternative foreign policy analysis (FPA) models, it is nonetheless important to provide an analytical framework which will help

---

[1] Memo, Harlow to the Republican Key Issues Committee, 'President Nixon and the Department of State: A Program to Ensure Control of Key Personnel by the New President,' 11 November 1968. Folder no. 28, *HAK Administrative and Staff Files*, Henry A. Kissinger Office Files (henceforth HAKOF), Box 1, National Security Council Files (henceforth NSCF), Nixon Presidential Materials Project (henceforth NPMP).

[2] Cited in P. W. Dickson, *Kissinger and the Meaning of History* (Cambridge: Cambridge University Press, 1978), 123.

generate more general observations about the interplay of structures, processes, and personalities in foreign policy crisis decision-making. Rather than providing alternative theoretical explanations to historical events or decisions, this book examines how the decision-making process within a particular crisis management group was facilitated by certain organisational structures that were put in place by the president. For this purpose, this chapter outlines pertinent approaches to the study of foreign policy decision-making in the FPA literature. This literature is particularly germane to this study as it deals with what is at the core of this book – human decision-makers, the decisions they make and the factors influencing their decisions.[3] The overview that follows includes three broad themes: (1) *crisis studies*, with reference to systemic and decision-making approaches to the subject; (2) *structure and U.S. foreign policy*, with focus on the interplay between the psychological make-up of the president and his chosen structure of management; and (3) *process and U.S. foreign policy*, with discussion of bureaucratic politics and small-group dynamics.

Crisis Studies

The phenomenon of crisis is central to the development of FPA. As Eric Stern noted recently, crises 'tend to capture the attention of leaders and scholars alike, sometimes to the neglect of other fundamental but less thrilling aspects of national and international politics.'[4] However, despite the prevalent interest in crises, and as is the case with other phenomena in international relations, there is little consensus amongst practitioners and observers alike on the precise definition of international crisis. The word 'crisis' is used widely to describe global phenomena ranging from drastic climatic changes to political tensions between nation-states. The complexity and diversity of the phenomenon thwart any attempt to construct a single, all-encompassing definition that could be embraced by the contending approaches to crisis studies.

[3] For a recent overview of the theoretical, methodological, and substantive contributions of FPA literature to IR theory, see V. M. Hudson, 'Foreign Policy Analysis: Actor-Specific Theory and the Ground of International Relations,' *Foreign Policy Analysis*, 1:1 (March 2005), 1–30.

[4] E. K. Stern, 'Crisis Studies and Foreign Policy Analysis: Insights, Synergies, and Challenges,' *International Studies Review*, 5:2 (June 2003), 183.

Definitions of crisis are therefore either precise and applicable to only a few cases, or they are so broad and inclusive that it becomes impossible to distinguish crisis from other phenomena in world affairs, such as conflict and war. It is not surprising that some have equated crisis with *trouble* in international relations, while others have found the term *situation* more accommodating.[5]

Definitions of international crises usually emerge from one of two broad approaches, commonly referred to as 'systemic' and 'decision-making.' Systemic approaches view international crises as the result of interaction *between* state actors in the global system, while decision-making approaches examine the actions of individuals or groups *within* the state as the *foci* of the decision-making process. To these can be added an emerging, though still rather marginal, alternative which emphasises the utilisation of symbols and rituals of power in crisis behaviour.[6] As this book examines the interplay between individuals (primarily Nixon and Kissinger), group dynamics (the WSAG), and institutional settings (the NSC apparatus) during four international crises, it is very much grounded in the decision-making approach to crisis studies and, therefore, the bulk of the following discussion will be focused on this perspective.

Given that the two approaches consider different variables and use different tools to explain the same phenomenon, any attempt to crown one of them as the 'correct' or 'right' approach is futile. While each approach makes some significant contribution to the study of crises, both are constrained by various conceptual and empirical limitations.

An early attempt to overcome the inherent flaws in each approach was made by McCormick, who suggested combining them to overcome their individual weaknesses, thus creating an 'integrated definition' which would explain international crisis as 'a situation between two (or more) nations that is characterized by perceptual conditions of high

[5] See, respectively, C. McClelland, 'Access to Berlin: The Quantity and Variety of Events, 1948–1963,' in D. J. Singer (ed.), *Quantitative International Politics: Insights and Evidence* (New York: Free Press, 1968), 159; and V. M. Hudson, *Foreign Policy Analysis: Classic and Contemporary Theory* (Lanham, MD: Rowman & Littlefield, 2007), 49–50.

[6] P. 't Hart, 'Symbols, Rituals and Power: The Lost Dimensions of Crisis Management,' *Journal of Contingencies and Crisis Management*, 1:2 (March 1993), 36–50; J. Weldes, *Constructing National Interests: The United States and the Cuban Missile Crisis* (Minneapolis: University of Minnesota Press, 1999).

threat, surprise, and short decision time, and by the behavioral conditions of marked change in their interaction patterns.'[7] Thus, according to McCormick, the two approaches complete each other in terms of the conditions required to identify an international crisis; the more conditions are present, the greater the justification to define a situation as a crisis. However, while McCormick's design is novel, it still fails to prevail over the inherent flaws in each approach; it is still unclear for example, how we should quantify changes in behavioural conditions, or why 'crisis' is only applicable to relations between nation-states. Similarly, the presence of a large number of conditions still does not necessitate the occurrence of a crisis, as the basic assumptions about what *are* the conditions for a crisis and how they should be measured are still debatable.

Decision-making and systemic approaches

At the core of the decision-making approach are three components: (1) a decision, (2) decision-makers, and (3) a decision-making process. The guiding assumption is that foreign policy is a series of decisions, and decisions are explained not merely as responses to external developments but rather as a unique process occurring among policy makers. This approach to foreign policy was first introduced by Snyder, Bruck, and Sapin, who argued that 'the key to explanation of why the state behaves the way it does lies in the way its decision-makers define their situation.'[8] This interpretation is closely linked to the distinction made by others during the 1960s between an operational environment which includes institutions and structures, and a psychological one, which includes ideas and values.[9] The assumption that foreign policy is in essence a series of decisions is central to this approach. Some argue that the notion of a 'process' or 'system' of decision-making can often

[7] J. M. McCormick, 'International Crises: A Note on Definition,' *Western Political Quarterly*, 31:3 (September 1978), 356.

[8] R. C. Snyder, H. W. Bruck, and B. Sapin, *Foreign Policy Decision-Making* (New York: Free Press, 1962), 65.

[9] H. Sprout and M. Sprout, 'Environmental Factors in the Study of International Politics,' in J. N. Rosenau (ed.), *International Politics and Foreign Policy: A Reader in Research and Theory* (New York: Free Press, 1969, rev. ed.), 41–56; J. Frankel, *The Making of Foreign Policy: An Analysis of Decision-Making* (London: Oxford University Press, 1963).

account for the difference in foreign policies between states. According to Rosenau, '*what* a state does is in no small way a function of *how* it decides what to do – in other words, foreign policy action is a product of decisions, and the way decisions are made may substantially affect their contents.'[10]

The approach assumes rational behaviour during the process of decision-making. This implies that decision-makers have clear objectives in mind at the start of the process, and that after carefully examining the likely costs and benefits of each possible policy, they will choose the one most likely to produce the 'best' outcome. Verba suggests that by assuming rationality on behalf of the decision-makers, the observer finds it easier to understand the process and even to predict the outcome: 'if the decision-maker behaves rationally, the observer, knowing the rules of rationality, can rehearse the decisional process in his mind, and if he knows the decision-maker's goals, can both predict the decision and understand why the particular decision was made.'[11] Nevertheless, there still remains the moot assumption that the observer is a rational actor, and that he or she has full access to the decision-maker's psyche. During crises however, policy makers often find themselves in an unfamiliar environment, where constraints of time, resources, and information are likely to impede the process of decision-making. In his highly regarded analysis of theories of accidents, Sagan argues that while it is naïve to assume the ability of human beings to behave with perfect rationality, organisations are expected to compensate for human imperfections by producing highly formalistic structures with clear objectives.[12] As the analysis in this book will later demonstrate, Nixon's highly formalistic and structured foreign policy system failed to counteract some human imperfections and the propensity of Nixon and Kissinger themselves to operate outside the formal system.

In contrast to decision-making approaches, the underpinnings of the various systemic approaches to international crises are neorealist theories of International Relations. The arena of action here is not a limited circle of policy makers; rather, it is the international system as a whole

---

[10] Rosenau, International Politics and Foreign Policy, 169.
[11] S. Verba, 'Assumptions of Rationality and Non-Rationality in Models of the International System,' in Rosenau (ed.), *International Politics and Foreign Policy*, 225.
[12] S. D. Sagan, *The Limits of Safety: Organizations, Accidents, and Nuclear Weapons* (Princeton, NJ: Princeton University Press, 1993).

and the interaction between nation-states. The emphasis is on power as a means to pursue the national interest. A crisis could, therefore, be viewed as a systemic variable, a fundamental facet of international relations. A crisis signifies a momentous change in the flow of events and is linked to other systemic phenomena in international relations such as conflict and war. As such, international crises fit into realist hypotheses on the anarchic nature of the international system. Central to this approach to crisis is the notion of *change* in the international system. Hermann's definition is representative of this theme, where a crisis 'disrupts the system or some part of the system . . . More specifically, a crisis is a situation that creates an abrupt or sudden change in one or more of the basic systemic variables.'[13]

A definition of crisis

While there is little consensus on the definition of international crisis, it is possible to identify a few themes that can be regarded as 'central crisis traits' that are shared by most definitions from both approaches. Notwithstanding the lack of consensus on the level of analysis and the conceptual boundaries, the majority of definitions link international crises to five main themes: (1) *threat* to basic values, (2) *time* constraints, (3) *surprise*, (4) the notion of *change*, and (5) a higher-than normal degree of *violence*.

Decision-making definitions such as Hermann's, for example, see an international crisis as 'a situation that (1) threatens high-priority goals of the decision-making unit, (2) restricts the amount of time available for response before the decision is transformed, and (3) surprises the members of the decision-making unit by its occurrence.'[14] Following this definition is the assumption that if all three traits are present, the decision-making process will be significantly different than if only one or two were present.

While Hermann's definition is compelling, it also has its critics. In a series of studies of the foreign policy system of Israel and the impact of stress on the decision-making process, Michael Brecher argues against the inclusion of surprise as a necessary trait and instead suggests the 'high probability of involvement in military hostilities' as a necessary

---

[13] C. F. Hermann, 'International Crisis as a Situational Variable,' in Rosenau (ed.), *International Politics and Foreign Policy*, 411.
[14] Ibid., 414.

condition.[15] Brecher's reasoning is persuasive: While often crises indeed surprise decision-makers by their occurrence (for example, the Cuban Missile Crisis or the Yom Kippur War), this is not a necessary trait as sometimes events develop into crises without taking the decision-making unit by surprise. Where it is possible to monitor the development of events and prepare adequate contingency plans for possible scenarios, the likelihood that decision-makers will be taken by surprise is then reduced significantly. Two immediate examples are the 1961 Berlin Crisis and the closing of the Tiran Straits by President Nasser just before the Six Day War.[16] Brecher's condition of likelihood of hostilities (violence) is particularly useful as it suggests a change in a state's behaviour. It signifies a dramatic shift in the decision-makers' perception of the situation and heightens the level of perceived threat.

This is a crucial point where decision-making and systemic approaches to crisis meet. Prominent students of the systemic approach, such as McClelland, Young, and Snyder and Diesing, emphasise this point – although it is worth noting that for them, the change refers to the interaction between states that might lead to war and not to the subjective perceptions of the decision-making unit.[17] For McClelland, a crisis implies a 'transition from peace to war. . . . Crises are most commonly thought of as interpositions between the prolongation of peace and the outbreak of war.'[18] In a similar fashion, Young describes a sudden change in the interaction between states which may push them toward confrontation. For Young, a crisis is a 'set of rapidly unfolding events which raises the impact of destabilizing forces in the general international system or any of its subsystems substantially

---

[15] M. Brecher with B. Geist (eds.), *Decisions in Crisis: Israel, 1967 and 1973* (Berkeley: University of California Press, 1980), 1. See also Brecher, *The Foreign Policy of Israel: Setting, Images, Process* (London: Oxford University Press, 1972); Brecher, *Decisions in Israel's Foreign Policy* (London, Oxford University Press, 1974).

[16] Brecher, *Decisions in Crisis*, 3.

[17] C. McClelland, 'The Beginning, Duration, and Abatement of International Crises: Comparison in Two Conflict Arenas,' in C. F. Hermann (ed.), *International Crises: Insights from Behavioural Research* (New York: Free Press, 1972), 83–105; O. Young, *The Intermediaries: Third Parties in International Crisis* (Princeton, NJ: Princeton University Press, 1967); G. Snyder and P. Diesing (eds.), *Conflict among Nations: Bargaining, Decision Making, and System Structure in International Crises* (Princeton, NJ: Princeton University Press, 1977).

[18] C. McClelland, 'The Beginning, Duration, and Abatement of International Crises,' 83.

above "normal" (i.e., average) levels and increases the likelihood of violence occurring in the system.'[19]

While many scholars from both approaches hold on to the likelihood of armed conflict as a necessary condition, still others hold opposing views. Holsti, for example, applies the decision-making approach to address the effect of stress on decision-makers and argues that this condition may be too restrictive.[20] Often, policy makers perceive a certain situation as a crisis which would not necessarily lead to violence or increase the likelihood of hostilities. What if, Holsti argues, Third World debtors were to confront the World Bank and demand that it erase all their external debts? World Bank officials would certainly perceive this development as threatening some important values, and time to address the problem would most likely be limited. However, the likelihood of escalation into an armed conflict is virtually non-existent. Similar arguments can be made for an 'environmental crisis' in industrialised societies or an 'AIDS crisis' in sub-Saharan Africa.

Holsti's argument is fairly convincing if we accept *a priori* that these examples are tantamount to crisis situations; however, in discussing these case studies, Holsti fails to address a fundamental question: Why are these cases viewed as crises? Would it be more appropriate to categorise them as developing disasters, emergencies, or conflicts? Recalling McClelland's point on the problems of definition, the wide use of the word 'crisis' in everyday life not only makes it impossible to generate a consensual definition, it also blurs the boundaries between crises and other global phenomena. The crux of the issue here is that we have come to associate 'crisis' with mainly military-security situations, whereas it is possible to conceptualise economic or environmental crises – but not from a decision-making perspective.

This book settles for a working definition that suits the boundaries set by the theoretical framework as well as the cases examined; one that accurately answers the questions raised here about the making of foreign policy and the decision-making process within a state. An international crisis is defined here as a situation that in the minds of the decision-makers (1) poses a threat to national interests which may endanger the status quo, (2) where time to respond to unfolding events

---

[19] Young, *The Intermediaries*, 10.
[20] O. R. Holsti 'Crisis Decision Making,' in P. Tetlock et al. (eds.), *Behaviour, Society, and Nuclear War* (Oxford: Oxford University Press, 1988), Vol. 1, 8–37.

is significantly limited, and (3) where the willingness to use force to defuse the situation increases, although force may not necessarily be used.

This definition clearly stems from the decision-making approach as it addresses perceptions of crisis that are born in the minds of the policy makers. Nonetheless, it also brings to the fore two notions which draw on the systemic approach – the national interest and the balance of power, described here as a situation of status quo. While the focus here is not on interstate interaction, policy makers are still guided by certain national priorities and clear objectives, which they aim to pursue. Therefore, when they perceive a situation as threatening these values or, indeed, threatening the status quo, it is likely to be treated as a crisis.

Like other definitions of crisis, this one is not impregnable. Its main weakness lies in the inherent assumption that a crisis, more often than not, poses a threat to the superpower. Stated differently, it assumes that international crises have the potential to disrupt the status quo, or the balance of power, thus implying that it threatens those who are in danger of losing a favourable position. Does it mean that medium or small powers do not experience crises? Crises can be used by policy makers to disturb the status quo, and because the superpower has more global resources and influence than smaller powers, it has more tools, or leverage, to 'start' a crisis. Indeed, it was Henry Kissinger who advocated the use of crises in foreign policy specifically for this purpose: 'If you act creatively you should be able to use crises to move the world towards the structural solutions that are necessary. In fact, very often the crises themselves are a symptom of the need for structural rearrangement.'[21] In this utilitarian outlook on crises, Kissinger masterfully combines the two theoretical approaches discussed earlier. Much like the definition of crisis used in this book, Kissinger sees the individual as the independent variable shaping the trajectory of the crisis but, at the same time, Kissinger the arch-realist, acknowledges the international environment in which the individual operates. Indeed, as the four case studies will later demonstrate, Kissinger rarely neglected to appreciate the delicate interplay between individual decisions and their reverberations on the international stage.

---

[21] Cited in H. Brandon, *The Retreat of American Power* (New York: Doubleday, 1973), 338.

The Structure of U.S. Foreign Policy: Does Personality Matter?

When we talk of the structure of foreign policy, we refer to the institutional settings that define the realms of foreign policy making and where the process of decision-making ultimately takes place.[22] Structure has a bearing not only on the process but also on the decision-makers themselves. Discussing the effects of structural settings on the decision-makers, Frankel argues that they 'not only determine their powers but also impose limitations upon them.'[23] Recent research has found that the impact of the decision setting is greater where it is well structured.[24] Henry Kissinger observed early on that structure was also necessary to ensure that personal instincts were left outside the process, especially in the modern age, where 'issues are too complex and relevant facts too manifold to be dealt with on the basis of personal intuition. An institutionalization of decision-making is an inevitable by-product of the risks of international affairs in the nuclear age.'[25] Interestingly, Kissinger wrote these words a few years before assuming the role of Nixon's national security advisor, where ultimately he and Nixon would repeatedly make decisions based on their intuition, outside the formal structure of decision-making.

Structure is particularly important during international crises. A crisis, by definition, is an event which constrains decision-makers by its occurrence. There is a perceived threat to national interests and time to respond to unfolding events is limited, the flow of information may be constrained, and resources are likely to be deficient. Structural safeguards are then put in place to 'routinise' the process and create a familiar, 'non-crisis' environment where the decision-makers are expected to perform their tasks based on clear procedures and objectives, thus bringing the effects of human frailties to a manageable minimum.

---

[22] P. J. Haney, 'Structure and Process in the Analysis of Foreign Policy Crises,' in L. Neack, J. Hey, and P. J. Haney (eds.), *Foreign Policy Analysis: Continuity and Change in Its Second Generation* (Englewood Cliffs, NJ: Prentice Hall, 1995), 99–116.

[23] J. Frankel, *The Making of Foreign Policy: An Analysis of Decision-Making*, 10.

[24] A. Astorino-Courtois, 'Clarifying Decisions: Assessing the Impact of Decision Structures on Foreign Policy Choices During the 1970 Jordanian Civil War,' *International Studies Quarterly*, 42:4 (December 1998), 733–754.

[25] H. Kissinger, 'Domestic Structure and Foreign Policy,' in Rosenau (ed.), *International Politics and Foreign Policy*, 263.

Presidential management of information and advice

Barber observed more than three decades ago that '[a] President's personality is an important shaper of his Presidential behavior on non-trivial matters,'[26] and Hermann later noted that a foreign policy decision 'may be the manifestation of the personal characteristics of a key decision-maker who is little affected by either the pulling and hauling of bureaucratic politics or the pressure of a small group to conform to its norm.'[27]

The American constitution grants the president the power and resources to structure the foreign policy machinery and enables him to become a central actor in foreign policy. The president can define his foreign policy roles and objectives, set up his decision-making system, and appoint senior and junior cabinet officials. In essence, then, the presidential system is hierarchical, wherein the conduct of foreign policy is ultimately derived from the president's management style and interest.[28]

Upon entering the White House, the president faces tough decisions regarding the conduct of foreign policy and the structuring of the foreign policy machine. A primary concern is how to manage the flow of information and advice from various agencies and departments to the Oval Office. In examining the linkage between a president's individual style of management and the advisory group in charge of providing the president with information, analysis, and advice, the group serves as the dependent variable, necessarily affected by the organisational settings put in place by the president. These settings can be institutionalised from the outset, before the outbreak of any crises, or they can be established on an ad hoc basis when a crisis looms, by implementing certain procedures that are suited to the particular circumstance. The president and the structure of his advisory system are important variables because they set the parameters within which the decision-making process takes place. In examining how the process works, we

[26] J. D. Barber, *The Presidential Character: Predicting Performance in the White House* (Englewood Cliffs, NJ: Prentice-Hall, 1972), 6.

[27] C. F. Hermann, 'What Decision Units Shape Foreign Policy: Individual, Group, or Bureaucracy?' *Policy Studies Journal*, No. 3 (Winter 1974), 166.

[28] For a useful account of the historical development of the foreign policy system and the growing influence of the president in foreign policy up to the Nixon administration, see A. M. Schlesinger, *The Imperial Presidency* (Boston: Houghton Mifflin, 1973).

should first look at the president and his management style as they shape the decision-making environment. In most policy arenas, the president can seek advice from external organisations or individuals, congressional leaders whose support is sought, or other 'wise men' whose opinion is valued. In the making of foreign policy, however, it is the circle of senior advisors whose counsel is most sought after and valued. As Destler noted, '[in] foreign affairs, official secrecy gives further advantages to insiders.'[29]

Most literature on the American presidency and the making of U.S. foreign policy tends to focus on either the structural arrangement of the advisory system or the management style of the president.[30] In their seminal studies of presidential styles of management, Richard Johnson and Alexander George present three distinct models: (1) formalistic, (2) competitive, and (3) collegial.[31] Both use similar typologies and characteristics, although each study examines different antecedents to presidential preferences. Johnson sees presidential choice as the product of four dilemmas: the president must choose (1) between the 'best' policy and the most 'feasible' policy; (2) between exclusion or inclusion of conflicting views; (3) between screening information or evaluating as much information as possible; and (4) between quick response and extensive deliberation. George, on the other hand, focuses on personality traits (cognitive style, orientation towards conflict, feelings of efficacy, and experience and competency) as explanatory variables of presidential choices between the three broad models of management. Each model has its strengths and weaknesses, and although this typology is broad and overlapping in some cases, it still provides the theoretical benchmark for succeeding scholars who wish to examine the organisation of American foreign policy. Since the publication

[29] I. M. Destler, 'National Security Advice to U.S. Presidents: Some Lessons from Thirty Years,' *World Politics*, 29:2 (January 1977), 145.

[30] On structural arrangements, see J. Pika, 'White House Boundary Roles: Marginal Men Amidst the Palace Guard,' *Presidential Studies Quarterly*, 16:4 (Fall 1986), 700–715; S. Hess, *Organizing the Presidency* (Washington, DC: Brookings Institution Press, 1988). On presidential management styles, see, for example, R. T. Johnson, *Managing the White House: An Intimate Study of the Presidency* (New York: Harper & Row, 1974); A. L. George, *Presidential Decisionmaking in Foreign Policy*; R. E. Neustadt, *Presidential Power and the Modern Presidents* (New York: Free Press, 1990).

[31] Johnson, *Managing the White House*; George, *Presidential Decisionmaking in Foreign Policy*.

of the works by Johnson and George, several attempts have been made
to reformulate their classic models: Hermann and Preston's focus on
the centralisation of the advisory system by the president; Preston's
expansion of presidential leadership styles based on sensitivity to information and desire for control; Haney's study of the quality of performance of the different classic models; and Mitchell's study of the effect
of presidential choice of management style on the process of decision-
making and its outcome.[32]

The organisation of foreign policy during the Nixon years follows
the traits of the formalistic model rather well. As will be shown later,
the theoretical design of the NSC system required a clear hierarchical chain of command intended to protect the president's time and
to screen information effectively, where the 'best' policy was sought,
policy making followed clearly defined procedures, and the president
was situated at the top of the pyramid and did not reach down for
information. Low-level committees reported to department heads, who
reported to Kissinger, who would in turn report to Nixon. The most
important decisions were made either by Nixon alone or in consultation with Kissinger. In accordance with the formalistic model, conflict in the Nixon administration was discouraged through the orderly
policy-making structure which relied on strict procedures and hierarchical lines of communication. However, as the four case studies
in this book will demonstrate, while the theoretical thrust of Nixon's
NSC system fit rather neatly into George's formalistic model, in reality,
decisions were rarely made along this highly formalistic model.[33]

George's collegial model is characterised by emphasis on teamwork
with less rigid procedures, where the president is located at the centre,
rather than at the top, and reaches down for information from the
bureaucracy. Information is not filtered in the process, and the most
'feasible' policy is sought. The competitive model is a distinct variation
of the collegial model in that rather than stimulate teamwork, the

---

[32] M. G. Hermann and T. Preston, 'Presidents, Advisors and Foreign Policy: The Effects
of Leadership Style on Executive Arrangements,' *Political Psychology*, 15:1 (March
1994), 75–96; T. Preston, *The President and His Inner Circle: Leadership Style and
the Advisory Process in Foreign Policy Making* (New York: Columbia University
Press, 2001); Haney, *Organizing for Foreign Policy Crises*; D. Mitchell, 'Centralizing
Advisory Systems: Presidential Influence and the U.S. Foreign Policy Decision-Making
Process,' *Foreign Policy Analysis*, 1:2 (July 2005), 181–206.
[33] Other examples of formalistic styles include the presidencies of Truman and Eisenhower.

president may manipulate his advisors in order to control and manage information. Despite the prominence of these models in the literature, they have proven less than adequate in explaining the effects of management choices on the policy process. The works of Johnson and George have been criticised for their broad nature and overlapping characteristics. Furthermore, in reality, there are some degrees of formality and informality in every administration, regardless of the type of structures put in place by the president. Perhaps most pertinent to this book, presidents often do not manage their foreign policy systems in accordance with these models.[34] Indeed, as subsequent chapters will show, the case of the Nixon administration suggests that there is some considerable discrepancy between the theoretical design of the foreign policy machinery and its actual performance during international crises.

The psychological make-up of the decision-makers

Any analysis of foreign policy decision-making must consider the human component and its impact on the overall process, as well as the outcome. But to what extent is the individual's personality influential in making decisions? Richard Nixon had no doubt about the importance of personality in crisis decision-making: 'reaction and response to crisis is uniquely personal in the sense that it depends on what the individual brings to bear on the situation – his own traits of personality and character, his training and religious background, his strengths and weaknesses.'[35] Studies into the psychological and cognitive make-up of leaders and decision-makers have played an important role in the development of foreign policy analysis literature from its early days in the late 1950s to the present.[36] While it is accepted that knowledge of belief systems cannot predict foreign policy behaviour,

---

[34] For more critical assessment of the typologies, see, for example, C. E. Walcott and K. Hult, 'Organizing the White House: Structure, Environment and Organizational Governance,' *American Journal of Political Science*, 31:1 (February 1987), 109–126; J. P. Burke, *The Institutional Presidency: Organizing and Managing the White House from FDR to Clinton* (Baltimore: Johns Hopkins University Press, 2000, 2nd ed.); D. E. Ponder, *Good Advice: Information & Policy Making in the White House* (College Station: Texas A&M University Press, 2000).

[35] R. Nixon, *Six Crises* (New York: Doubleday, 1970), xiii.

[36] Some of the early works in the field include those by H. Sprout and M. Sprout, *Man-Milieu Relationship Hypotheses in the Context of International Politics* (Princeton, NJ: Princeton University Press, 1956), and 'Environment Factors in the Study of

most observers agree that cognitive processes are an integral part of the decision-making process and, as such, should be understood and studied further.[37] Gaining an insight into the mind of the decision-maker is crucial, as the mind contains belief systems, national and self-images, experience, memory, and emotions. These individual characteristics invariably determine how the decision-maker understands, processes, and ultimately chooses policy options. Under conditions of crisis, where stress, uncertainty, and time constraints shape the boundaries of the process, the psychological make-up of the leader is particularly important to our understanding of foreign policy decisions. As the discussion of processes of foreign policy making will show, while policy makers are motivated individuals who pursue certain goals and make decisions from an array of alternatives, they are never truly 'rational,' as their ability to make rational choices is constrained by certain cognitive structures or processes, such as their need to maintain their image or position among the decision-making group or the desire to win the attention and respect of the president.[38] At the extreme, top advisors may use an array of structural, procedural, and interpersonal manoeuvres to manipulate the president and the overall process of policy making.[39] This behaviour stems from the individual's unique bases of knowledge and belief systems, and makes the policy makers into what is known in social cognition theory as 'cognitive misers' – individuals who rely on simplified schemes and structures to process

International Politics,' *Journal of Conflict Resolution*, 1:4 (December 1957), 309–328. See also N. Leites, *The Operational Code of the Politburo* (New York: McGraw-Hill, 1951).

[37] N. Geva and A. Minz (eds.), *Decision Making on War and Peace: The Cognitive-Rational Debate* (Boulder, CO: Lynne Rienner Press, 1997); M. G. Hermann and J. D. Hagan, 'International Decision Making: Leadership Matters,' *Foreign Policy*, No. 110 (Spring 1998), 124–137; H. E. Purkitt and J. W. Dyson, 'The Role of Cognition in U.S. Foreign Policy Toward Southern Africa,' *Political Psychology*, 7:3 (September 1986), 507–532.

[38] B. Farnham, 'Political Cognition and Decision-Making,' *Political Psychology*, 11:1 (1990), 83–111; S. Fiske and S. Taylor, *Social Cognition* (New York: McGraw-Hill, 1991); W. H. Riker, 'The Political Psychology of Rational Choice Theory,' *Political Psychology*, 16:1 (1995), 23–44; H. Simon, 'Rationality in Political Behavior,' *Political Psychology*, 16:1 (1995), 45–61.

[39] J. A. Garrison, *Games Advisors Play: Foreign Policy in the Nixon and Carter Administrations* (College Station: Texas A&M University Press, 1999); S. B. Redd, 'The Influence of Advisers on Foreign Policy Decision Making,' *The Journal of Conflict Resolution*, 46:3 (June 2002), 335–364, and 'The Influence of Advisers and Decision Strategies on Foreign Policy Choices: President Clinton's Decisions to Use Force in Kosovo,' *International Studies Perspectives*, 6:1 (February 2005), 129–150.

and organize new information.[40] These structures or schemes enable decision-makers to draw upon experiences or past behaviours to interpret the present and prepare for complex scenarios in the future.

These observations are crucial to our understanding of foreign policy making during times of crisis, when levels of anxiety and uncertainty are particularly high. Irvin Janis has identified three coping mechanisms which policy makers resort to during such situations: (1) *cognitive,* (2) *affiliative,* and (3) *egocentric.*[41] Cognitive decision rules are best understood as the use of simplified images of reality and the selective treatment of incoming information to bolster these simplified portraits of the more complex reality, to the extent of ignoring evidence which may not fit into the policy maker's constructed image of reality. Perhaps the most common of these cognitive methods is the use of historical analogies, which shall be discussed in detail later in this chapter. Janis's affiliative heuristics refer to modes of thinking which seek a solution to the problem at hand, but one that will not endanger relationships with subordinates or superiors. The emphasis here is on the preservation of harmony and the discouragement of conflict or tension amongst policy makers. As will be shown, the pursuit of unanimity and collegiality may provide a fertile ground for the most adverse symptoms of groupthink, where existing group norms may exacerbate inherent individual flaws. Finally, Janis's self-centric and emotive (eccentric) mechanism which policy makers may resort to in times of stress is designed to satisfy the personal motives or emotional needs of the policy maker, which may include the need for power or desire to control – often explained as compensation mechanisms for insecurity or lack of confidence in one's ability to manage the crisis successfully. It is likely then that leaders with deep egocentric needs or desires will harden their positions and put forward more hawkish policies.[42]

---

[40] O. R. Holsti, 'Cognitive Dynamics and Images of the Enemy: Dulles and Russia,' in D. J. Finlay, O. R. Holsti, and R. Fagen (eds.), *Enemies in Politics* (Chicago: Rand McNally, 1967), 25–96, and 'Crisis Decision Making,' in B. Glad (ed.), *Psychological Dimensions of War* (Beverly Hills, CA: Sage, 1999), 116–142; R. Jervis, *Perception and Misperceptions in International Politics* (Princeton, NJ: Princeton University Press, 1976); M. A. Milburn, *Persuasion and Politics: The Social Psychology of Public Opinion* (Pacific Cove, CA: Brooks/Cole, 1991).

[41] I. L. Janis, Crucial Decisions: Leadership in Policymaking and Crisis Management (New York: Free Press, 1989).

[42] R. N. Lebow and J. G. Stein, *We All Lost the Cold War* (Princeton, NJ: Princeton University Press, 1994); C. Parker and E. K. Stern, 'Blindsided? September 11 and the Origins of Strategic Surprise,' *Political Psychology*, 23 (2002), 601–630.

Understanding how personality traits affect policy choices are particularly important in relation to leaders because of the responsibility associated with the role. As the overview of George's and Johnson's types of presidential management has shown, the combination of role and personality results in unique styles of management, as presidents differ in how they store, process, and evaluate information and advice. This, in turn, has important implications for the structuring and processing of decision-making in foreign policy, particularly during international crises. Furthermore, recent studies of presidential management and the advisory system support the basic premise of George's and Johnson's studies about the linkage between the nature of the advisory system and the individual make-up of the decision group.[43]

The Process of U.S. Foreign Policy: Rationality, Bureaucratic Politics, and Small-Group Decision-Making

Rationality and alternative decision models

How do leaders make decisions? What are the defining characteristics of the process of foreign policy decision-making? Assumptions of rationality in foreign policy have long been the conventional wisdom. Indeed, at first glance, the rational actor model of foreign policy seems attractive, as Allison and Halperin pointed out more than three decades ago: It 'permits a quick, imaginative sorting out of problems of explanation or prediction. It serves as productive shorthand, requiring a minimum of information. It can yield an informative summary of tendencies, for example, by identifying the weight of strategic costs and benefits.'[44]

At the core of the model lies the assumption that the nation-state is a unitary, rational utility–maximising actor. Accordingly, state actions are motivated by the 'conscious calculation of advantages, calculation that in turn is based on an explicit and inherently consistent value-system.'[45] The rational process of decision-making begins with the survey of objectives and their ranking in order of preference. All

[43] Garrison, 'Games Advisors Play'; Preston, *The President and His Inner Circle*.

[44] G. Allison and M. H. Halperin, 'Bureaucratic Politics: A Paradigm and Some Policy Implications,' in R. Tanter and R. H. Ullman (eds.), *Theory and Policy in International Relations* (Princeton, NJ: Princeton University Press, 1972), 44.

[45] G. Allison, 'Conceptual Models and the Cuban Missile Crisis,' *American Political Science Review*, 63:3 (September 1969), 693.

alternative courses of actions are then considered according to their
expected benefits and costs. Finally, a decision is made based on value-
maximising choice. Conversely, a bad foreign policy decision is likely
to be the product of inappropriate values or lack of foresight, conditioned by uncertainty, misperceptions, bias, or incomplete information.[46]

Despite its theoretical prominence over the years, the notion of rationality in decision-making has become somewhat of a moot assumption.
Like the typologies of presidential styles of management, the rational
actor model is closer to the ideal than the real. Rather than an orderly,
clearly defined, and well-informed process of decision-making, foreign
policy making is often characterised by a plethora of institutional and
organisational constraints, further compounded by human errors of
perception and judgment. An alternative to the idea of optimum rationality is Herbert Simon's notion of *bounded rationality*. The complexity of foreign policy, coupled with the invariable limitations of
knowledge and cognitive capacities of policy makers, cannot produce
an optimum outcome, as only a limited number of aspects of each
alternative can be properly evaluated at any given time. Furthermore,
policy makers will often settle for the first option which is satisfactory
enough, rather than searching endlessly for the 'best' option. Accordingly, argues Simon, choices of foreign policy decisions are based on
picking the least unsatisfactory course of action.[47]

A more recent alternative to the rationality model is the advancement of poliheuristic (PH) theory which bridges the gap between
rational-choice theories and cognitive approaches to foreign policy
analysis. This alternative approach to decision-making postulates a
two-level stage of the decision process. First, the set of possible policy
options is reduced by applying a simplified noncompensatory analysis which eliminates those options deemed unacceptable. Second, the
remaining options are then calculated in a cost-benefit analysis to max-
imise benefits and minimise costs.[48] A key contribution of this theory

[46] S. D. Krasner, 'Are Bureaucracies Important? (Or Allison Wonderland),' *Foreign Policy*, 7 (Summer 1972), 159–179.
[47] H. Simon, *Administrative Behavior* (New York: Macmillan, 1957), and *Models of Bounded Rationality* (Cambridge, MA: MIT Press, 1982).
[48] A. Mintz, 'The Decision to Attack Iraq: A Noncompensatory Theory of Decision Making,' *Journal of Conflict Resolution*, 37:4 (December 1993), 595–618, and 'How Do Leaders Make Decisions? A Poliheuristic Perspective,' *Journal of Conflict*

is the assumption that decision-makers use a mixture of decision models, some of which are less efficient than others. Moreover, it has been successfully applied to situations outside the experience of U.S. presidential systems, including democratic and nondemocratic polities, as well as various phases during international crises.[49]

The *bureaucratic politics* model of decision-making offers a more acute challenge to notions of rationality. The basic assumption is that the process of decision-making is inherently irrational. Foreign policy is not the product of a logical, coherent process but rather a battleground between various interests, where a decision is the result of bargaining and compromise between officials with incompatible interests and unequal influence.[50] Furthermore, the rational assumption of the state as a unitary actor is also dropped. According to Halperin, governmental decisions are

> more often an amalgam of a number of coincidental occurrences: actions brought about by presidential decisions (not always those intended), actions that are really manoeuvres to influence presidential decisions, actions resulting from decisions in unrelated areas, and actions taken at lower levels by junior participants without informing their superiors or the president.[51]

By far, the most widely cited study of bureaucratic politics is Graham Allison's *Essence of Decision*, which examines American decision-making during the Cuban Missile Crisis through three alternative theoretical models: (1) rational actor, (2) organisational process, and (3) governmental politics. Allison's work was a landmark in the study of the role of bureaucracy in foreign policy making and presented for

Resolution, 48:1 (February 2004), 3–13, and 'Applied Decision Analysis: Utilizing Poliheuristic Theory to Explain and Predict Foreign Policy and National Security Decisions,' *International Studies Perspectives*, 6:1 (February 2005), 94–98.

[49] A. Astorino-Courtois and B. Trusty, 'Degrees of Difficulty: The Effect of Israeli Policy Shifts on Syrian Peace Decisions,' *Journal of Conflict Resolution*, 44:3 (June 2000), 359–377; B. J. Kinne, 'Decision Making in Autocratic Regimes: A Poliheuristic Perspective,' *International Studies Perspectives*, 5:1 (February 2005), 114–128; A. Maleki, 'Decision Making in Iran's Foreign Policy: A Heuristic Approach,' *Journal of Social Affairs*, 19:73 (Spring 2002), 39–53; M. Ye, 'Poliheuristic Theory, Bargaining, and Crisis Decision Making,' *Foreign Policy Analysis*, 3:3 (July 2007), 317–344.

[50] Allison, *Essence of Decision*, 162.

[51] M. H. Halperin, *Bureaucratic Politics and Foreign Policy* (Washington, DC: Brookings Institution, 1971), 293.

the first time a purposeful theoretical framework to enable a more analytically rich approach. Allison's formulation of three theoretical models helped to develop alternative explanations for decisions and to provide more scientific foundations to the study of the bureaucracy and foreign policy. The study's primary contribution is in demonstrating the relevance of theory to the explanation of tangible events. In particular, Allison's Model II and Model III proved groundbreaking in explaining how organisational behaviour and internal bargaining among advisors affect the making of foreign policy. Since its publication, many scholars have extended Allison's theoretical approach, and some have applied it to noncrisis situations as well.[52]

Despite their wide applicability, Allison's models have faced growing criticism over the years. Model I has been criticised for the simplified and inadequate application of the assumption of nation-states as unitary rational actors to the Cuban Missile Crisis, and Model III in particular has been attacked for being too complex and for ignoring the importance of hierarchical chain of command within the bargaining process, as well as for failing to explain adequately initiatives taken by the president without bureaucratic involvement.[53] More broadly, while notions of bureaucratic politics tell us why certain actors propose certain policy positions ('where you stand depends on where you sit'), they fail to provide a cogent account of how the consequences of those alternative courses of actions are evaluated.[54] In reality, the model's basic proposition – 'positions dictate actions' – may sit rather loosely

[52] See J. Steinbruner, *The Cybernetic Theory of Decision* (Princeton, NJ: Princeton University Press, 1974); W. Kohl, 'The Nixon-Kissinger Foreign Policy System and U.S.-Europe Relations,' *World Politics*, 28:1 (October 1975), 1–43; Snyder and Diesing, *Conflict among Nations*; Z. Maoz, 'The Decision to Raid Entebbe: Decision Analysis Applied to Crisis Behavior,' *Journal of Conflict Resolution*, 25:4 (December 1981), 677–707.

[53] See, in particular, J. Bendor and T. H. Hammond, 'Rethinking Allison's Models,' *American Political Science Review*, 86:2 (June 1992), 301–322; D. A. Welch, 'The Organizational Process and Bureaucratic Politics Paradigm: Retrospect and Prospect,' *International Security*, 17:2 (Autumn 1992), 112–146. See also Krasner, 'Are Bureaucracies Important?'; S. Smith, 'Allison and the Cuban Missile Crisis: A Review of the Bureaucratic Politics Model of Foreign Policy Decision Making,' *Millennium*, 19:1 (1980), 21–40.

[54] R. Axelrod, 'Argumentation in Foreign Policy Settings: Britain in 1918, Munich in 1938 and Japan in 1970,' *Journal of Conflict Resolution*, 21:4 (December 1977), 728.

on the actors.[55] A policy maker may argue for a policy position not because of his or her bureaucratic position but because of certain cognitive or psychological conditioning. As various studies have shown, the 'pure' explanation of policy preferences as the product of bureaucratic positions fails to account for the role of individuals and their personal experiences.[56] Perhaps the most pertinent policy implication of bureaucratic politics is the prospect of presidential decisions not being followed through by the bureaucracy. The bureaucracy's career officials may not share a sense of loyalty to the president and his policies, and they may have different interests and views. The potential threat to the president is that while he or she has the power to make decisions, the bureaucracy is in charge of the ultimate task of implementation.

The power of the bureaucracy to resist presidential authority was particularly acute during the Nixon years. Remarkably, the potential danger of a rebellious State Department sabotaging Nixon's foreign policy initiatives was first raised on 11 November 1968, less than a week after Nixon's election. Bryce Harlow, one of Nixon's campaign aides, observed that 'Mr Nixon's candidacy not only was unsupported by nearly 90% of the personnel of the Department of State – it was opposed, at least passively.'[57] As the cases of Cambodia and India-Pakistan will demonstrate, the inevitable result was a dissenting bureaucracy that rebelled against the policies emanating from the White House.

While the works by Allison and Halperin on bureaucratic politics remain hugely influential, foreign policy analysis literature since the 1990s has attempted to move beyond the holistic models of decision-making, such as bureaucratic politics and groupthink, by building bridges between foreign policy analysis and constructivist schools of international relations, with considerable emphasis on the role of

[55] M. Hollis and S. Smith, 'Roles and Reasons in Foreign Policy Decision Making,' *British Journal of Political Science*, 16:3 (July 1986), 275.

[56] Two recent examples are D. P. Houghton, *U.S. Foreign Policy and the Iran Hostage Crisis* (Cambridge: Cambridge University Press, 2001); and S. A. Yetiv, *Explaining Foreign Policy: U.S. Decision-Making and the Persian Gulf War* (Baltimore: Johns Hopkins University Press, 2004).

[57] Memo, Harlow to the Republican Key Issues Committee, 'President Nixon and the Department of State.'

images, ideas, and identities as explanatory factors of foreign policy behaviour.[58]

Small-group decision-making: groupthink and historical analogies

Almost regardless of regime type or the personality traits of the leader, most foreign policy choices are processed and prioritised in small groups, especially during international crises. The structural settings put in place by the president are designed to facilitate decision-making in the advisory group and to ensure the orderly procedures within the bureaucracy. Furthermore, as has been discussed, these structural settings and the make-up of the advisory system are dependent on the president's personality. Nevertheless, as various studies have shown, small groups often fail to perform well because of inherent impediments in the decision-making process.[59] Amongst the most common malfunctions in small-group decision-making process are excessive conformity and insufficient diversity amongst advisors, on the one hand, and overly competitive group process to the degree of explicit conflict among advisors, on the other. Indeed, many studies have attempted to provide 'recipes for success' and ways to overcome these all-too-common malfunctions in the advisory process.[60] The risk of vicious competition among advisors for presidential attention is a common problem is the making of U.S. foreign (as well as domestic) policies. This tension is particularly evident in the relationship between

---

[58] D. P. Houghton, 'Reinvigorating the Study of Foreign Policy Decision Making: Toward a Constructivist Approach,' *Foreign Policy Analysis*, 3:1 (January 2007), 24–45.

[59] See, for example, J. de Rivera, *The Psychological Dimension of Foreign Policy* (Columbus, OH: Charles E. Merrill, 1968); George, *Presidential Decisionmaking in Foreign Policy*; P. 't Hart, E. K. Stern, and B. Sundelius (eds.), *Beyond Groupthink: Political Group Dynamics and Foreign Policy-Making* (Ann Arbor: University of Michigan Press, 1997); G. R. Hess, *Presidential Decisions for War: Korea, Vietnam, and the Persian Gulf* (Baltimore: Johns Hopkins University Press, 2001); Haney, *Organizing for Foreign Policy Crises*.

[60] See, in particular, Janis, *Groupthink*; A. L. George, 'The Case for Multiple Advocacy in Making Foreign Policy,' *American Political Science Review*, 66:3 (September 1972), 751–785; A. L. George and E. K. Stern, 'Harnessing Conflict in Foreign Policy Making: From Devil's to Multiple Advocacy,' *Presidential Studies Quarterly*, 33:4 (September 2002), 484–508.

national security advisors and secretaries of states, which for several decades has shaped various institutional and organisational patterns of foreign policy making.[61]

Perhaps the most widely cited work on small-group decision-making is Janis's study of *groupthink*. Groupthink is 'a mode of thinking that people engage in when they are deeply involved in a cohesive in-group, when the members' strivings for unanimity override their motivation to realistically appraise alternative courses of action.'[62] In this situation, existing group norms may exacerbate inherent individual flaws. The decision-making process within the advisory group can be seriously damaged when group loyalty and cohesion are so strong that important tasks such as evaluation of alternatives are not performed effectively. Some of the antecedents that are likely to bring about groupthink are high group cohesiveness, directive leadership, high stress from external threat, and homogeneity of members' social background. These conditions may lead to overconfidence, cognitive rigidity, and pressure on dissenters to conform. Janis lists seven defects in the decision-making process that can result from groupthink: (1) incomplete survey of alternatives, (2) incomplete survey of objectives, (3) failure to examine risks of preferred courses of action, (4) failure to reevaluate initially rejected courses of action, (5) poor information search, (6) selection bias in processing information at hand, and (7) failure to work out contingency plans.[63] A suboptimal performance is thus not a product of individual flaws or irrational behaviour on the part of the group members but rather the result of group dynamics. As the economist Kenneth Arrow suggested in his *impossibility theorem*, individual rational behaviour cannot be aggregated to produce an overall rational outcome.[64] Furthermore, as Janis himself admitted, the link

---

[61] See I. M. Destler, L. H. Gelb, and A. Lake, *Our Own Worst Enemy: The Unmaking of American Foreign Policy* (New York: Simon and Schuster, 1984); C. V. Crabb and K. V. Mulchay, *Presidential and Foreign Policy Making: From FDR to Reagan* (Baton Rouge: Louisiana State University, 1986).

[62] Janis, *Groupthink*, 9.

[63] Ibid., 175. In a similar fashion to Janis, George identifies nine possible malfunctions in the advisory process, among them premature consensus on the nature of the problem and on responses to it; failure to cover the full range of options; and presidential failure to ascertain how firm the consensus is among the advisors. See George, *Presidential Decisionmaking in Foreign Policy*, 121–136.

[64] K. Arrow, *Social Choices and Individual Values* (New Haven, CT: Yale University Press, 1970, 2nd ed.).

between defective process and defective outcomes is rather intangible, as 'defective decisions based on misinformation and poor judgment sometimes lead to successful outcomes.'[65] As the case of the Yom Kippur War will show, guided largely by instinct, policy makers are often right for the wrong reasons.

Groupthink tendencies can be counteracted in several ways. Janis recommends encouraging individuals in the group to be more critical, adopting a neutral stand by the leader, and working several groups simultaneously.[66] Another mechanism to overcome the problem of group conformity, which has been further elaborated by Alexander George, is the *devil's advocate*, which requires a preselected individual in the group to take the role of presenting dissenting views, thereby encouraging others in the group to present their genuine views and point out flaws in others.'[67] As excessive conformity was a rare trait in WSAG meetings, there was little reason to appoint a devil's advocate. Although Kissinger's views tended to dominate group meetings, other members might have felt obliged to present opposing views for that purpose exactly, which was particularly evident in meetings during the India-Pakistan War.

While George's *devil's advocate* is designed to overcome excessive conformity in the advisory group, his alternative model, *multiple advocacy*, confronts another malfunction in small-group dynamics, namely, explicit conflict between advisors. This model is designed 'to moderate tendencies toward pathological conflict/competition among advisers such as those associated with more vicious forms of cabinet and bureaucratic politics.'[68] Although the model is designed to counteract conflict among advisors, a certain degree of diversity is nevertheless important to create an atmosphere of critical and creative thinking.[69] George's *multiple advocacy* calls for presidential involvement in the decision-making process early on, before final recommendations

[65] Janis, *Groupthink*, 11.

[66] Ibid., 260–271.

[67] George, 'The Case for Multiple Advocacy in Making Foreign Policy'; George and Stern, 'Harnessing Conflict in Foreign Policy Making.'

[68] George and Stern, 'Harnessing Conflict in Foreign Policy Making,' 485.

[69] See Janis, *Groupthink*; K. M. Hult, 'Advising the President,' in G. C. Edwards, J. H. Kessel, and B. Rockman (eds.), *Researching the Presidency: Vital Questions, New Approaches* (Pittsburgh, PA: University of Pittsburgh Press, 1993), 111–160; D. Gergen, *Eyewitness to Power* (New York: Simon & Schuster, 2000).

are agreed upon. However, it is the national security advisor who is
assigned the central role in this model. Acting as a *neutral custodian*,
the national security advisor's task is to ensure that staff resources,
information, power, and access to the president are distributed appro-
priately amongst the advisors or the governmental departments. The
model accepts that conflict among advisors over policy issues is
inevitable in any complex organisational process of policy making,
but the aim is to build on the diversity of views to produce a wide
range of policy options, in the hope that this carefully managed and
structured advisory system would result in adequate consideration of
policy alternatives. This ideal mechanism rarely resembled the realities
of the policy-making process during the Nixon years.

    Second-generation FPA studies have attempted to refine our under-
standing of small-group dynamics.[70] Herek, Janis, and Huth build
upon Janis's *groupthink* to draw conclusions about the relationship
between decision-making and outcome in U.S. foreign policy crises.[71]
Examining nineteen crises in U.S. foreign policy during the Cold
War, and building upon Janis's aforementioned seven malfunctions
in decision-making, they conclude that a relationship between high-
quality decision-making process (with few or no malfunctions) and
successful outcome of crises can be established. High-quality process
can be achieved if decision-makers follow the *vigilant problem-solving*
model of Janis and Mann, which assumes rational behaviour and
includes a careful search for information and alternatives and planning of contingencies.[72] However, not only is the notion of 'high-
quality' process extremely subjective and arbitrary, the study also fails
to address the importance of external factors in shaping the outcomes
of international crises, even though the authors themselves point out
that crisis outcome is also dependent on decisions made by adversary

---

[70] Representative of this second generation of FPA literature are the works of Herek,
Janis, and Huth, 'Decision Making During International Crises,' and 'Quality
of Decision Making During the Cuban Missile Crisis: Major Errors in Welch's
Reassessment,' *Journal of Conflict Resolution*, 33:3 (September 1989), 446–459;
C. McCauley, 'The Nature of Social Influence in Groupthink: Compliance and Inter-
nalization,' *Journal of Personality and Social Psychology*, 57:2 (1989), 250–260;
Hart, Stern, and Sundelius, *Beyond Groupthink*.
[71] Herek, Janis, and Huth, 'Decision Making During International Crises.'
[72] I. L. Janis and L. Mann, *Decision Making: A Psychological Analysis of Conflict,
Choice, and Commitment* (New York: The Free Press, 1977).

governments, as well as chance factors. As Welch noted, 'one side's decision-making process...will never determine absolutely the outcome.'[73] In a recent study of the linkage between process and outcome in foreign policy making, Schafer and Crichlow suggest that structural factors (such as group insulation and the use of methodological procedures) and information processing (including survey of objectives and alternatives) are related to outcomes in terms of national interest and level of international conflict, while situation variables, such as stress and time restraints, have only marginal impact on outcomes and the quality of information processing.[74]

Policy makers frequently deal with the complexities and uncertainties that are associated with crises by simplifying their strategies and the difficult decisions they have to make. These strategies may include rigidity in accommodating new information and reluctance to modify preconceptions, avoiding hard decisions, and dependence on simple models to assess the future behaviour of adversaries.[75] Indeed, the four crises examined in this book suggest that all of these mechanisms have been used on various occasions. Perhaps the most popular strategy that policy makers may resort to in their effort to minimise the risks of uncertainty is the use of historical analogies.[76] While the simplification of the lessons from similar precedents may help policy makers to deal with the uncertainty of a current crisis, this strategy often has detrimental effects on the quality of the decision-making process and the overall outcome. In his study of U.S. foreign policy in the Middle East, Dowty points out that policy makers tend to learn from crises that were handled poorly, while past examples of effective management are often disregarded. In other words, 'the bigger the success, the

---

[73] D. A. Welch, 'Crisis Decision Making Reconsidered,' *Journal of Conflict Resolution*, 33:3 (September 1989), 440. Welch also criticises the authors' methodology. See their rebuttal in Herek, Janis, and Huth, 'Quality of U.S. Decision-Making during the Cuban Missile Crisis.'

[74] M. Shafer and S. Crichlow, 'The Process-Outcome Connection in Foreign Policy Decision-Making.'

[75] Jervis, *Perception and Misperception in International Politics*; George, *Presidential Decisionmaking in Foreign Policy*.

[76] A recent study suggests that a third of proposals for the first U.S. programme for development and aid were based on analogies. See M. Breuning, 'The Role of Analogies and Abstract Reasoning in Decision-Making: Evidence from the Debate over Truman's Proposal for Development Assistance,' *International Studies Quarterly*, 47:2 (June 2003), 229–245.

less the learning process.'[77] Lessons are usually drawn from traumatic, significant events in the past; thus, when policy makers are confronted with alternative options, often 'continuity of policy follows success, while innovation follows failure.'[78] Furthermore, policy makers tend to keep the analogies simple, as complexity often constrains their applicability to the current crisis. Therefore, the case of German aggression in the 1930s and the disastrous consequences of appeasement have proven popular analogies over the years, despite their questionable applicability to Cold War crises.[79] By emphasising the abstracted similarities between current and past crises, policy makers undermine the crucial differences between the occurrences, which inevitably impede the quality of the advice submitted to the president at the end of the process. Nixon's peculiar reference to the 1930s during the incursion into Cambodia, or the use of no less than a dozen historical analogies by President Carter's group of advisors during the Iran hostage crisis, illustrate the point made by various studies: Regardless of the issue, the misuse of analogies may lead to poor forecasts of policy actions which leaders may contemplate. A structured and controlled approach to using historical analogies is needed, which should include description of the target situation and possible analogies, as well as rating similarities and deriving forecasts.[80]

As noted previously, recent FPA studies have attempted to move beyond one-dimensional models of decision-making, such as groupthink, that fail to acknowledge the complex, multidimensional environment in which decisions are made.[81] Accordingly, it is accepted

---

[77] A. Dowty, *Middle East Crisis: U.S. Decision-Making in 1958, 1970, and 1973* (Berkeley: University of California Press, 1984), 376.

[78] D. Reiter, 'Learning, Realism, and Alliances: The Weight of the Shadow of the Past,' *World Politics*, 46:4 (July 1994), 490.

[79] Y. F. Khong, *Analogies at War: Korea, Munich, Dien Bien Phu, and the Vietnam Decisions of 1965* (Princeton, NJ: Princeton University Press, 1992); S. MacDonald, 'Hitler's Shadow: Historical Analogies and the Iraqi Invasion of Kuwait,' *Diplomacy & Statecraft*, 13:4 (December 2002), 29–59.

[80] See J. S. Armstrong, *Long-Range Forecasting* (New York: John Wiley, 1985, 2nd ed.); R. E. Neustadt and E. R. May, *Thinking in Time: The Use of History for Decision Makers* (New York: The Free Press, 1986); M. Pei, 'Lessons of the Past,' *Foreign Policy*, 137 (July–August 2003), 52–55; Houghton, *U.S. Foreign Policy and the Iran Hostage Crisis.*

[81] S. Fuller and R. Aldag, 'Challenging the Mindguards: Moving Small Group Analysis beyond Groupthink,' in Hart, Stern, and Sundelius, *Beyond Groupthink*, 55–94;

today that groupthink is just one of many possible models of small-group dynamics and that what is needed is a better understanding of how different individual characteristics interact and influence across different levels of analysis to produce a policy at the end of the process. Future research on small-group dynamics must move beyond the American experience. The most influential works by Allison, Halperin, Janis, and George are heavily grounded in the hierarchical, presidential system of the United States, and as Jean Garrison has noted recently, 'the critical issue in this instance is not nationality, but the degree of power-sharing in the policymaking group,' and, as such, future research must focus on political systems where power is distributed more horizontally than vertically (such as cabinet systems).[82]

   As the following chapter will demonstrate, the advisory group's dual task is to help the president reach a decision that is based on sound, well-informed advice and then to provide support in implementing the chosen policy. Often, however, there is tension between 'full consideration of all options' and 'perseverance in a policy course.'[83] Destler surmised correctly more than three decades ago that faced with the dilemma between policy choice and policy execution, presidents often enter the White House with unfavourable views of existing policies and procedures and are eager to make an impact in their search for better alternatives. In due course, however, the realities of the tasks at hand sink in and the president settles for a more pragmatic approach. Indeed, the transformation of the Nixon-Kissinger foreign policy system 'from an open process, oriented toward widening Presidential options, to a very closed implementation system' provides the quintessential example of the divergence between theory and practice in the making of U.S. foreign policy.[84]

C. F. Hermann et al., 'Resolve, Accept, or Avoid: Effects of Group Conflict on Foreign Policy Decisions,' *International Studies Review*, 3:2 (Summer 2001), 133–168.

[82] J. A. Garrison, 'Foreign Policymaking and Group Dynamics: Where We've Been and Where We're Going,' *International Studies Review*, 5:2 (June 2003), 181.

[83] Destler, 'National Security Advice to U.S. Presidents,' 166.

[84] Ibid.

2

The Making of U.S. Foreign Policy During the Nixon-Kissinger Years

> Certain day-to-day problems are held up because [Kissinger] will not allow the inter-agency machinery to go to work on them... Dr. Kissinger's references to the representatives of the State Department, Defence Department etc at Under Secretary level as 'my advisers' do not contribute to a smooth working of the policy machine.[1]
>
> Research Department, British Foreign and Commonwealth Office, 9 February 1972

Students and observers of the Nixon administration are faced with particular difficulty when attempting to evaluate foreign policy making during this period, as the president's remarkable achievements in foreign affairs are sometimes hard to reconcile with his less remarkable personality. President Truman described Nixon as 'a no-good lying bastard. He can lie out of both sides of his mouth at the same time, and if he ever caught himself telling the truth, he'd lie just to keep his hand in.'[2] Even Henry Kissinger warned in 1968: 'Richard Nixon's being nominated by the Republican party is a disaster and thank God he can't be elected president or the whole country will be a disaster area.'[3]

---

[1] Memo, Research Department, FCO, 'The US Policy-Making Process under the Nixon Administration,' 9 February 1972. FCO 51/262, National Archives, London (henceforth NA).

[2] Cited in W. A. DeGregorio, *The Complete Book of U.S. Presidents: From George Washington to Bill Clinton* (New York: Wings Books, 1996, 5th ed.), 600.

[3] Cited in J. Hoff, *Nixon Reconsidered* (New York: Basic Books, 1994), 154.

While Kissinger's remark should be placed in context – it was made while he was advising Nelson Rockefeller, Nixon's chief rival in the 1968 Republican presidential elections – it nevertheless suggests that Nixon's disgraceful resignation from office in 1974 following the Watergate affair merely completed the demonization of Nixon, and that adverse publicity had accompanied the man since the beginning of his political career, in the immediate aftermath of World War II.

Nevertheless, as Joan Hoff accurately observed, the one area in which Nixon's achievements have mostly obscured his notorious personality traits has been foreign policy.[4] By the time of his resignation in August 1974, Nixon had achieved some extraordinary feats in the global arena against a background of domestic turmoil and a fierce superpower rivalry. These achievements include the opening of relations with China, détente with the Soviet Union, ending the war in Vietnam, brokering unprecedented agreements in the Middle East between bitter foes, and enhancing America's position and leverage in the Arab world.[5] While none of these achievements is impervious to criticism, in strict foreign policy terms, the Nixon years are undoubtedly the most pro-active and dynamic of the Cold War presidencies.

However, in parallel to these achievements, some less glorious facets of Nixon the man and his policies were readily apparent, even in the foreign policy arena. His fixation with secrecy and back-channelling in the conduct of foreign policy, his disregard of bureaucratic advice in favour of gut instincts, his exclusion of cabinet members from important policy decisions, his unremitting mistrust and suspicion of those close to him, all cast a shadow over Nixon's foreign policy achievements.

Perhaps one of the most intriguing aspects of the making of foreign policy during this period concerns Nixon's complex yet incredibly prolific partnership with his Special Assistant for National Security Affairs, Henry Kissinger. Indeed, so closely are the two men associated in the historiography of the period that it is often referred to as

---

[4] Ibid., 147.
[5] Moreover, students of the Nixon presidency often tend to ignore Nixon's domestic achievements. In her groundbreaking study of the Nixon presidency, Joan Hoff argues that academics and journalists alike tend to underrate Nixon's success on a variety of domestic policies (for example, welfare and health and economic reforms), while attributing foreign policy successes almost solely to Henry Kissinger.

the 'Nixinger' years. Building on the theoretical themes of structures, processes, and personalities in U.S. foreign policy making, this chapter shall now examine how this tripartite worked in practice to produce perhaps the most ambitious design of an advisory system in the history of the National Security Council (NSC). Furthermore, the chapter will explain how Kissinger came to dominate the national security agenda by making himself indispensable to the president as a source of information and advice. Through this study of their personalities and the structures they imposed on the foreign policy machinery, we can understand the workings of the Washington Special Actions Group (WSAG) – one of the most active interagency groups, though hitherto little known – during four major foreign policy crises.

The bulk of the following discussion is dedicated to the reorganisation of the advisory system and the institutionalisation of the WSAG and is based almost solely on primary sources such as recently declassified governmental records and interviews. The contribution of personalities to the make-up of this national security system will be examined in reference to specific examples and where appropriate. Over the years, the literature on Nixon's and Kissinger's personalities and the enthralling nature of their relationship has reached mammoth proportions, and there is little new that can be said about Kissinger's drive for power or Nixon's dark side *per se*. The main contribution of Jussi Hanhimaki's excellent recent book on Kissinger, for example, is not in telling us something new about the personality traits of the national security advisor but rather in discovering new archival material that confirms what we already know. The first dedicated book on Henry Kissinger appeared as early as 1972 with David Landau's *Kissinger: The Uses of Power*, which was followed by studies of Kissinger by Stephen Graubard, the Kalb brothers, Bruce Mazlish, John Stoessinger, Roger Morris, Coral Bell, Peter Dickson, and others in the 1970s who were quick to speak of that decade as the 'Kissinger era.' Since then, more studies followed, including those by Robert Schulzinger, Seymour Hersh, Walter Isaacson, Jussi Hanhimaki, Jeremi Suri, and others.[6] Biographical and introspective accounts of Nixon are equally

---

[6] D. Landau, *Kissinger: The Uses of Power* (Boston: Houghton Mifflin, 1972); S. Graubard, *Kissinger: Portrait of a Mind* (New York: Norton, 1973); M. Kalb and B. Kalb, *Kissinger* (Boston: Little, Brown, 1974); B. Mazlish, *Kissinger: The European*

ubiquitous and include the works by Jules Witcover; Fawn Brodie; Stephen Ambrose; Tom Wicker; Jonathan Aitken; Joan Hoff; Volkan, Itzkowitz, and Dodd; Monica Crowley; Melvin Small; Anthony Summers; Richard Reeves; and Robert Dallek.[7]

A common trait of many of these works is the effort to decipher the minds of the two thespians: What was the source of Kissinger's appetite for power? What drove Nixon to the abyss of Watergate? Why did they work so well together despite the mutual suspicion and rancour? A crucial story which is often neglected, however, is how did the psychological make-up of this odd couple affect the organisation of foreign policy and, in turn, the making of foreign policy, particularly during international crises wherein personalities played a particularly important role in the shaping of the nature and outcome of the decision-making process. Therefore, rather than narrowly focusing on personalities, this chapter offers an original analysis of the product

Mind in American Policy (New York: Basic Books, 1976); J. Stoessinger, *Henry Kissinger: The Anguish of Power* (New York: W. W. Norton, 1976); R. Morris, *Uncertain Greatness: Henry Kissinger and American Foreign Policy* (New York: Harper & Row, 1977); C. Bell, *The Diplomacy of Détente: The Kissinger Era* (New York: St. Martin's Press, 1977); Dickson, *Kissinger and the Meaning of History*; S. Hersh, *The Prince of Power: Kissinger in the Nixon White House* (New York: Summit Books, 1983); W. Isaacson, *Kissinger: A Biography* (New York: Simon & Schuster, 1992); J. Hanhimaki, *The Flawed Architect: Henry Kissinger and American Foreign Policy* (New York: Oxford University Press, 2004); J. Suri, *Henry Kissinger and the American Century* (Cambridge, MA: Belknap Press of Harvard University Press, 2007). For an excellent review of Kissinger's historiography, see J. Hanhimaki, '"Dr. Kissinger" or "Mr. Henry"? Kissingerology, Thirty Years and Counting,' *Diplomatic History*, 27:5 (November 2003), 637–676.

7 J. Witcover, *The Resurrection of Richard Nixon* (New York: G. P. Putnam's Sons, 1970); F. M. Brodie, *Richard Nixon: The Shaping of His Character* (New York: W. W. Norton, 1981); S. E. Ambrose, *Nixon: The Education of a Politician, 1913–1962* (New York: Simon & Schuster, 1987), *Nixon: The Triumph of a Politician, 1962–1972* (New York: Simon & Schuster, 1989), and *Nixon: Ruin and Recovery, 1973–1990* (New York: Simon & Schuster, 1991); T. Wicker, *One of Us: Richard Nixon and the American Dream* (New York: Random House, 1991); J. Aitken, *Nixon: A Life* (Washington, DC: Regency Publishing, 1993); J. Hoff, *Nixon Reconsidered*; V. D. Volkan, N. Itzkowitz, and A. W. Dodd, *Richard Nixon: A Psychobiography* (New York: Columbia University Press, 1997); M. Crowley, *Nixon in Winter: The Final Revelations* (New York: I. B. Tauris, 1998); M. Small, *The Presidency of Richard Nixon* (Lawrence: University Press of Kansas, 1999); A. Summers, *The Arrogance of Power: The Secret World of Richard Nixon* (New York: G. P. Putnam's Sons, 2000); R. Reeves, *President Nixon: Alone in the White House* (New York: Touchstone, 2001); R. Dallek, *Nixon and Kissinger: Partners in Power* (New York: Harper Collins, 2007).

of this interaction between the personal characteristics of the two men and their visions of foreign policy.

The Early Days

In May 1968, Richard Nixon made a public statement about his plans for organising his presidency should he be elected. Some six months before his election, Nixon emphasised the importance of delegating responsibilities to other people and departments. His watchword was not to concentrate too much power in the White House:

> For one thing, I would disperse power, spread it among able people. Men operate best only if they are given the chance to operate at full capacity ... instead of taking all power to myself, I'd select cabinet members who could do their jobs, and each of them would have the stature and the power to function effectively ... [W]hen a President takes all the real power to himself, those around him become puppets. They shrivel up and become less and less creative ... [a]nd your most creative people can't develop in a monolithic, centralized power set-up.[8]

Only days after his inauguration, however, press reports suggested that Nixon found it difficult to make foreign policy decisions within the executive branch. *The New York Times* reported in February 1969 that 'the first sign of trouble' for the administration had appeared, suggesting some tension in the relationships between the White House and the State Department, the Defense Department, and the Senate Foreign Relations Committee.[9] These early tensions would come to epitomise the making of U.S. foreign policy during the Nixon administration.

This chapter will review how and, more important, why Nixon and Kissinger's complex yet effective design of the NSC system was often at odds with the realities of foreign policy making. Specifically, this chapter will demonstrate that while Nixon and Kissinger had a solid thesis about America's role in the world, they found it difficult to apply it to the formalistic, orderly structure which they introduced. Ironically, whereas the NSC system was reformed as an instrument to serve Nixon and Kissinger's grand design of U.S. foreign policy,

[8] E. Mazo and S. Hess, *Nixon: A Political Portrait* (New York: Harper & Row, 1968), 314–315.
[9] J. Reston, 'Mr. Nixon's First Whiff of Trouble,' *New York Times*, 9 February 1969.

ultimately this powerful dyad not only took foreign policy decision-making outside the formal system, but they also manipulated the very system that they had created.

Upon entering the White House, Richard Nixon was well aware of the importance of a centrally managed foreign policy system in generating effective foreign policy initiatives. One of the main changes he sought in reorganising the foreign policy machinery was a shift from a cabinet-oriented system to a staff-oriented system. Early in his presidency, Nixon recognised that the cabinet was not the most efficient forum for decision-making. Meetings often dragged on, and some of the participants talked too much or found it difficult to adjust to their new roles as cabinet members.[10] Indeed, Nixon's post-presidential criticism of the cabinet-oriented system was rather blunt: 'Cabinet government is a myth and won't work. A president should never rely on his cabinet . . . no [president] in his right mind submits anything to his cabinet . . . it is ridiculous . . . it is boring.'[11] Nixon also found the task of finding 'good people' arduous. White House Chief of Staff H. R. 'Bob' Haldeman recalled that one day Nixon 'got into problem of where you find people for government service. Must have judgment, character, loyalty, patriotism. Most lack at least two of these, especially the Eastern intellectuals.'[12]

Nixon's desire to make the White House the lynchpin of U.S. foreign policy making is well documented.[13] Following his election and before entering the White House in January 1969, Nixon had already laid plans for a White House–centred foreign policy machine. Accordingly, the first eight months of the Nixon administration were not only a period of policy formulation, they also marked a significant change in national security architecture. From mid-1970, the balance of power

[10] B. Glad and M. Link, 'President Nixon's Inner Circle of Advisers,' *Presidential Studies Quarterly*, 27:1 (Winter 1996), 14–15.

[11] Cited in Hoff, *Nixon Reconsidered*, 52.

[12] H. R. Haldeman, *The Haldeman Diaries: Inside the Nixon White House* (New York: G. P. Putnam's Sons, 1994), 145.

[13] See, for example, Kohl, 'The Nixon-Kissinger Foreign Policy System and U.S.-Europe Relations'; George, *Presidential Decisionmaking in Foreign Policy*; Hess, *Organizing the Presidency*; W. Bundy, *A Tangled Web: The Making of Foreign Policy in the Nixon Presidency* (New York: Hill and Wang, 1998); R. C. Thornton, *The Nixon-Kissinger Years: The Reshaping of American Foreign Policy* (St. Paul, MN: Paragon House, 2001, 2nd ed.).

within the administration had started to shift decisively in favour of the White House staff at the expense of the bureaucracy and cabinet members.

The effect of this change on the making of U.S. domestic and foreign policies was that, gradually, department heads found it almost impossible to access the president. Nixon's time was carefully protected by three 'gatekeepers': Bob Haldeman, John Ehrlichman, and Henry Kissinger. In his memoirs, Nixon explained the importance of imposing strict access to the president: 'I wanted to keep the Cabinet meetings in my administration to a minimum. I felt that the better each Cabinet member performed his job, the less time I should have to spend discussing it with him except for major questions of politics or policy.'[14] As Nixon's Chief of Staff, Haldeman shielded the president from 'the unending flow of government officials who "just wanted to see the president" . . . or worse: long, time-wasting discussions of some minor departmental gripe.'[15] The second member of Nixon's troika was John Ehrlichman, who was responsible for controlling cabinet and staff members' access to Nixon on the domestic front.

Henry Kissinger was the third gatekeeper. On foreign policy issues, he exercised even stricter control in preventing department heads from taking the president's time. Kissinger excluded State Department officials from certain meetings, and even kept Secretary William Rogers out of the loop on important foreign policy issues, such as the opening to China and the peace negotiations with the North Vietnamese. Questions in the press about who would lead U.S. foreign policy – Kissinger or Rogers – appeared as early as February 1969. The London-based *The Economist*, for example, reported that 'the peculiar nature of the Kissinger–State Department relationship poses problems, which will have to be sorted out if American diplomacy is to function smoothly.'[16] These observations later turned into open allegations in the U.S. Congress that Kissinger's pre-eminent position in the administration had downgraded the prestige and power of the secretary of

[14] R. Nixon, *RN: The Memoirs of Richard Nixon* (New York: Simon & Schuster, 1978), 338.

[15] In his memoirs, Haldeman adds that Nixon needed protection 'from himself' as well, with reference to Nixon's temperament and 'petty vindictive orders.' H. R. Haldeman (with J. DiMona), *The Ends of Power* (New York: Times Books, 1978), 58.

[16] 'Kissinger versus the State Department,' *The Economist*, 6 February 1969.

state and his department. Senator Stuart Symington (D-MO) complained: 'Wherever one goes in the afternoon or evening around this town, one hears our very able Secretary of State laughed at. People say he is Secretary of State in title only.'[17]

Those allegations were inevitable given the shift from a cabinet-oriented to a staff-oriented system. The hub of the new foreign policy machinery was now placed at the White House, where Henry Kissinger, in his role as the Assistant to the President for National Security Affairs (henceforth the national security advisor), would ultimately be in charge of providing the president with information and advice. Indeed, one year after entering the White House, Nixon spoke in a different tone about his foreign policy design. In his first Foreign Policy Report to Congress, Nixon described the new NSC system as one

designed to make certain that clear policy choices reach the top, so that the various positions can be fully debated in the meeting of the Council . . . I refuse to be confronted with a bureaucratic consensus that leaves me no options but acceptance or rejection, and that gives me no way of knowing what alternatives exist.[18]

The ultimate objective of the new system was to centralise decision-making on key foreign policy issues and to minimise bureaucratic meddling, particularly with regard to the three cornerstones of the new foreign policy: Vietnam, China, and the Soviet Union. The NSC staff played an important role in the new system and around fifty staff members were responsible for collecting data, processing study memoranda, organising interdepartmental groups, preparing studies, and presenting Kissinger with detailed analysis.[19] The central role of the NSC staff in the new system allowed Nixon and Kissinger to keep control of the agenda and the bureaucracy. Kissinger would also reinforce his personal views in private talks with Nixon and by monitoring

---

[17] John Osborne, 'Kissinger and Rogers,' *New Republic*, 27 March 1971.

[18] R. M. Nixon, 'First Annual Report to Congress on United States Foreign Policy for the 1970s, February 18, 1970,' *Public Papers of the Presidents of the United States* (henceforth *PPPUS*): *Richard Nixon, 1970* (Washington, DC: U.S. Government Printing Office, 1971), 122.

[19] H. Sonnenfeldt, 'Reconstructing the Nixon Foreign Policy,' in K. Thompson (ed.), *The Nixon Presidency: Twenty-Two Intimate Perspectives of Richard M. Nixon* (Lanham, MD: University Press of America, 1987), 315–334.

the flow of information and advice to the president. When necessary, Kissinger's staff would also amend policy recommendations generated by the bureaucracy. For example, William Quandt, who joined the NSC Middle East Office in 1972, recalls:

> When I first got there one of the things I learned was not to take memos from the State Department too seriously. If Rogers would write to the President, you couldn't not send it to the President, but you always sent it in with Kissinger's memo on top of it. Our job would be to write the draft of the Kissinger memo on top of the State Department memo, and then we would write our memo to Kissinger, saying 'here is what Rogers says, and here is what we think you should say.' So the President would get something from Kissinger saying, 'we received the following memo from the State Department – see Tab A, and they recommend so and so; here is what *I* think and here is what *I* recommend,' and Nixon would read the first two pages and wouldn't even look at the rest of the memo.[20]

Chairing the interdepartmental meetings also helped Kissinger to 'shape' the attitudes of the bureaucracy along the lines of his realist, power-centred worldview. Quandt again explains:

> [Kissinger] thought that through the process of having these endless meetings and engaging people – he was dominating every meeting he was in – he would end up shaping their worldview. They began to see the world as he and Nixon did; a strategic, cold war prism. So partly the meetings were to ensure that his and Nixon's worldview was given the stamp of approval.... and people did begin to say phrases and see things in this way.[21]

Quandt's account is supported by Kohl, who argues that although during the first year of the administration the NSC system performed rather effectively, by the time important developments with China unfolded, the decision-making pattern had transformed and important policy issues were now made almost exclusively in private discussions between Nixon and Kissinger.[22] A growing obsession with secrecy accelerated this metamorphosis. Thus, by 1973, NSC meetings with Nixon were a rare occasion, and as the following chapters will

---

[20] Interview with W. B. Quandt, 26 August 2004, Charlottesville, VA.
[21] Ibid.
[22] Kohl, 'The Nixon-Kissinger Foreign Policy System and U.S.-Europe Relations,' 7–9. This account is supported by Destler, 'National Security Advice to U.S. Presidents,' 154–155.

demonstrate, they proved particularly ineffective during international crises. Indeed, during the four crises examined in this book, it would be hard to point to a single case in which a decision came out of NSC meetings to have a significant impact on U.S. foreign policy.

Another important mechanism which Nixon and Kissinger used early on to cement the power of the White House at the expense of the foreign policy bureaucracy was their constant request for study papers on a variety of issues. During the first months of the administration, the bureaucracy was flooded with requests for studies that were generated at Kissinger's office. This occurred to such an extent that the prevailing view amongst bureaucrats was that it was Nixon's intention to overload the bureaucracy with paperwork so he could make foreign policy with Kissinger without too much disruption. Moreover, it soon became apparent that the sheer volume of completed studies exceeded the capacity of the NSC system to review and submit them for Nixon's consideration.[23] To add insult to injury, Nixon and Kissinger often made important policy decisions with little regard to the advice that had reached them from the bureaucracy. Even on broader policy issues that were less sensitive than Vietnam, China, and the Soviet Union, decisions were often made outside the formal process of the NSC and on an ad hoc basis. Helmut Sonnenfeldt, a former senior member of Kissinger's NSC staff, describes this pattern precisely:

The orderliness of the process was there in certain respects but not in others, and it doesn't mean that it was disorderly, it just meant that it was not in the formal manner in which the meeting structure operated. A lot of things were settled in conversations between people... A lot of decisions were made that were not the product of formal process. They may fit into the theory and the thrust of the formal process, but they were made in terms of the necessities and requirements of the moment.[24]

Notwithstanding Sonnenfeldt's observation about Nixon and Kissinger's propensity to make policy outside the formal NSC system, they were nevertheless aware that good working relations with the

---

[23] Ibid., 154. Destler reports that no less than sixty-nine studies were ordered in the first six months.

[24] Interview with H. Sonnenfeldt, 13 August 2004, the Brookings Institution, Washington, DC.

bureaucracy were conducive to the success of their foreign policy initiatives. Echoing the observations made by Allison and Halperin about bureaucratic power, Quandt suggests that maintaining good working relations with the bureaucracy was important to Nixon and Kissinger, not so much because of the advice it generated but because of its central role in the implementation process:

There was no doubt whatsoever in my mind that it was Nixon and Kissinger who through some complex way made foreign policy decisions; it was not the State Department. One might ask why did they go through all this effort to have these interagency meetings, and to some extent I think that Kissinger was realistic enough to know that if you don't have at least some degree of buy-in by the bureaucracy they can sabotage the process. You can make decisions but you can't implement them. Bureaucracy exists not to tell you what to do as much as help you implement it once you have decided. Kissinger realized that even if they didn't quite trust the State Department and had thoughts about the Defence Department, or they were worried about the quality of intelligence, you couldn't ignore these enormous agencies. And from time to time they could actually help you do some of the stuff.[25]

Somewhat inevitably, then, the decline in the power of the foreign policy bureaucracy saw the rise to prominence of the NSC staff. Indeed, according to Destler, this was perhaps the most important legacy of the Nixon administration. Destler identifies three major functions that the NSC can perform in the foreign policy arena, deriving from the substantive objective of effective coordination of foreign policy information and advice: (1) a forum for senior advisors to review foreign policy issues for the president; (2) a formal process for the development of policy planning and decision-making process; and (3) an institutional base for the creation of a presidential foreign policy staff.[26] Tellingly, Brent Scowcroft, who succeeded Kissinger and later served as national security advisor under George H. W. Bush, recognised the danger in the increasing size of the NSC staff: 'I wanted to cut the NSC staff, and I did. I took twenty percent out when I came in because I thought it was too big [during the Bush administration]... it creeps back up... I think there is a real danger in turning the NSC into another large

---

[25] Interview with Quandt.
[26] Destler, 'National Security Advice to U.S. Presidents.'

bureaucracy.'[27] Furthermore, while the NSC staff indeed grew in numbers and in influence during the Nixon administration, as subsequent chapters will demonstrate, by the administration's second year, the role of the NSC as a forum for top advisors to debate major foreign policy issues had reduced significantly.

The National Security Advisor

Nixon's decision to assign primary responsibilities for foreign policy to the White House must be examined within the broader context of U.S. foreign policy making. The decision whether to place the main tasks of foreign policy in the State Department or the NSC has occupied the minds of American presidents since the early 1960s, when the rivalry between the national security advisor and the secretary of state first emerged.[28] However, while personal rivalries between the national security advisor and the secretary of state should not be discounted, often it is the management style of the president that dictates where the power lies. During the transition period between the Johnson and the Nixon administrations, Walt Rostow, Johnson's national security advisor, acknowledged the impact of the president's personal preferences on the shaping of foreign policy: 'First – and above all – the organization should meet the working style and convenience of the President. No two Presidents are the same. The only right way to organize is to serve the President's needs.'[29]

During the Eisenhower administration, the national security advisor was not a policy advisor and was rather constrained to a more neutral role of manager of a process. It was McGeorge Bundy under President

---

[27] Despite Scowcroft's cut to around forty NSC professionals, the number jumped to nearly 100 during President Clinton's second administration. See Center for International Security Studies at Maryland (henceforth CISS) and the Brookings Institution, 'Oral History Roundtable: The Role of the National Security Advisor,' *National Security Council Project* (25 October 1999), 27–28, http://www.brookings.edu/fp/research/projects/nsc/transcripts/19991025.pdf.

[28] J. Dumbrell, *The Making of U.S. Foreign Policy* (Manchester: Manchester University Press, 1997, 2nd ed.), 88–93.

[29] Memo, Rostow to Johnson, 'Talking Points for LBJ with Kissinger,' 5 December 1968. Document no. 8, National Security File (NSF) – Walt Rostow Files, Box 14, Lyndon Baines Johnson Presidential Library.

Kennedy who gradually acquired the new role of policy advisor and later on challenged the traditional division of responsibilities between policy planning (NSC) and operations (State Department).[30] This pattern of power shift in favour of the national security advisor continued during the Johnson administration, with Walt Rostow as national security advisor.[31] However, it was in the Nixon years that the power of the national security advisor reached an unprecedented, never to be repeated zenith. Kissinger's Harvard associate Morton Halperin observed that Kissinger's active engagement in matters which were clearly beyond the traditional boundaries of his job was rapidly growing. At the same time, Nixon became increasingly reliant on Kissinger as an alternative source of information and advice on a broad range of military and national security issues.[32]

Still, this reliance did not translate into anything more than a businesslike relationship between the two men, as Nixon himself acknowledged: 'I don't trust Henry, but I can use him.'[33] Nixon's announcement in December 1968 of his decision to appoint Kissinger as his national security advisor surprised many people, not least Kissinger himself. Until then, Kissinger had worked as the foreign policy advisor of Nelson Rockefeller, Nixon's chief rival during the Republican presidential campaign, and before that, as Kissinger explained in his memoirs, 'I had taught for over ten years at Harvard University, where among the faculty disdain for Richard Nixon was established orthodoxy.'[34]

Nevertheless, Nixon and Kissinger had a lot more in common than one would have assumed in 1968. Both men believed that the key to equilibrium in international politics was the threat of force, and that

[30] See, for example, George, *Presidential Decisionmaking in Foreign Policy*, 162–163; Hoff, *Nixon Reconsidered*, 147–148.
[31] For a useful account of the historical development of the NSC system, see J. Prados, *Keepers of the Keys: A History of the National Security Council from Truman to Bush* (New York: William Morrow, 1991); D. J. Rothkopf, *Running the World: A History of the National Security Council and the Architects of American Power* (New York: Public Affairs, 2005).
[32] M. H. Halperin, 'The President and the Military,' *Foreign Affairs*, 50:2 (January 1972), 316.
[33] Cited in Hoff, *Nixon Reconsidered*, 155.
[34] H. Kissinger, *White House Years* (London: Weidenfeld and Nicolson and M. Joseph, 1979), 3–4.

American credibility in the world rested on its impressive military capabilities. The making of successful foreign policy, therefore, depended on America's ability to honour its commitments and to maintain its credibility anywhere in the world vis-à-vis the Soviet Union, as failure in one region would ultimately lead to capitulation in other areas. Such a forceful policy of threat, which hinged on the careful coordination of various policy issues, explicitly demanded a centralised, hierarchical system managed from the White House.[35]

Nixon and Kissinger's grand yet simple view of world politics resonates well with Isaiah Berlin's proverbial metaphor of the hedgehog. In his recent study of expert political judgement, Philip Tetlock uses Berlin's metaphor of the hedgehog and the fox to show why some people are better than others at forecasting political events.[36] While hedgehogs see international relations as driven by a single explanatory force, such as the balance of power or the clash of civilisations, foxes, on the other hand, see international affairs as a mixture of self-fulfilling and self-negating prophecies. While there is no clear political distinction between hedgehogs and foxes, Tetlock shows that hedgehogs perform worse in predicting events in their areas of expertise, partly because they also over-predict – in other words, they are quicker than foxes to develop great theories about the future of mankind and possible shifts in international affairs. Extrapolating Tetlock's findings to the main themes of this book, one could rather convincingly talk about the tenacious dogmatism of two hedgehogs (Nixon and Kissinger) regarding the preservation of American interests in international affairs and the means to achieve them (*realpolitik*, triangular diplomacy, balance of power). In the context of WSAG crisis decision-making process, as chapters 3–6 will show, it is possible to picture (in most cases) a spar between a Kissingeresque hedgehog, who could always make the link to Soviet aggression and manipulation regardless of the nature of the individual crisis, and a group of foxes, who attempted – often futilely – to depict a more complex scenario of events and possible outcomes. But, to answer accurately why the hedgehog and the foxes

---

[35] Ibid., 55–70; Hersh, *The Price of Power*; Bundy, *A Tangled Web*, 56; Hanhimaki, *The Flawed Architect*, 23–24.
[36] P. E. Tetlock, *Expert Political Judgment: How Good Is It? How Can We Know?* (Princeton, NJ: Princeton University Press, 2005).

had conflicting assessments of future moves of adversaries and possible ramifications of U.S. policies, the broader spectrum of FPA literature on structures, processes, and personalities must be considered.

Nixon and Kissinger also shared more personal traits – although as one observer noted, they enhanced rather than compensated for each other's worst characteristics.[37] They shared disdain for the bureaucracy and viewed Congress as an impediment to the successful conduct of great power diplomacy. Both were fond of secrecy and back-channelling and were overly suspicious in their pursuit of their own interests – they even eavesdropped on themselves.[38] Jonathan Aitken, Nixon's biographer, summed up the psychological traits of this partnership: 'the two men shared a child-like enthusiasm for springing surprises, a conspirator's love of secrecy, a guerrilla's contempt for the regular force of the bureaucracy, and a manipulator's enjoyment of power politics.'[39]

It is hardly surprising, then, that relations between the president and his national security advisor were far from harmonious, especially as Kissinger gradually became a cause célèbre in Washington. Columnist Joseph Kraft reported on Kissinger's celebrity status for *Harper's Magazine* in 1971: 'He began going out with well-known glamour girls... His luncheon dates at the Sans Souci became a regular subject of press gossip – the basic rule being that the more hairy the crisis is, the more often Kissinger had a long-stemmed lovely to lunch.'[40] The key issue underscoring this awkward relationship was Nixon's concern that Kissinger was building up his own reputation at the expense of the president's. Nixon's resentment and suspicion were apparent as early as September 1970, when John Ehrlichman informed Kissinger that he was not to give any more televised press briefings on policy issues. Ehrlichman and Haldeman's misgivings about Kissinger were public knowledge in the administration. The two could not tolerate his 'headline grabbing, arrogance, counterfeit anguish, and indiscriminate

[37] Hoff, *Nixon Reconsidered*, 150.
[38] J. Sisco, 'Nixon's Foreign Policy: The NSC and State Department,' in K. Thompson (ed.), *The Nixon Presidency: Twenty-Two Intimate Perspectives of Richard M. Nixon* (Lanham, MD: University Press of America, 1987), 394–395.
[39] Aitken, *Nixon: A Life*, 379.
[40] Kraft, 'In Search of Kissinger,' *Harper's Magazine*, January 1971, 61.

threats to resign.'[41] Indeed, Nixon's concern with Kissinger's growing status in the press almost led him to fire Kissinger in the winter
of 1971/72. The president was also worried about Kissinger's mental
stability – musing aloud whether 'Henry needed psychiatric care.'[42]
Kissinger, for his part, was contemplating whether to resign. However, once Nixon's attention began to be consumed by Watergate in
1973, the balance of power between the two had changed. Not only
did Kissinger remain in the administration, he also replaced Rogers as
secretary of state in October 1973, while retaining his role as national
security advisor. As chapter 6 will demonstrate, this put Kissinger in a
particularly propitious position to design, manage, and make foreign
policy almost single-handedly.

It is therefore hardly surprising that Kissinger was gradually depicted in public as the architect and executor of U.S. foreign policy.
His remarkable diplomatic achievements in the early 1970s led George
Shultz, secretary of state under President Reagan, to conclude: 'There's
only one Henry Kissinger. They broke the mold after they made him.'[43]
Referring to Kissinger's dramatic ascendance to power in Washington,
David Landau of *The Washington Post* found parallels between the
shrewd and highly able national security advisor and Prince Metternich, the hero of Kissinger's Ph.D. thesis in Harvard: 'Like the Aus-
trian minister who became his greatest political hero, Kissinger has
used his position in government as a protective cloak to conceal his
larger ambitions and purposes. Far from being the detached, objective
arbiter of presidential decision-making, he has become a crucial molder
and supporter of Mr. Nixon's foreign policy.'[44] Of course, Metternich
also played a great role in Kissinger's realist outlook on international

[41] J. Ehrlichman, *Witness to Power: The Nixon Years* (New York: Simon & Schuster,
    1982), 311; Hoff, *Nixon Reconsidered*, 153.
[42] Hanhimaki, *The Flawed Architect*, 188. The reason for Nixon's concern followed
    Kissinger's discovery that the Pentagon had been spying on him and his NSC staff.
    See chapter 5, n. 2.
[43] Cited in R. Schulzinger, *Henry Kissinger: Doctor of Diplomacy* (New York:
    Columbia University Press, 1989), 238.
[44] D. Landau, 'Henry Kissinger: Nixon's Metternich,' *Washington Post*, 11 July 1971. A
    growing body of literature challenges this traditional image of Henry Kissinger as the
    'lone ranger' of U.S. foreign policy and instead accredits Nixon a more central role in
    devising and shaping U.S. foreign policy. See, for example, Hoff, *Nixon Reconsidered*,
    chapters 5–8; Hanhimaki, '"Dr. Kissinger" or "Mr. Henry"? Kissingerology, Thirty
    Years and Counting.'

affairs and the importance of creating equilibrium between interests. Indeed, many have come to consider Kissinger as the embodiment of political realism, a reputation which Kissinger himself rarely tried to shake off.[45]

Kissinger employed various tactics to mold U.S. foreign policy to his and Nixon's liking. One of them concerned the entanglement of the bureaucracy in what Landau described as 'a web of useless projects and studies, cleverly shifting an important locus of advisory power from the Cabinet departments to his own office.'[46] Another method was less subtle but just as effective in disciplining the bureaucracy. In a conversation with George Shultz, Director of the White House Office of Management and Budget, President Nixon described in colourful terms his ideas on how to ensure that the bureaucracy and the White House were on the same wavelength:

You've got to get us some discipline, George. You've got to get it, and the only way you get it, is when a bureaucrat thumbs his nose, we're going to get him ... They've got to know, that if they do it, something's going to happen to them, where anything can happen ... There are many unpleasant places where Civil Service people can be sent. We just don't have any discipline in government. That's our trouble. Now I'm getting a little around the White House, uh, but we got to get it in these departments ... So whatever you – well, maybe he is in the regional office. Fine. Demote him or send him to the Guam regional office. There's a way. Get him the hell out.[47]

By far, the most effective tool used to ensure control of U.S. foreign policy was Kissinger himself. Kissinger's position at the top of the NSC system allowed Nixon to run U.S. foreign policy with only limited bureaucratic interference. However, as the next section demonstrates, Kissinger's indispensable position in the system also proved to be the greatest obstacle to the prospects of a smooth and efficient policy-making process.

---

[45] H. Kissinger, *Diplomacy* (New York: Simon & Schuster, 1994); R. D. Kaplan, 'Kissinger, Metternich and Realism,' *The Atlantic Monthly*, 283 (June 1999), 72–81; W. M. Mead, *Special Providence: American Foreign Policy and How It Changed the World* (New York: Routledge, 2002), 139.

[46] Landau, 'Henry Kissinger: Nixon's Metternich.'

[47] Cited in J. D. Aberbach and B. A. Rockman, 'Clashing Beliefs within the Executive Branch: The Nixon Administration Bureaucracy,' *American Political Science Review*, 70:2 (June 1976), 457.

The Reorganisation of the NSC

In November 1968, only days after Nixon's election, Kissinger submitted to the president-elect an extensive report concerning the restructuring of the NSC. Kissinger asked his Harvard associate Morton Halperin to conceptualise a new structure for the NSC system, in which major foreign policy issues were to be managed from the White House.[48]

Ironically, Kissinger's initial aim was to move away from the overly hierarchical and cumbersome Eisenhower system. Still, he proposed a system where one man – the national security advisor – effectively controlled the flow of information and advice to the president. Outlining NSC practices during the Eisenhower and Johnson administrations, Kissinger proposed a new system which should:

- combine the best features of the two systems; to develop a structure, using the NSC, which will provide the President and his top advisers with:
- all the realistic alternatives;
- the costs and benefits of each;
- the views and recommendations of all interested agencies.[49]

President Johnson's attempt at reform, Kissinger argued, failed to do the job, since the main decision-making body, the 'Tuesday Lunch' group, had no formal agenda or formal institutional follow-up. Consequently, Kissinger observed, 'decisions [were] covered orally to the Departments, with frequent uncertainty about precisely what was decided.'[50] While Kissinger acknowledged that the decision-making system of the outgoing administration was flexible and permitted 'a

---

[48] Interview with Sonnenfeldt. Kissinger also asked Halperin to devise a new Vietnam strategy. In May 1969, after a series of leaks to the press over the secret bombing of Cambodia, the White House had ordered wiretapping Halperin's phone line. In late 1969, Halperin resigned, and in June 1973 he filed a damage suit against Kissinger and Attorney General John Mitchell. See Hersh, *The Price of Power*, 83–97.
[49] Memo, Kissinger to Nixon, 'Memorandum on a New NSC System,' 27 November 1968. Folder no. 1, *Subject Files FG (Federal Government)*, EX FG6-6, Box 1, White House Central Files (henceforth WHCF), NPMP. Nixon approved the memo on 30 December 1968.
[50] Ibid. The 'Tuesday Lunch' was an informal grouping that had developed alongside the formal NSC system during the Johnson administration.

free and frank discussion unencumbered by a large group of second-level staff,' he also noted the lack of formal methods for assuring that all relevant alternatives were examined and all decisions adequately implemented. In that respect, Kissinger's conclusion that 'in recent years the NSC has not been used as a decision-making instrument' was correct.[51] While President Kennedy issued no less than 272 National Security Action Memorandums (NSAM) in his 1,000 days in office, his successor issued only 100 NSAMs between 1963 and 1969.[52]

Kissinger was also critical of the Eisenhower system, arguing that between 1953 and 1961, the excessive formality of the system 'tended to demand too much of the principals' time, while giving insufficient priority to issues of primary Presidential concerns.'[53] Indeed, Eisenhower himself acknowledged that 'this [NSC] work could have been better done by a highly competent and trusted official with a small staff of his own.'[54] It was with these lessons from the past in mind that Kissinger proposed a new system, composed of various interdepartmental groups and ad hoc committees, in which the role of the national security advisor was critical to the successful organisation of the foreign policy system and to the effective flow of information and advice to the president. He suggested that the new NSC would be 'the principal forum for issues requiring interagency coordination, especially where Presidential decisions of a middle and long-range nature are involved.' Kissinger also emphasised the central role of the national security advisor in the process, outlining his responsibility for 'determining the agenda and ensuring that the necessary papers are prepared' by the relevant departments.[55] To perform this seemingly modest role effectively, Kissinger proposed a NSC structure which included the following bodies:

---

[51] Ibid.
[52] The NSAM was an earlier version of the National Security Decision Memoranda (NSDM) discussed later. See B. K. Smith, *Organizational History of the National Security Council during the Kennedy and Johnson Administrations* (Washington, DC: National Security Council, 1988), 23.
[53] Memo, Kissinger to Nixon, 'Memorandum on a New NSC System.'
[54] D. D. Eisenhower, *The White House Years: Waging Peace, 1956–1961* (London: Heinemann, 1965), 634.
[55] Memo, Kissinger to Nixon, 'Memorandum on a New NSC System.'

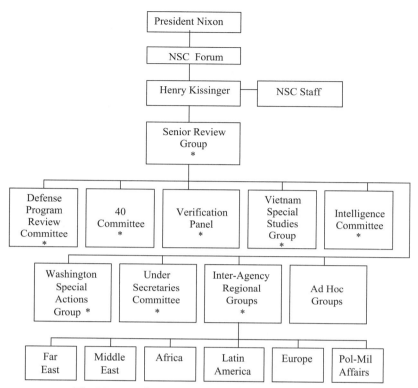

FIGURE 2.1 The Nixon Administration's NSC Structure.
*Chaired by Henry Kissinger.

The Review Group (later renamed Senior Review Group) was placed at the top of the NSC pyramid, and its role was to act as the key nexus between the Council and the various groups below it. Its responsibilities included ordering policy papers from the different NSC interdepartmental groups, reviewing them before submission to the consideration of the council, and coordinating the works of the various interdepartmental groups. Importantly, Kissinger emphasised that it was vital 'not to achieve a compromise or consensus which hides alternatives.'[56] The group was chaired by Kissinger, and its core members included the senior State and Defense Departments officials below the

---

[56] Ibid.

secretary level, the Chairman of the Joint Chiefs of Staff (JCS), and the Director of Central Intelligence (DCI). Other officials would participate when appropriate. Often the group would be used on sensitive issues where Kissinger wanted to limit access and knowledge of NSC staff and nonessential officials.[57]

In addition to the WSAG (responsible for crisis management), other specialist groups included the Defense Program Review Committee (responsible for defense policy and budget), the 40 Committee (covert operations), the Verification Panel (strategic arms talks), the Vietnam Special Studies Group, and the Intelligence Committee. As with the Senior Review Group (SRG) and the WSAG, these groups were chaired by Kissinger, and the membership in them was identical.

The Under Secretaries Committee dealt with issues referred to by the Review Group that did not require presidential decision. It was chaired by the Under Secretary of State, and its members included the Deputy Secretary of Defense, the Chairman of the JCS, and the DCI.

Several Inter-Agency Regional Groups handled issues that could be settled at the assistant secretary level. They would draft policy papers for the NSC and prepare contingencies for possible crisis situations for review by the NSC. Membership would be at the assistant secretary level and the groups would be chaired by the relevant assistant secretary of state (i.e., for Latin America, Middle East, Far East, Europe, Africa, and Political-Military Affairs).

Ad Hoc Working Groups were established where the problem could not fit into any of the previous geopolitical groups. Composition of the group would depend on the issue and, in any case, interagency coordination would be required. Additionally, outside consultants would participate in preparation of papers for the NSC, depending on their expertise. In addition to the structural reorganisation of the NSC system, Kissinger also brought two important procedural changes to the new system: the National Security Decision Memoranda (NSDMs) and National Security Study Memoranda (NSSMs). The first would inform the various departments and agencies of presidential decisions which may or may not result from NSC meetings, whereas the latter

---

[57] Interview with Quandt.

would direct the bureaucracy that studies of certain issues should be undertaken, normally for the consideration of the NSC.

Notwithstanding this dramatic structural and procedural overhaul, as the next section will demonstrate, there were serious discrepancies between the theoretical underpinnings of the NSC process envisaged by Nixon and Kissinger and the practicalities of implementation.

The NSC Process in Theory

Nixon presented the thrust of the NSC process in his first Foreign Policy Report to Congress in February 1970.[58] This process is strikingly similar to theoretical notions of rationality in foreign policy – namely, the need to survey all possible objectives and alternatives with their associated benefits and costs and the emphasis on achieving the 'best' policy at the end of the process. A typical process would begin with a NSSM coming out of Kissinger's office with Nixon's approval. The NSSM would request that a specific issue be studied and that alternative courses of action be surveyed. It would then be referred to the relevant interdepartmental group, and if no suitable group existed, an ad hoc working group would be established. The completed study would include the available courses of action and their respective costs and benefits; however, it would not indicate preferences or recommendations.

When issues required specialist studies, they would be referred to one of the several NSC subject-specific groups – namely, the Defense Program Review Committee, the 40 Committee, the Verification Panel, the WSAG, the Vietnam Special Studies Committee, and, after 1971, the NSC Intelligence Committee.

The completed study would then be referred to the SRG to make sure that all relevant points had been addressed. If the study was found to be inadequate, the SRG could revise it or send it back to the interdepartmental group. Once the SRG had approved the study, it would then be sent to the NSC forum, whose statutory members included the president, the vice president, secretaries of State and Defense, and the director of the Office of Emergency Preparedness, as well as the

---

[58] See Nixon, 'First Annual Report to Congress on United States Foreign Policy for the 1970s,' 18 February 1970, *PPPUS 1970*, 122–126.

national security advisor, chairman of the JCS, and the DCI. The forum would examine the study and choose the most appropriate course of action. Once Nixon had made his final decision, a NSDM would be sent to the secretaries of State and Defense and the DCI. This would signal the end of the policy stage and the beginning of the operational stage. The execution of the presidential decision would ultimately be supervised by the Under Secretaries Committee, also responsible for reviewing policy implementation.

The NSC Process in Practice

While the process seemed smooth and efficient in theory, in practice it was anything but. Interestingly, Nixon himself suggested that 'the policies of this Administration will be judged on their results, not on how methodically they were made.'[59] Nevertheless, it is important to pay attention to these methods, as ultimately they affected the policies selected. To that extent, the British Foreign Office's view of the tension between theory and practice in the NSC process is telling:

> The system of policy-making that has evolved during the Nixon Administration is not as business-like and efficient in practice as its theoretical structure might suggest. The system is too much dominated by personalities. In the case of foreign policy the State Department and other departments and agencies have become seriously demoralised through lack of consultation and the feeling that their traditional powers have been usurped . . . On the whole, the Cabinet feels left outside the charmed inner circle where decisions are made . . . never before have the President's staff controlled the policy-making process to such a degree at the expense of members of the Cabinet.[60]

Criticism from home of the new system was also prevalent, and early reservations were voiced even before Nixon entered the White House. In January 1969, designated-Secretary of Defense Melvin Laird informed Kissinger that he feared the new system would institute a 'close loop, where all intelligence inputs would be channelled through a single source.' Not only was Laird concerned that the national security

---

[59] Ibid., 126.
[60] Memo, Research Department, Foreign and Commonwealth Office 'The US Policy-Making Process under the Nixon Administration,' 9 February 1972. FCO 51/262, NA.

advisor would in effect isolate the president from important input from the bureaucracy, he also raised fears that the system would give the national security advisor the power and the responsibility to implement NSC policy without adequate consultation or even notification of NSC principals.[61]

This was exactly what happened as the administration entered its second year. Kissinger's desire to control the system, however, was evident even in the early days of the administration. Less than a week before Nixon entered the White House, Kissinger directed that to preclude bureaucratic 'misunderstandings,' all national security matters originating in the executive departments and agencies (including those from department and agency heads) should be delivered to his NSC office. The implication of this order, as Kissinger himself outlined, was that the national security advisor would establish secretarial control of all incoming papers before forwarding them to the president's office.[62]

Unsurprisingly, Kissinger's burgeoning control over the flow of information and advice to Nixon and his increasing role as the lynchpin of the new NSC system attracted criticism from various quarters. On one such occasion, Rear Admiral Rembrandt Robinson, the liaison officer between the NSC and the JCS, expressed concerns raised by the Joint Staff regarding Kissinger's frequent absence from important interdepartmental meetings:

We have looked into the Joint Staff complaint of difficulty in getting authoritative NSC information and guidance from the White House in the absence of Dr. Kissinger... The real criticism should be directed at Dr. Kissinger's difficulty in attending promptly and remaining throughout the many meetings of the NSC sub-structure (Review Group, Washington Special Action Group, etc.). This practice has a disruptive effect on the meetings, results in inefficient utilization of the time of the other participants, and has become a source of irritation within the interagency committee. Unfortunately, there is no suitable substitute for the Assistant to the President at most of these meetings. Dr. Kissinger alone enjoys both the intimate day-to-day contact and confidence of

---

[61] Memo, Laird to Kissinger, 'Your Memorandum Dated January 3, 1969 Concerning a New NSC System,' 9 January 1969. Folder no. 32, *HAK Administrative and Staff Files*, HAKOF Box 1, NSCF, NPMP.

[62] Memo, Kissinger to Haldeman, 'Arrangements for Secretariat Control of National Security Papers,' 16 January 1969. Folder no. 27, *HAK Administrative and Staff Files*, HAKOF, Box 1, NSCF, NPMP.

the President. Furthermore, he is able to chair National Security meetings with relative neutrality, or at least with an unannounced position.[63]

Accordingly Robinson recommended that the NSC should 'correct or at least ameliorate some of the more obvious problems' inherent in the system in order to 'protect [Kissinger's] schedule and to induce in him a greater sense of punctuality and attendance.'[64] Robinson's observation provides a telling insight into the indispensable position Kissinger had acquired for himself within the NSC system. Kissinger's chairmanship of the various NSC groups, although designed to facilitate the flow of information and advice to the president, in effect made the process of decision-making within the NSC more cumbersome. In effect, his complete control over the system limited the capacity of the NSC machine to the volume of work that one man could absorb and respond to which he could.

The new NSC system and Kissinger's central role in it were also easy targets for the press, and reports in the media about 'turmoil' in the NSC were not uncommon. Following the departure of eleven of Kissinger's staff in late 1969, the *Houston Chronicle* cited a staff member criticising Kissinger's inability to delegate responsibilities: 'When a memo goes to the President from the National Security Council Staff, it carries one name, and only one name – Henry Kissinger. It doesn't make any difference who wrote it.' Another observed: 'Those who can accept Henry's style are staying on. Others, like myself, have said, "The hell with it," and are getting out.'[65]

The WSAG: Early Roots and Institutionalisation

The issue of crisis management was institutionalised early on in the life of the new administration. In March 1969, Nixon ordered that

---

[63] Memo, Robinson to Wheeler, 'NSC Organization and Procedures,' 19 January 1970. Folder no. 5, *Miscellaneous Files of the Nixon Administration*, NSC System, Box H-300, National Security Council Institutional Files (henceforth NSCIF), NPMP. In the memo, he also pointed to Kissinger's private acquaintances as another cause for concern, concluding that 'we hope to prevent his academic friends and visitors of opportunity from pre-empting his time just prior to NSC-related meetings.'

[64] Ibid.

[65] The eleven staff members represented more than a third of Kissinger's original staff. J. McCarthy, 'One-Third of Kissinger Staff Has Quit,' *Houston Chronicle*, 19 October 1969.

'increased emphasis be placed on the anticipation of potential crisis situations that may affect the interests of the United States.'[66] Nixon directed the existing interdepartmental groups to 'prepare contingency studies on potential crisis areas for review by the NSC.' The studies should include a careful orchestration of political and military actions.[67] Once again, the benefits of such procedures epitomised the case for rational decision-making. According to the presidential directive (NSDM-8), the potential advantages of such contingency planning included the following:

- a clearer assessment of U.S. interests and possible need for U.S. action in a particular situation;
- an increased likelihood that U.S. actions taken will be timely and will minimize risks or losses;
- the possible discovery of actions which might resolve or head off a crisis; and
- the familiarization of key officials with factual material and alternative courses of action in event of a crisis.[68]

The first format of a crisis management group along the lines of NSDM-8 was initiated after an incident in April 1969, in which a U.S. EC-121 reconnaissance plane was shot down over the Sea of Japan by a North Korean aircraft. The group was interdepartmental at the deputy level and was chaired by Kissinger. This was the first international crisis that the new administration had faced, and the format of the WSAG appeared here first. Following the incident, Kissinger asked members of the group for a critique of the way the crisis was managed. Vice Admiral Nels Johnson, Director of the Joint Staff, praised Kissinger's chairmanship of the group as vital to the successful management of the crisis, concluding that procedures 'were good ones and worked well,' highlighting particularly the size of the group and the expertise of its members.[69]

---

[66] Memo, Kissinger to the Secretary of State, Secretary of Defense, and DCI, 'Crisis Anticipation and Management' (NSDM-8), 21 March 1969. Folder no. 6, *Miscellaneous Files of the Nixon Administration*, NSC System, Box H-300, NSCIF, NPMP.
[67] Ibid.
[68] Ibid.
[69] Memo, Johnson to Kissinger, no title, 21 April 1969. Folder no. 1, *Washington Special Actions Group Meetings*, Meeting Files (henceforth MF), Box H-070, NSCIF, NPMP.

Others, like Warren Nutter, Assistant Secretary of Defense for International Security Affairs, were more critical. In his memorandum to Kissinger, Nutter highlighted constant delays in the gathering of information which impeded the process – and in a similar fashion to Janis's symptoms of defective decision-making (*groupthink*), he identified a failure to survey alternatives and objectives:

The most pertinent observation about these procedures is that virtually no progress was made on preliminary analysis of alternative military responses to the EC121 incident... After long hours of discussion and drafting, the options already outlined early in the [following] morning remained virtually the same... Twenty-six hours elapsed between the shoot-down and a systematic presentation of possible responses.[70]

Perhaps the most poignant part of Nutter's critique concerned the composition of the group. While Vice Admiral Johnson reported to Kissinger that the group was 'interdepartmental in the most effective way,'[71] Nutter concluded that 'Interdepartmental Groups do not seem to be suited to contingency planning and crisis management when our national security is seriously in danger.'[72]

Kissinger submitted his own assessment to Nixon ten days after the crisis concluded. He acknowledged that there were some shortcomings but concluded that, in general, 'the bureaucracy functioned well, especially during the initial stages of the crisis,' partially due to the use of an interdepartmental group, which 'made it possible to bring about a rapid and intimate exchange of views and maximum security in the development of highly sensitive options.'[73] Based on the experience of the EC-121 incident, Nixon accepted Kissinger's recommendation to institutionalise an interagency group for future crisis management at the beginning of May 1969. Alternative names for the new group which were rejected included Washington Operations Coordinating

---

[70] Memo, Nutter to Kissinger, 'Critique of EC121 Planning Exercise,' 26 April 1969. Folder no. 1. Ibid.

[71] Memo, Johnson to Kissinger, no title.

[72] Memo, Nutter to Kissinger, 'Critique of EC121 Planning Exercise.'

[73] Some of the shortcomings were the result of 'inter-service rivalry.' In one case, the Air Force and the Navy could not agree on whether to attack an airfield with B-52s or A-6s. See Memo, Kissinger to Nixon, 'After-Action Report on the Korean Shootdown Incident,' 29 April 1969. Folder no. 1, *Washington Special Actions Group Meetings*, MF, Box H-070, NSCIF, NPMP.

Committee, the Washington Executive Group, and the Washington Coordinating Group.

The familiar tensions between the NSC and the State Department were visible during the institutionalisation of the WSAG. Alexander Haig, Kissinger's deputy, suggested approaching Secretary of State Rogers in private before disseminating the memorandum on WSAG to all parties concerned:

While I foresee no problems with signing this memorandum and dispatching it directly to the Departments, I think especially in the case of [sic] State it would be politic to inform Secretary Rogers or Under Secretary Richardson that the President had directed the institutionalization of the group of the same composition as the group which dealt with the EC-121 incident.[74]

The group was officially established on 16 May 1969, and its role within the NSC system was institutionalised two months later, in NSDM-19. In the memo, Nixon (via Kissinger) directed that 'henceforth political-military contingency plans prepared by NSC Interdepartmental Groups in accordance with NSDM 8 shall be forwarded to the NSC Washington Special Actions Group.'[75]

In the following months, the issue of international crisis management had been discussed extensively in various NSC channels. Evidence suggests that careful attention had been given to the planning and executing of clearly defined orderly procedures of international crisis decision-making. Procedural guidelines for WSAG work were established in a series of memos in the summer of 1969. In one of them, NSC senior staff member Morton Halperin raised important questions about the desired end product of WSAG deliberations, suggesting that discussions should ideally produce a concise contingency plan, to carry the following functions: 'a) States the likely contingencies which might arise; b) Summarizes the available courses of military action and their pros and cons; c) Provides a real time scenario of

---

[74] Memo, Haig to Kissinger, 'Interagency Coordinating Group for Future Crisis Management,' 12 May 1969. Folder no. 1, *Washington Special Actions Group Meetings*, MF, Box H-070, NSCIF, NPMP.

[75] Kissinger to the Secretary of State, Secretary of Defense, and DCI, 'Washington Special Actions Group' (NSDM-19), 3 July 1969. Folder no. 7, *Washington Special Actions Group Meetings*, MF, Box H-070, NSCIF, NPMP.

military and diplomatic moves to implement some or all of the courses of action.'[76]

With regard to the method in which these contingency papers would be prepared, Halperin considered Interagency Groups (IGs) or Task Forces unsuitable for this task and instead suggested the creation of a WSAG Working Group, a special ad hoc group chaired by the NSC staff. Following this recommendation, Halperin outlined a clear procedure of work for crisis contingencies, according to which the WSAG Working Group would act between IGs (who were responsible for drafting contingency papers) and the WSAG (responsible for producing the final plan).[77] In a similar fashion, Colonel Robert Behr, who chaired the WSAG Working Group, suggested several tasks concerning the organisation of WSAG as a crisis management group. These tasks included, amongst others, determining the preferred bureaucratic level of the Working Group, developing criteria which defines the end-product, developing a six-month-long agenda for the WSAG, and assessing the relevance of WSAG to NSDM-8 and other NSC directives.[78]

The last point is particularly important since NSDM-8 did not define clear boundaries for crisis anticipation, contingency planning, and management. The existing body which resembled most the crisis activities associated with the new WSAG was the Under Secretaries Committee, which according to NSDM-8 was to 'determine the organization and procedures for crisis management.'[79] It was therefore crucial, Behr concluded, to make a clear distinction between the responsibilities of the two bodies.

It is evident that careful consideration has been given to the structure and procedures of the NSC system and to the functioning of the new crisis management group within it. The previous discussion suggests a very hierarchical structure that placed great weight on the decision-making process. At least by design, then, policy formulation and advice within the new system were given high priority.

[76] Memo, Halperin to Kissinger, 'WSAG Meeting, July 11, 1969,' 8 July 1969. Ibid.
[77] Ibid.
[78] Memo, Behr to Haig, 'WSAG Activities,' 18 July 1969. Folder no. 7, *Washington Special Actions Group Meetings*, MF, Box H-070, NSCIF, NPMP.
[79] Memo, Kissinger to the Secretary of State, Secretary of Defense, and DCI, 'Crisis Anticipation and Management.'

Since its institutionalisation in July 1969, the WSAG was convened whenever an international event threatened to escalate into a full crisis. Between July 1969 and November 1973, the group met nearly 200 times and addressed a range of issues, from Middle East crises to developments in the Vietnam War.[80] Indeed, the WSAG met more than any other group in the NSC – a clear indication that in the words of Winston Lord, former member of the NSC staff, 'WSAG got more and more important as time went on. Other [groups] got less important.'[81]

That careful attention was given to the structure of policy advice and policy making in the new NSC system is indisputable. Nevertheless, while the system of NSSMs and NSDMs was perhaps the most sophisticated attempt since the creation of the NSC in 1947 to provide the president with a wide range of well-informed policy alternatives, the execution of the orderly procedures was at some variance with the structured system designed by Kissinger in late 1968. Although Nixon favoured orderly procedures, and despite the meticulous planning of the process by people like Halperin and Behr, in reality the most important decisions were made during informal, outside-the-system deliberations. Over time, one of the original designs of the NSC – a discussion forum for the senior advisors – fell into disuse. Even when NSC meetings were convened, it was evident to all the participants that Nixon had already reached a decision, or that he would make a decision following the meeting in private consultation with Kissinger. To that extent, the NSC forum could not be considered a decision-making body but rather merely a discussion body.[82] While this pattern can be explained as an inevitable consequence of Nixon and Kissinger's personality traits and cognitive schemes, such as their appetite for secrecy and power and mistrust of the bureaucracy, the more interesting question is why did they bother devising a sophisticated advisory system which they had no intention of using in the

---

[80] Index, 'Washington Special Actions Group Meetings,' no date. Folder no. 1, *Washington Special Actions Group Meetings*, MF, Box H-070, NSCIF, NPMP.

[81] CISS and the Brookings Institution, 'Oral History Roundtable: The Nixon Administration National Security Council,' *National Security Council Project* (8 December 1998), 31. http://www.brookings.edu/fp/research/projects/nsc/transcripts/19981208.pdf.

[82] Interview with Sonnenfeldt.

first place? As noted earlier, the evidence here suggests that the system worked rather well during the first eighteen months of the administration and when Nixon *wanted* to utilise it to its full potential (as the case of the Jordanian Crisis will show). The fact of the matter is that personalities did dominate the advisory system, for good and for bad. To a large extent, the discrepancies between the quality of decisions or performance of the WSAG in the four crises can be explained as a derivative of the way in which Nixon and Kissinger chose to use the system. In this analysis, the system was as important as the personalities who managed it, and a testimony to its effective design lies in the fact that when used properly, it produced more favourable results than when it was abused. Recalling Quandt's earlier comment on the need for a cooperative bureaucracy, even when Nixon and Kissinger ignored or bypassed the advice emanating from the NSC machinery, they nevertheless relied on it to carry out their decisions, making it an indispensable component of the process.

Returning to the eminent role of personalities in this discussion, perhaps the most disturbing element of the new NSC system, which participants as well as observers were quick to point a finger at, was the pivotal position that Kissinger had secured for himself as the national security advisor. Encouraged by a president who eschewed large-group deliberations, Kissinger carefully designed a system which ensured that Nixon would not have to reach down for information and advice. At the same time, Kissinger made sure that department heads would find it impossible to reach up for the president without prior approval. As the following four case studies will now demonstrate, while in theory this system was designed to protect the president's time and to save him from protracted and sterile discussions in the bureaucracy by producing coherent advice and ultimately the 'best' policy, in practice it placed the burden of running U.S. foreign policy on the shoulders of one man.

3

The Incursion into Cambodia, Spring 1970

> I think we need a bold move in Cambodia ... We are going to find out
> who our friends are now, because if we decide to stand up here some of
> the rest of them had better come along fast.[1]
>
> Nixon to Kissinger, 22 April 1970

Nixon's bold move in Cambodia resulted in the first major international crisis of his administration. Following a military coup in Cambodia that saw the ruler, Prince Sihanouk, ousted, the number of North Vietnamese attacks from Cambodian sanctuaries on U.S. forces in South Vietnam had risen dramatically in the spring of 1970. In response, Nixon ordered more than 30,000 U.S. ground troops into the neutral country to eliminate enemy sanctuaries along the border, disrupt supply lines, and capture the Communist headquarters in Cambodia. Importantly, the incursion followed more than a year of secret bombing of targets in Cambodia which became public knowledge only in May 1970. The 'widening down' of the Vietnam War to include attacks on a neutral country led to unprecedented upheaval in the United States, which culminated in the deadly shooting of four students in Kent State University by the National Guard. The controversial invasion of Cambodia also saw the beginning of a congressional process which resulted in the 1973 War Powers Act, which repealed

---

[1] *Foreign Relations of the United States (henceforth FRUS)*, 1969–1976, Volume I: Foundations of Foreign Policy, 1969–1972, 209–210 (doc. 64).

the 1964 Gulf of Tonkin Resolution that had given President Johnson a carte blanche to expand the war in Vietnam. The War Powers Act (which was passed over Nixon's veto) placed limitations on the president's power to deploy U.S. forces abroad without a prior consultation with Congress. The ground operation in Cambodia ended within two months with only a modest military success but exacted high political and diplomatic costs on the administration.

This crisis contains much evidence to support the central proposition of this book, that more often than not during the Nixon administration, the careful planning of a well-structured, formalistic foreign policy system with clearly defined procedures for effective decision-making, failed to produce the 'best' policy outcomes. The most important decisions during this crisis were made by Nixon and Kissinger either by bypassing the formal policy-making process or by ignoring the advice of the foreign policy bureaucracy. This pattern is particularly alarming given that the crisis provided Nixon with his first real opportunity to implement the new procedures for crisis decision-making which were put in place following the EC-121 incident the previous year. Decision-making during the Cambodia episode therefore provides us with a first example of the disproportional weight of the Nixon-Kissinger dyad in the tripartite relationship of structures–processes–personalities. Although the WSAG was convened several times during the spring of 1970, its input proved rather marginal to the overall strategy, as the most important decisions during the Cambodia crisis were conceived in the mind of the president before the decision-making process had been exhausted with relation to the careful examination of the relevant policy alternatives and their associated costs and benefits. It is hardly surprising, then, that the result fell short of the 'best' policy outcome envisaged by the architects of the new NSC system.

This chapter begins by placing the crisis in the broader context of the Vietnam War and then proceeds to examine U.S. decision-making during this period with reference to the main episodes of the crisis – namely, the secret bombing and the subsequent invasion of Cambodia. The chapter then provides a more detailed analysis of the performance of the WSAG as the designated crisis-management group. The concluding observation – that the consequences of Nixon's key decisions during the crisis were tragically evident *before* they were taken – perhaps provides the most telling evidence of a flawed decision-making process. These flaws could have largely been avoided had it not been for the constraints which were placed on the process by the president's cognitive approach to the crisis – namely, his perception of threat and of the enemy and, perhaps more important, his self-image of the beleaguered leader overcoming insurmountable obstacles on the path to eventual glory and self-vindication, much like Nixon's source of inspiration during the crisis – General Patton in the Battle of the Bulge a generation earlier.

The Nixon Administration and the Vietnam War

Upon entering the White House, Richard Nixon's most urgent and difficult task was to bring an end to the fighting in Vietnam. He gradually came to realise that it was not possible to win the war militarily and was aware of the political costs of an endless war. A Gallup poll from early 1969 suggested that the American public was becoming increasingly sceptical of the prospects of securing a peaceful settlement in Vietnam. More than half (52 percent) believed that the United States had made a mistake sending troops to fight in Vietnam, while a startling 70 percent did not believe that the Paris Peace Talks were making headway.[2] Notwithstanding the obvious public concern, Nixon feared that a unilateral withdrawal might be interpreted as a sign of weakness. Accordingly, Nixon's Vietnam policy rested on three pillars: (1) the Vietnamization programme, (2) the 'madman theory,' and (3) linkage diplomacy.

The Vietnamization programme was born in the mind of Defense Secretary Melvin Laird, who was perhaps the most sensitive of the cabinet members to public opinion and relations with Congress.[3] Apart from saving the lives of U.S. troops in Vietnam, his plan aimed to gradually transfer to the South Vietnamese the primary responsibility for their own defence and replace military assistance with financial aid.[4]

---

[2] *The Gallup Poll: Public Opinion, 1935–1971* (New York: Random House, 1972), 218–219.

[3] Bundy, *A Tangled Web*, 63.

[4] While most accounts suggest that the plan was originally devised by Laird following a visit to Vietnam in March 1969, the Kalbs claim that Nixon had considered the pull-out of troops months earlier. Kalb and Kalb, *Kissinger*, 127.

Vietnamization helped Nixon achieve two objectives: first, appeasing the anti-war critics at home who called for a substantial withdrawal of troops – when Nixon took office the number of U.S. troops in Vietnam reached a peak of nearly 550,000;[5] and second, sending a clear signal that the United States would never abandon its allies, by continuing to support Saigon financially. Ultimately, the rationale behind Vietnamization seemed fairly convincing, as Hanhimaki explains: 'while fewer body bags were likely to mean fewer moratoriums, more material aid [sic] should satisfy the concerns of those who could not stomach the reality that the United States was being gradually smoked out of Vietnam.'[6]

Kissinger, however, thought differently. In a *Foreign Affairs* article in early 1969, he brought forward a two-tier approach to achieve 'peace with honour' in Vietnam, by separating the political and military elements of a future settlement. First, the United States would negotiate the military issues with the North Vietnamese in order to achieve a cease-fire. Second, a political solution would be negotiated with the South Vietnamese. Should Hanoi reject the plan, Kissinger called for a unilateral American action to minimise casualties and strengthen the South Vietnamese army.[7] While Nixon and Secretary of State William Rogers were supportive of Laird's plan, Kissinger was sceptical of its chances of success.[8] Kissinger believed that not only would Vietnamization weaken U.S. leverage in future negotiations with Hanoi but was also doubtful of Saigon's ability to control the political and military situation once American forces had left. In September 1969, he expressed his concern to Nixon: 'Withdrawal of U.S. troops will become like salted peanuts to the American public: the more U.S. troops come home, the more will be demanded. This could eventually result, in effect, in demands for unilateral withdrawal – perhaps within a year.'[9] Indeed, Kissinger later conceded that he got it wrong: 'I saw

---

[5] Kissinger, *White House Years*, 235.
[6] Hanhimaki, *The Flawed Architect*, 43.
[7] H. Kissinger, 'The Viet Nam Negotiations,' *Foreign Affairs*, 47:2 (January 1969), 211–234.
[8] In his memoirs, Nixon acknowledged that '[i]t was largely on the basis of Laird's enthusiastic advocacy that we undertook the policy of Vietnamization.' *RN*, 392.
[9] *FRUS*, Volume I, 106 (doc. 36).

it as a bargaining ploy, a negotiating tool, but really I never thought it would work.'[10]

Despite Kissinger's reservations, the Vietnamization programme worked very well. The number of U.S. troops in Vietnam almost halved by the end of 1970 to 280,000, further reduced to 140,000 by late 1971, and by the end of 1972, the last year of Nixon's first term, U.S. troops in Vietnam amounted to only 24,000.[11] In fact, Vietnamization was so successful that much to Kissinger's irritation, it soon became a declared policy that could not be separated from the overall planning and budgeting of the Vietnam War.[12] This was truly a rare episode. On very few occasions were Kissinger's views overlooked in favour of cabinet members' advice. However, this anomaly can be fairly easily explained by the fact that Kissinger, unlike Nixon and Laird who owed their jobs to their constituents, paid little attention to the importance of public opinion. Moreover, in the early months of the administration, Kissinger had not yet solidified his position as the president's key advisor and, at that point, Nixon was more disposed to listen to the bureaucracy. In fact, Kissinger himself acknowledged that during the first year of the administration, 'the NSC machinery was used more fully before my authority was confirmed, while afterward tactical decisions were increasingly taken outside the system in personal conversations with the president.'[13] This remarkable admission suggests that Kissinger himself was aware of the inevitable conflict between his pre-eminent position in the NSC system and the prospects of achieving a smoothly run NSC apparatus. In fact, Nixon's use of the NSC as an advisory tool was rather modest on the two most important decisions during the Cambodia crisis, and what quickly emerged was a Nixon-Kissinger front facing a dissenting bureaucracy.

The second pillar of Nixon's Vietnam policy – the 'madman theory' – was largely a tool to deflect any claims that his withdrawal programme meant that he had gone soft on communism. The 'theory' was an extension of Nixon's Cold War realist worldview which saw

[10] Kalb and Kalb, *Kissinger*, 128.
[11] Hanhimaki, *The Flawed Architect*, 496 (fn. 23).
[12] Bundy, *A Tangled Web*, 64.
[13] Hoff, *Nixon Reconsidered*, 161.

power as the centrepiece of international relations. Originally devised for the negotiations with the North Vietnamese, the notion centered on the importance of threat as a reliable tool in foreign policy. During the secret negotiations with Hanoi, Kissinger often played the role of the 'good messenger,' deliberately playing off against Nixon's well-established reputation as an anti-communist and referring to the president's volatile and unpredictable personality.[14] Alongside the bombing of and incursion into Cambodia, Nixon took several decisions during the Vietnam War to give further credence to this theory, including the bombing of Hanoi and the mining of Haiphong harbour in 1972. 'Bob' Haldeman, Nixon's Chief of Staff, recalled in his memoirs how Nixon explained to him the essence of the theory:

> I call it the Madman Theory, Bob. I want the North Vietnamese to believe I've reached the point where I might do *anything* to stop the war. We'll just slip the word to them that, 'for God's sake, you know Nixon is obsessed about Communism. We can't restrain him when he's angry – and he has his hand on the nuclear button' – and Ho Chi Minh himself will be in Paris in two days begging for peace.[15]

Unlike the madman theory, the idea behind Nixon's third pillar – linkage diplomacy – was aimed more at Moscow than at Hanoi and was a key element in Nixon and Kissinger's geopolitical approach to world politics and to the Vietnam War in particular. For a long time, Nixon believed that the road to peace in Vietnam must pass through Moscow. Closely linked to the idea of détente – the relaxation in superpower relations – the objective of linkage was to woo the Soviets into the Vietnam negotiations by demonstrating the potential benefits to be obtained through cooperation. Over the course of the negotiations, Nixon offered several incentives to the Soviets to put pressure on Hanoi to compromise, such as the SALT (Strategic Arms Limitations Talks) negotiations, European affairs, and trade.[16] Nixon had no illusions about the central role that Moscow could play in ending the war. Even during the 1968 presidential campaign, he suggested that 'If the Soviets were disposed to see the war ended and a compromise

---

[14] Ibid., 177.
[15] Haldeman, *The Ends of Power*, 83.
[16] Kalb and Kalb, *Kissinger*, 126–127. For a detailed account of linkage diplomacy, see Kissinger, *White House Years*, 247–249.

settlement negotiated, they have the means to move Ho Chi Minh to the conference table.'[17]

Kissinger did not share the president's vision at first but quickly changed his tune once the benefits of the approach became apparent. In his 1969 *Foreign Affairs* article, Kissinger suggested that the United States should ignore the Soviets in its quest for peace in Vietnam, since '[for] a long time now, Moscow has seemed paralyzed by conflicting considerations and bureaucratic criteria.' Kissinger also noted that the events in Czechoslovakia in 1968 'have reduced Moscow's usefulness even further.'[18] In fact, as Hoff suggests, there was little agreement between Nixon and Kissinger on most geopolitical matters in 1969, and pretty much the only ideas they shared in foreign policy concentrated on 'their distrust of bureaucracy in formulating policy and their belief that it was time to get out of Vietnam, although neither had any specific notion about how to accomplish the latter.'[19]

The Unfolding Crisis over Cambodia: Bombing, Coup, and Incursion

Hoff's observation about Nixon and Kissinger's inability to work out a coherent and feasible plan to end the war in Vietnam goes some distance in explaining the flawed decision-making during the Cambodia crisis. The secret decisions taken by the two in early 1969 largely contradicted the administration's proclaimed objectives of ending the war by 'winning the peace' and the unilateral withdrawal of U.S. troops through the Vietnamization process. Similarly, the decision to send ground troops to Cambodia seemed almost suicidal given the evident military and political costs. However, given Nixon's predisposition to view the world in the prism of *realpolitik* and his 'madman' theory, his decisions during the crisis were somewhat inevitable. Indeed, as one observer noted: 'Not to retaliate was for Nixon a painful choice...however irrational it might appear and however far from

---

[17] Kalb and Kalb, *Kissinger*, 124.

[18] Kissinger, 'The Viet Nam Negotiations,' 220.

[19] Hoff, *Nixon Reconsidered*, 152. Kissinger was also sceptical of Nixon's plan to review relations with China, partly because of his lack of China expertise, but also because he viewed relations with Moscow and the Vietnam War as more pressing matters. See Hanhimaki, *The Flawed Architect*, 32–33.

the norms of American behavior during even the greatest Cold War crises in 1948 and 1962.'[20]

Nixon took his first 'irrational' decision on Cambodia only months after entering the White House. On 18 March 1969, American B-52 bombers went on their first 'hot pursuit' mission across the border of Cambodia to destroy supply routes and sanctuaries used by the Vietcong (VC) and the North Vietnamese Army (NVA) to launch attacks against U.S. troops and the South Vietnamese forces (Army of the Republic of Vietnam, or ARVN). By May 1970, when the White House officially acknowledged the bombing, more than 3,600 sorties had been sent on similar missions, which gradually expanded in their objectives and scope.[21] Between March 1969 and March 1970, 91,363 tons of bombs were dropped on Cambodia. The 3,000-odd sorties dispatched over this period represented 17 percent of the total B-52 missions in South East Asia.[22]

This massive air campaign followed the dramatic increase in the number of North Vietnamese forces in the area. Following the 1968 Tet Offensive and the increase in retaliatory attacks by American and ARVN forces, many North Vietnamese forces fled to the border areas in Cambodia to seek refuge. By early 1969, they numbered 40,000 and were served by various supply bases and routes, many of which were supported by China. General William Westmoreland, Army Chief of Staff, estimated that between 1966 and 1969 military and non-military shipments from North Vietnam to the Cambodian sanctuaries amounted to 21,600 and 5,000 tons, respectively.[23] Most important, these facilities were thought to include the North Vietnamese headquarters, the Central Office of South Vietnam (COSVN).[24] The ever-growing presence of North Vietnamese troops in Cambodia not only undermined Cambodian claims to neutrality, but it also posed a real threat to American forces operating in neighbouring South Vietnam,

[20] Bundy, *A Tangled Web*, 73.
[21] C. Hitchens, *The Trial of Henry Kissinger* (London: Verso, 2001), 35.
[22] Memo, Wheeler to Laird, 'Assessment of MENU Operation,' 12 March 1970. *Declassified Documents Reference System (henceforth DDRS)*, Fiche no. 398C, Fiche issue date 01/10/1979, Document no. 00204.
[23] W. C. Westmoreland, *A Soldier Reports* (New York: Doubleday & Co., 1976), 182.
[24] Bundy, *A Tangled Web*, 71; W. Shawcross, *Sideshow: Kissinger, Nixon and the Destruction of Cambodia* (London: Andre Deutsch, 1979), 113.

who came under frequent attacks from the North Vietnamese sanctuaries in Cambodia.

Nixon was concerned about the increase in VC activities in Cambodia even before entering the White House. On 8 January 1969, he ordered Kissinger to report on the situation in Cambodia and the policy options available, as part of a comprehensive study on Vietnam. Nixon concluded, most ominously, 'I think a very definite change of policy toward Cambodia probably should be one of the first orders of business when we get in.'[25] Five days later, Kissinger reported that the enemy had established eleven known base areas at points along the Cambodia-Vietnam border from Laos south to the Mekong delta. He added, 'All are well documented. They are employed for rest and sanctuary; for training, resupply and logistical storage; and for medical care of the sick and wounded.'[26] At that point, American actions against the sanctuaries amounted to no more than air reconnaissance and very restricted ground reconnaissance. Kissinger reported to Nixon that all requests by the military command in South Vietnam to enter Cambodia for pre-emptive operations 'have been denied, or are still pending without action.'[27]

Soon, however, the overzealous commanders in Saigon got what they asked for and more. On his first day in office, Nixon asked the Pentagon to prepare contingency plans for action against the North Vietnamese sanctuaries in Cambodia. A month later, General Creighton Abrams, Commander of U.S. forces in Vietnam, reported to General Wheeler, Chairman of the Joint Chiefs of Staff, that an intense B-52 bombing raid against COSVN will 'have its effect on future military offensives which COSVN may desire to undertake.' For that purpose, Creighton suggested that the assault would be 'a short-duration, concentrated B-52 attack of up to 60 sorties, compressing the time interval between strikes to the minimum.' Although the scale of the operation was too large for the targeted area, Creighton concluded that 'in this case it would be wise to ensure complete destruction.'[28] On 23 February, Nixon made his mind up on the matter and, as Kissinger recalls, 'he

---

[25] Memo, Nixon to Kissinger, no title, 9 January 1969. Folder no. 25, *HAK Administrative and Staff Files*, HAK Office Files, Box 1, NSCF, NPMP.

[26] Memo, Kissinger to Nixon, no title, 9 January 1969. Ibid.

[27] Ibid.

[28] Cited in Shawcross, *Sideshow*, 20.

suddenly ordered the bombing of the Cambodian sanctuaries.'[29] The
following day, Kissinger, his deputy Alexander Haig, White House
Chief of Staff Haldeman (representing Nixon who was speaking at
NATO headquarters in Brussels), and a Pentagon planning officer went
over the operational guidelines on board Air Force One. According to
the guidelines, the bombing of the Cambodian sanctuaries 'would be
limited to within five miles of the frontier; we would not announce the
attacks but acknowledge them if Cambodia protested, and offer to pay
compensation for any damage to civilians.'[30] Code-named Breakfast,
this bombing mission was the first of six 'Menu' bombing operations
in Cambodia, followed by Dessert, Snack, Supper, Lunch, and Dinner.

Surprisingly, although Kissinger convinced Nixon to postpone his
order for forty-eight hours so that relevant officials could be consulted, the NSC was not convened. Nor was there a proper consultation among the president's top advisors. Instead, Secretaries Laird and
Rogers were only informed of the decision and the operational guidelines post factum. Nixon later met Rogers in London and gave him 'a
cryptic account of his thinking but no details.'[31] Rogers opposed the
operation because of the likelihood of domestic opposition. Laird too
was quick to sound his reservations. After a short brief by Haldeman
back in Washington, Laird cabled his views to Brussels. He also
expressed to Rogers his fear that it would be difficult to handle the
media and the public, and that it would be impossible to keep the
bombing secret. However, Laird was proved wrong in his assessment.
The fourteen-month-long bombing of Cambodia was kept under heavy
secrecy, and even Vietnam specialists in the NSC were not aware of
operation Menu. At the same time, Prince Norodom Sihanouk of
Cambodia and the NVA forces in the sanctuaries knew all too well
about the bombing that was kept secret from the American public and
Congress.

This remarkable situation supports prevalent assumptions about
Kissinger's aversion to public opinion and domestic policies. Referring
to his Harvard book, *A World Restored*, David Landau of *The Washington Post* explained that in Kissinger's view, 'popular opinion was

---

[29] Kissinger, *White House Years*, 243.
[30] Ibid.
[31] Ibid.

little more than an encumbrance on those few who were capable of making decisions.'[32] The Kalb bothers – perhaps the most sympathetic of Kissinger's many biographers – have added that Kissinger feared that domestic scrutiny would only complicate further the administration's efforts for a settlement in Vietnam:

Kissinger had no trouble justifying the deception. He felt that if it became known that the United States was widening the war geographically, extending the bombing into Cambodia, this would prompt a wave of angry denunciations from an increasingly disillusioned Congress and from antiwar critics across the country. This kind of nationwide uproar would only complicate the Administration's plans for peace in Vietnam.[33]

In fact, so afraid were Nixon and Kissinger of the public reaction that the White House did not officially acknowledge the bombing until May 1970, when U.S. ground troops were already operating in Cambodia. The incursion was the result of the gradual disintegration of Cambodia, which in the space of a few months experienced the overthrow of Prince Sihanouk, a civil war with the Khmer Rouge, relentless American bombing, and then clashes between Cambodian, South Vietnamese, and NVA forces. Ironically, in large part this disintegration was an inevitable result of the Menu bombing, which drove the North Vietnamese away from their sanctuaries and deeper into Cambodia. The secret bombing campaign also had a debilitating effect on the regime of Prince Sihanouk. In March 1970, while he was abroad, an organised military coup led by his Prime Minister, General Lon Nol, had taken place. Sihanouk learned of the coup while in Moscow, where he appealed for support against the increasing presence of North Vietnamese forces in Cambodia. The prince was quick to blame the CIA for recruiting Cambodians to turn the country away from neutrality and into the hands of the United States.[34] For some time, Sihanouk

---

[32] Landau, 'Henry Kissinger: Nixon's Metternich.'

[33] Kalb and Kalb, *Kissinger*, 132. Furthermore, Nixon and Kissinger feared that domestic protest might undermine the regime of Prince Sihanouk. J. M. Blum, *Years of Discord: American Politics and Society, 1961–1976* (New York: W. W. Norton & Company, 1991), 322–323.

[34] Some suggest an active CIA assistance in the coup against Sihanouk, although concrete evidence for such involvement is hard to find. Thornton, *The Nixon-Kissinger Years*, 39–41; Hersh, *The Price of Power*, 176–183; Bundy, *A Tangled Web*, 149. Kissinger maintains in his memoirs that the administration 'neither encouraged

had managed to keep his country out of direct involvement in the war by turning a blind eye on the NVA use of border areas of Cambodia to launch attacks on South Vietnam, while doing exactly the same with regard to the continuous bombing of his country by American B-52s. Now he decided to align himself with China, in direct opposition to the pro-American regime of Lon Nol. While in Beijing on 23 March, he announced the establishment of a National United Front with the Khmer Communists, which immediately brought him closer to Hanoi.[35] Meanwhile, his successor turned Cambodia's neutrality into anti-communism, and demanded that Hanoi pull out all its forces from the country. However, the poorly trained and ill equipped 30,000-strong Cambodian army could not match the NVA forces, which by then amounted to 60,000 in Cambodia alone.[36] He also announced the permanent closure of Sihanoukville port, which was the main supply route to the NVA forces in Cambodia, thus seriously damaging Hanoi's war efforts.[37]

News of the events in Cambodia led to varied assessments in Washington. On the one hand, civilian officials in the State and Defense Departments, including Secretaries Rogers and Laird, believed that diplomatic prudence and Cambodia's return to neutrality were the best courses of action. Any military action in Cambodia would be unacceptable. The State Department advised Kissinger that the administration 'should emphasize that our policy is to continue to support Cambodia's independence, neutrality and territorial integrity. We should not try to force Cambodia into our camp, and should be careful to keep

---

Sihanouk's overthrow nor knew about it in advance.' *White House Years*, 563. Nixon noted that the coup 'came as a complete surprise. The CIA had received no indication that the opposition to Sihanouk had gone so far.' He also recalled that his response to the news was somewhat edgy: '"What the hell do those clowns do out there in Langley" I asked Bill Rogers impatiently.' See *RN*, 447. For a comprehensive account of the roots of the coup and the possible CIA involvement, see Shawcross, *Sideshow*, 112–127.

[35] Bundy, *A Tangled Web*, 149–150.

[36] This number, presented by Lon Nol to provincial governors in Phnom Penh, was 20,000 more than his estimate six months earlier. The high number was designed to 'stir up public anger.' See Shawcross, *Sideshow*, 116.

[37] A CIA report estimated that up to 80 percent of Hanoi's war supplies came through the port. Thornton, *The Nixon-Kissinger Years*, 35. By mid-April, 70,000 men had enlisted in the Cambodian Army – 60,000 more than the Lon Nol government had called for. Shawcross, *Sideshow*, 131.

a low and somewhat detached posture with the Cambodians for the present.'[38] On the other hand, military officials in the Pentagon, as well as Kissinger's deputy Alexander Haig, argued that a measured intervention was essential to help the outnumbered and poorly trained Cambodian Army. Preventing the fall of Cambodia into Communist hands thus seemed imperative.[39]

As far as Richard 'madman' Nixon was concerned, the events presented him with an opportunity to crush Communist presence in Cambodia once and for all and to demonstrate to Hanoi and Moscow that unlike his predecessor, he did not shy away from military escalation in Vietnam. To that extent, there was no real dilemma for the president about which course of action to endorse. Marshall Green, Assistant Secretary of State for East Asian and Pacific Affairs, confirmed that 'From day one, Nixon was insistent on building Lon Nol.'[40]

As discussed in the previous chapter, Nixon's management style was characterised by aversion to 'reaching down' for information. He wished to avoid confrontation with his cabinet. He much preferred to consult with Kissinger and increasingly Alexander Haig, whose support for intervention was well known to his superiors. Rogers and Laird were left out of the decision-making process until the president had made up his mind. Accordingly, Kissinger recalls that upon hearing of the overthrow of Sihanouk, Nixon asked him to work out a plan to help Lon Nol, without informing the bureaucracy: 'I want Helms to develop and implement a plan for maximum assistance to pro-US elements in Cambodia. Don't put this out to 303 or the bureaucracy. Handle like our [Menu] air strike.'[41] Nixon then ordered CIA Director Richard Helms to set up an office in Phnom Penh, but his order was not carried out for several weeks because of Secretary Rogers's continuous objection over possible outcry in Congress. It took nearly a month before Nixon personally intervened and unleashed his rage on the State Department, which included a vindictive decision to recall one

[38] Memo, Eliot to Kissinger, 'Political/Diplomatic Initiatives on Laos and Cambodia,' 19 March 1970. Folder no. 4, *WSAG Meetings*, MF, Box H-073, NSCIF, NPMP.
[39] Bundy, *A Tangled Web*, 151.
[40] Cited in Shawcross, *Sideshow*, 129.
[41] Kissinger, *White House Years*, 465. The 303 Committee preceded the 40 Committee as the NSC interdepartmental group charged with overseeing covert activities by the CIA and other agencies. Like the other NSC groups, it was chaired by Kissinger.

State Department official from Phnom Penh in order to clear desk space for the incoming CIA personnel.[42]

Nixon was not the only one who was jittery about the news from Cambodia. Kissinger too was evidently worried that the situation might develop into a crisis. Haldeman recalls that Kissinger contemplated cancelling his much-needed holiday and returning to Washington early. Haldeman's diary entry from 30 March reads: 'Now K[issinger] is all stirred up. Had him stashed away at Paradise Island for a week's vacation, but he's afraid to be away if crisis breaks, and Cambodia is brewing one. After numerous calls, I finally talked him into staying, much to P[resident]'s relief. He knows K needs time off and rest.'[43] Kissinger's holiday was indeed timely, as he would soon work hard to protect Nixon from a dissenting bureaucracy and an agitated American public.

Nixon's insistence on carrying on with his decision to act forcefully against NVA strongholds in Cambodia despite the political costs and the reservations of the bureaucracy was remarkable. However, it was during such times of crisis that Nixon, by his own admission, was working to his full potential. Nixon always thought of himself as the beleaguered leader who had to overcome challenges to an eventual triumph. As Hoff observed, Nixon's 'risk taking, street fighting, and attack and overkill tactics' were shaped in a Cold War era of 'gut-level' approach to crisis management.[44] Indeed, in his first book, *Six Crises*, Nixon's cognitive approach to crisis is rather telling: 'The easiest period in a crisis situation is actually the battle itself. The most difficult is the period of indecision – whether to fight or run away. And the most dangerous period is the aftermath. It is then, with all his resources spent and his guard down, that an individual must watch out for dulled reactions and faulty judgment.'[45] Recalling the discussion on personal characteristics and threat perceptions, for Nixon, indecision in the face of a looming crisis was far worse than making a wrong decision. Add to this the crisis constraints of time and information and it becomes clear why Nixon acted swiftly and resolutely,

[42] Ibid., 466–467.
[43] Haldeman, *The Haldeman Diaries*, 143.
[44] Hoff, *Nixon Reconsidered*, 52.
[45] Nixon, *Six Crises*, xv.

based on his gut instincts and without full consultation with the advisory system. It is this anxiety about indecisiveness in crises that best explains Nixon's determination to act the way he did on Cambodia, without allowing doubts or reservations (on behalf of the bureaucracy) to challenge his gut reaction. This gut reaction was evidently fuelled by experience, which is invaluable during crises. In *Six Crises*, Nixon went on to explain that once the leader recognised and accepted the physical symptoms that accompanied a crisis situation, then he would make the right decision and look forward to the end of the battle:

When a man has been through even a minor crisis, he learns not to worry when his muscles tense up, his breathing comes faster, his nerves tingle, his stomach churns, his temper becomes short, his nights are sleepless. He recognizes such symptoms as the natural and healthy signs that his system is keyed up for battle. Far from worrying when this happens, he should worry when it does not. Because he knows from experience that once the battle is joined, all these symptoms will disappear – unless he insists on thinking primarily of himself rather than the problem he must confront.[46]

Nixon was therefore under no illusion that he was facing an uphill battle during the last week of April 1970. The tense period leading to the decision to invade Cambodia saw Nixon finding solace in the film *Patton*, about the defiant World War II general who overcame challenges to eventual triumph in the Battle of the Bulge. Secretary Rogers recalled that Nixon was so heavily influenced by the tragic portrait of Patton that he turned into 'a walking ad for the movie . . . it comes up in every conversation.'[47] When Chief of Staff Bob Haldeman did not feel 'inspired,' he recalled that Nixon 'said I should see [*sic*] movie *Patton*. He inspired people, charged them up, chief of staff has to do this.'[48] Kissinger too could not ignore the president's obsession. When Nixon invited him to yet another screening of the film, Kissinger told a friend, 'If I have to see that movie one more time, I'll shoot myself.'[49]

Nixon felt that like the beleaguered and misunderstood Patton, he too was confronted by challenges and crises. He clearly had Patton on

[46] Ibid.
[47] Kalb and Kalb, *Kissinger*, 154.
[48] Haldeman, *The Haldeman Diaries*, 147.
[49] Prados, *Keepers of the Keys*, 297.

his mind when he announced his decision to send 32,000 troops into Cambodia in a televised address to the nation on 30 April 1970. The president compared his decision on Cambodia to historical decisions made by Wilson during World War I, Roosevelt in World War II, Eisenhower during the Korean War and the Suez Crisis, and Kennedy during the Cuban Missile Crisis.[50] While there is no documented evidence to suggest that these historical analogies informed his decision on Cambodia, it is clear that Nixon was desperate to have history on his side. Overall, the tone of Nixon's address was rather apocalyptic. He began by warning of the possible consequences of American inaction in the face of communist threat:

If, when the chips are down, the world's most powerful nation, the United States of America, acts like a pitiful, helpless giant, the forces of totalitarianism and anarchy will threaten free nations and free institutions throughout the world... If we fail to meet this challenge all other nations will be on notice that despite its overwhelming power, the United States, when a real crisis comes, will be found wanting.[51]

While the secret bombing and the large-scale commitment of U.S. ground forces clearly suggested a widening of the war, Nixon went to great lengths to reassure the American public that this was not the case: 'This is not an invasion of Cambodia... Our purpose is not to occupy the area. Once enemy forces are driven out of these sanctuaries and their military supplies destroyed, we will withdraw.'[52] This was merely an exercise in semantics. Nixon was well aware of the political costs of his decision. He concluded his address: 'I would rather be a one-term President and do what I believe is right than to be a two-term President at the cost of seeing America become a second-rate power and to see this nation accept the first defeat in its proud 190-year history.'[53]

Still, it seemed that Nixon was not ready for what was to come – the domestic outcry that followed his address reached unprecedented proportions that went well beyond the most pessimistic assessments harboured by the bureaucracy. Anti-war demonstrations quickly spread

---

[50] Nixon, 'Address to the Nation on the Situation on Southeast Asia, April 30, 1970,' *PPPUS 1970*, 409.
[51] Ibid.
[52] Ibid., 407–408.
[53] Ibid., 410.

all over the country, calling for the president's resignation. Emotions ran high on the campuses, particularly after four students were killed by the National Guard at Kent State University. Five days later, nearly 100,000 demonstrators arrived in Washington to protest against Nixon's Cambodia's policy. By the end of the week, a third of the colleges in the country were shut down by angry students and teachers. The White House was besieged by protestors, and the media's treatment of Nixon was more critical than ever. Another cause for concern for Nixon was a move in the Senate, led by two prominent members of the Senate Foreign Relations Committee, John Cooper (R-KY) and Frank Church (D-ID), to cut off funds for the Cambodia operation.[54]

Evidently alarmed by the nationwide protest, Nixon finally yielded to the pressure, and on 8 May, he announced that the ground operation would be completed by the end of June with the withdrawal of 'all Americans of all kind, including advisers.'[55] As scheduled, on 30 June, the last American soldier left Cambodia. The same day, the Senate passed the Cooper-Church amendment which prohibited any American activity in Cambodia. It was meaningless since Nixon had already announced the completion of the Cambodia operation, but its historic significance could not be undermined. It was the first-ever decision by Congress to restrict presidential war powers.[56]

Crisis Decision-Making

Not surprisingly, there were no WSAG meetings on Cambodia prior to the March coup. The extreme secrecy surrounding the bombing of Cambodia meant that no interdepartmental meetings had taken place on that issue. Following the coup, however, and with the increase in North Vietnamese activities in Cambodia, the need for coherent information and advice led to no less than twenty-four meetings of the group between 19 March and 15 June.[57] Most of the meetings took place during the last week of April and the first week of May – the run-up to the incursion and the first week of the operation, respectively.

---

[54] Bundy, *A Tangled Web*, 155–156; Shawcross, *Sideshow*, 152–153; Blum, *Years of Discord*, 367–368.
[55] 'The President's News Conference of May 8, 1970,' *PPPUS 1970*, 417.
[56] Bundy, *A Tangled Web*, 160–161.
[57] These data were collected from the various archival records and the Kissinger memoirs.

Once the wheels were in motion, the group convened less frequently, indicating a 'routinization' of crisis management. This was in stark contrast to the Jordanian Crisis, for example, where short crisis duration combined with almost daily developments led to fourteen meetings in as many days.

The performance of the WSAG during the Cambodian crisis is unique amongst the cases examined in this book. There was a noticeable difference in the group's performance before and after Nixon's decision to send U.S. forces into Cambodia. Kissinger's view of this difference is telling: 'The WSAG meetings, which in previous weeks had been nightmares of evasion and foot-dragging, now turned crisp and precise.'[58] Kissinger's account supports Nixon's assertion quoted earlier about the perils of indecisiveness in the face of crisis. Furthermore, it reinforces a key argument about the necessity of the advisory system – once the president set out the parameters of the problem and the policy priorities, the contribution of the WSAG was significant and 'crisp.' Until that point however, with little presidential guidance and being kept in the dark, the group's meetings were ineffective. In other words, when the president wants the system to work, it will do its job, and do it well. Part of the failed management of the Cambodia episode, however, lies in the fact that it was not until the last days in April that Nixon finally decided to turn to his advisory system. By then, however, the disastrous decision to invade Cambodia had already been taken by the president. Indeed, his decision on 28 April followed weeks of intense deliberations within the administration about how to come to the aid of the pro-western regime of Lon Nol in the face of growing NVA attacks. However, it did not result from a coherent process of decision-making where alternative contingencies were carefully evaluated within a defined decision-making group. Rather, the decision was made by Nixon with little consultation with his top advisors. The few WSAG meetings between 14 and 27 April were of little substance but with seemingly endless discussions on relatively straightforward issues, such as the shipment of several thousand rifles to Phnom Penh. In stark contrast, once a presidential directive had been issued on 28 April, WSAG meetings became more constructive, with more

---

58 Kissinger, *White House Years*, 503.

substantive output. Kissinger's explanation for this improvement provides an insightful account of the power – and limitations – of bureaucratic politics: 'Once a Cabinet department recognizes that a decision is irrevocable and cannot be altered by artful exegesis or leaks, it can become a splendid instrument, competent, efficient, thoughtful.'[59]

The incursion into Cambodia proved to be infinitely more complex than the secret bombing. The invasion of more than 30,000 ground troops could not have been done covertly and required close co-operation and coordination between the various government agencies. Additionally, the White House had to work hard to defend its decision in front of the media and Congress. Nevertheless, in authorizing the operations against the Cambodian sanctuaries, it seemed that Nixon paid little attention to the domestic ramifications of his decision. Not even Kissinger could rein in the president's desire to deliver a massive blow to Hanoi's military operations. According to Haldeman, Kissinger was concerned about Nixon's almost reckless management of the crisis. On 24 April, Haldeman noted that 'K[issinger] was very worried last night, and still is, to a lesser degree, that [the] P[resident] is moving too rashly without really thinking through the consequences.'[60] Perhaps more than any other case examined in this book, the decision-making process during the Cambodia episode was ultimately shaped by Nixon's personal anxieties and gut feelings. Undoubtedly, Nixon's decision was fuelled by his self-image of the beleaguered leader fighting against the odds, much like General Patton. Unlike Patton's however, Nixon's enemies were 'Those senators [who] think they can push me around but I'll show them who's tough' and, of course, the liberals, who were waiting 'to see Nixon let Cambodia go down the drain just the way Eisenhower let Cuba go down the drain.'[61]

Nixon's last comment is particularly telling since it provides at least partial explanation for the faulty decision-making process during the crisis. Although the issue of Cuba did not come up during meetings, it is evident that it affected or shaped, at least cognitively, Nixon's perception of what was at stake in Cambodia. Indeed, this crisis provides

[59] Ibid.
[60] Haldeman, *The Haldeman Diaries*, 154.
[61] Morris, *Uncertain Greatness*, 174.

several cases of references to analogical reasoning. Following the invasion, Nixon also referred to the failure of appeasement in the 1930s
to justify his order to send troops into Cambodia,[62] and Nixon's references to past presidents and momentous events in the twentieth century in his Address to the Nation on 30 April were already mentioned.
This type of analogical reasoning could have detrimental effects on
the quality of the decisions made, as by oversimplifying the similarities
between past and present crises, policy makers risk ignoring the crucial
differences between the cases. The crisis in Cambodia in the spring of
1970 was patently different from the events surrounding the 'fall'
of Cuba in the 1950s or European affairs in the 1930s. Nixon's
reluctance to see beyond the simple labels of 'aggression' or 'defeat'
undoubtedly contributed to his faulty perception of the crisis, which
in turn affected the way in which he was prepared to engage with the
decision-making machinery.

In addition to Kissinger, who chaired the meetings, usually present
at the WSAG forum were U. Alexis Johnson and Marshall Green
from the State Department (under secretary for political affairs and
assistant secretary for East Asian and Pacific Affairs, respectively),
David Packard and Warren Nutter from the Defense Department
(deputy secretary of defense and assistant secretary for international
security affairs, respectively), General Earle Wheeler and Admiral
Thomas Moorer (chairman and acting chairman of the JCS, respectively; Moorer succeeded Wheeler in the summer of 1970), Richard
Helms and Thomas Karamessines from the CIA (director and deputy
director for plans, respectively), and Colonel Richard Kennedy (NSC
staff). The first substantial WSAG meeting took place on 14 April in
response to Lon Nol's request for 'unconditional foreign aid from all
sources.'[63] The purpose of the meeting was to work out a level and
type of military aid sufficient to reassure Lon Nol but at the same time
not to aggravate Hanoi. That meeting signalled a dramatic turn in the
administration's view of the situation, as well as the preferred way
to handle it. Hitherto, issues concerning Cambodia were discussed in

---

[62] Hanhimaki, *The Flawed Architect*, 78.
[63] Kissinger, *White House Years*, 472. The group had met previously on 19 March after
the overthrow of Sihanouk but spent most of the meeting discussing developments in
Laos. As Kissinger noted in his memoirs, that meeting reflected the administration's
'priorities' at the time. See *White House Years*, 465.

meetings of the 40 Committee or other informal, secret intelligence channels.[64] Indeed, Kissinger acknowledged that the 14 April meeting indicated that 'the problem of Cambodia had grown beyond the intelligence framework. A major policy decision was likely to be required in the near future.'[65]

The group recommended sending to Lon Nol up to 3,000 captured Soviet AK-47 rifles from South Vietnamese stocks in order to maintain, at least publicly, American dissociation from Cambodia. For this reason, the shipment of heavier or American equipment was not discussed. The State Department refused to deliver even medical supplies.[66] The following day, the group met to recommend the establishment of a $5 million fund to Cambodia, which would be channelled through Australia. This decision was taken following Lon Nol's appeal for economic and military assistance to expand his army.[67] Clearly alarmed by the rising number of NVA attacks in Cambodia and acting out of character, Nixon decided to reach down and personally intervene in the process. Following the WSAG meeting, he met with Helms and his deputy, Robert Cushman. Nixon ordered them to send to Phnom Penh military aid, an option which had been rejected the previous day by the WSAG. Several days later, he ordered the group to double the level of assistance funding to Cambodia to $10 million.[68]

Somewhat surprisingly, the increasing number of NVA attacks did not deter Nixon from his decision to continue with his Vietnamization programme. On the contrary, on 20 April, he announced the largest pullout of U.S. forces yet. In a televised speech from his presidential retreat in San Clemente, California, he declared that by the end of spring 1971, 150,000 U.S. troops would return home. At the same time, however, not to appear weak or indecisive, Nixon referred to the looming crisis in Cambodia and sent a direct warning to Hanoi that 'they will be taking grave risks should they attempt to use the occasion to jeopardize the security of our remaining forces in Vietnam.'[69]

---

[64] To date, all minutes of the 40 Committee meetings remain classified.
[65] Kissinger, *White House Years*, 472.
[66] Ibid., 473.
[67] Prados, *Keepers of the Keys*, 293.
[68] Kissinger, *White House Years*, 473.
[69] Nixon, 'Address to the Nation on Progress toward Peace in Vietnam, April 20, 1970,' *PPPUS 1970*, 374–375.

However, even on this important decision, Nixon did not consider it necessary to consult his cabinet. Only hours before Nixon made his speech, 'too late for leaks to the evening newscasts,' Kissinger informed secretaries Laird and Rogers of Nixon's decision.[70] Nixon also refused to allow Kissinger to give a backgrounder on general foreign policy because he feared it would help the press. As Haldeman recalled, Nixon 'gave K a lecture about playing only to your friends in the press, those that will give you a 40–50 percent chance of a fair story.'[71]

Surprisingly, despite Nixon's decision to exclude his top advisors from the decision-making process, he was clearly concerned by the prospect of Kissinger overshadowing the assessments and views of Rogers and Laird. While Kissinger was on holiday in early April, Nixon had a rare opportunity to speak with Secretary Rogers in private. As Haldeman's diary entry shows, the president expressed serious doubts about Kissinger's tactics of exclusion:

[Nixon] had a meeting with Rogers this morning, and concluded he's got to have more of these without K. Feels K doesn't give him accurate picture of Laird's and Rogers' views. Always puts it in black and white. P talked a long time with E[hrlichman] and me about this problem, trying to figure out how to handle this. Basically, it's impossible because of the characters, especially K. But Rogers clearly manoeuvres to clobber Henry.[72]

However, good intentions aside, immediately after his 20 April address, Nixon reverted to his old self. Fearing that Secretary Laird would take advantage of the withdrawal announcement to speed up the schedule, Nixon opened a back channel to the military command in Vietnam. Haldeman recalled that while on the flight back to Washington, Nixon talked to Kissinger 'about problem of dealing with Cabinet people. Wants to set up back channel to issue orders to military not through Secretary of Defense. Said he's not going to let Laird kill this by pulling out too fast. Said will pull all together tomorrow, will decide without Rogers. P[resident] will personally take over responsibility for war in Cambodia.'[73] The decision to keep Laird and Rogers out of the loop had seemed to work. Haldeman jubilantly recalled: 'All the

---

[70] Kissinger, *White House Years*, 481.
[71] Haldeman, *The Haldeman Diaries*, 152.
[72] Ibid., 145.
[73] Ibid., 152.

commentators, etc., still off balance about speech. Weren't expecting 150,000 withdrawal, and it left them without a line. One time we really kept a secret. Only way is not to tell anyone.'[74]

That Nixon was averse to use the foreign policy machine that he himself had set up is evidenced by the fact that he convened a meeting of the NSC only once during the crisis, on 22 April. Kissinger arrived at the meeting equipped with a memo by General Westmoreland, listing alternative courses of action in Cambodia.[75] Westmoreland reported that although the intelligence coming from Cambodia was 'fragmentary,' it was clear that the enemy was moving 'to isolate Phnom Penh by the systematic interdiction of all the major roads and waterways leading into the city.' He was also confident that the United States 'can, and must, do everything possible to provide appropriate equipment' for the Cambodian forces, suggesting that the shipment of thousands of captured Soviet AK-47s was not enough and would 'probably fall far short of altering the military situation.'[76] Following this assessment, Westmoreland's advice was inevitable. To 'stem the deterioration within Cambodia,' he recommended that plans should be developed for attacks by the South Vietnamese air force (RVNAF) on enemy positions. Most important, Westmoreland suggested a greater role for U.S. forces – this would include placing them 'on the border to provide logistic and artillery support for the RVNAF forces engaged in operation within Cambodia.' By doing this 'expediently' (the monsoon season was approaching), Westmoreland assessed that it would allow the United States to 'exploit the situation to our overall advantage without any substantial involvement by United States forces on the ground.'[77] Thus relying on a single source to base his recommendations upon, Kissinger was apparently elated by the prospect of stepping up the war effort against the North Vietnamese. Haldeman recalled that before the NSC meeting, Nixon turned back to him 'with a big smile and said, "K's really having fun today, he's playing Bismarck."'[78]

---

[74] Ibid., 153.

[75] Westmoreland sent the report to Secretary Laird on 21 April. Laird sent a copy to Kissinger the following day.

[76] Memo, Westmoreland to Laird, 'Courses of Action with Regard to Cambodia,' 21 April 1970. Folder no. 8, *WSAG Meetings* MF, Box H-073, NSCIF, NPMP.

[77] Ibid.

[78] Haldeman, *The Haldeman Diaries*, 153.

While notionally the NSC meeting on 22 April was the pinnacle
of weeks of intense deliberations among Nixon's top advisors, it is
more than likely that by then Nixon had already made up his mind
about sending U.S. troops into Cambodia. If this was indeed the case,
as Jeffery Kimball suggests, then everything that had happened up to
28 April (when Nixon made his 'final' decision) was nothing but 'an
elaborate charade.'[79] Kissinger believed that this time frame gave 'all
parties an opportunity to express themselves,' whereas Nixon 'needed
time to steel himself for an inevitable adverse congressional and anti-
war reaction to an American invasion of Cambodia.'[80] Present at the
meeting were Nixon, Kissinger, Vice President Spiro Agnew, Rogers,
Laird, Admiral Moorer, Helms, Attorney General John Mitchell, and
Director of the Office of Emergency Preparedness Brig. Gen. George
Lincoln. Kissinger presented the group three basic options: (1) taking
no military action (which was supported by State and Defense Departments); (2) attacking the sanctuaries with ARVN forces, as Kissinger
had recommended; and (3) using whatever force was necessary against
the sanctuaries, as proposed by the JCS, the CIA, and Military Assistance Command in Vietnam (MACV, which controlled all U.S. units in
Vietnam).[81] The general feeling at the meeting was that the NVA had
expanded its resources and capabilities in Cambodia enough to inflict
significant casualties on U.S. forces. The group considered the situation too dangerous to slow down the planned withdrawal of American
troops from Vietnam and considered it a possible threat to the success
of the entire process of Vietnamization. While avoiding a concrete
decision, the group supported the use of ARVN forces for ground
operations and recommended that the U.S. role should be limited to
air support.[82] Two border areas in particular were considered for
attack at the meeting. The first, called 'Parrot's Beak,' was located
less than 40 miles from Saigon, from which NVA forces shelled the
South Vietnamese capital. The second, 'Fishhook,' was farther north
and was believed to be home to the elusive COSVN. Since Fishhook

---

[79] J. Kimball, *Nixon's Vietnam War* (Lawrence: University Press of Kansas, 1998), 206.
[80] Ibid. By the time of the meeting, General Abrams had already recommended combined
US-ARVN operations against the sanctuaries along the border area. Prados, *Keepers
of the Keys*, 294–295.
[81] Kissinger, *White House Years*, 490–491.
[82] Shawcross, *Sideshow*, 138–139.

was heavily defended, the majority view was that it was not feasible to attack both areas simultaneously.[83]

During the Nixon years, NSC meetings were not used as a decision-making forum. This time, however, perhaps because of the mounting pressure or perhaps because he wished to 'steel' himself, as Kimball suggests, Nixon told the group that he had decided in favour of using ARVN forces with U.S. support. The heated debate which ensued about the preferred role of U.S. forces probably convinced Nixon that this ought to be the last time he revealed his decisions in this forum. His irritation was particularly apparent when Vice President Agnew spoke up. As Kissinger noted, 'If Nixon hated anything more than being presented with a plan he had not considered, it was to be shown up in a group as being less tough than his advisers'[84] – a perfect example of what Janis termed eccentric, or self-centric, and emotive coping mechanism which leaders may resort to during times of crisis (see chapter 1). The result of lack in one's confidence or ability to steer the crisis is often the hardening of positions so as not to appear soft in front of one's peers. Agnew's input thus clearly hit a raw nerve for Nixon. Arguing that if eliminating the NVA strongholds was necessary for the success of the Vietnamization process, Agnew concluded that he did not understand 'all the pussyfooting about the American role or what we accomplished by attacking only one.'[85] He therefore recommended attacking both areas, using U.S. forces. Nixon was furious with Agnew for showing him up in front of his top advisors, and on the spot authorised U.S. air support for the ARVN attack on Parrot's Beak only, to be launched on Sunday, 26 April. He then rounded on Kissinger for not forewarning him of Agnew's views before the meeting.

However, while the WSAG met twice the following day, 23 April, to work out plans for the implementation of Nixon's decision to attack Parrot's Beak, the president was already considering an attack on Fishhook.[86] During this period (23–28 April), it was plain to those around

---

[83] Kissinger, *White House Years*, 490.

[84] Ibid., 491.

[85] Ibid.

[86] During the 23 April meetings, the WSAG recommended committing U.S. 'air assets' to support the ARVN attack in Cambodia. The WSAG emphasised that the objective of the operation would be a limited involvement and that American assets would be used 'only if absolutely required – first reliance would be on the South Vietnamese.'

him that Nixon was under a great deal of pressure, consumed by stress and alcohol. Kissinger and Haldeman provide similar accounts of his erratic behaviour during the last week of April. Nixon was roaring on with very little sleep, was in 'high gear' and 'very much absorbed in Cambodia'; he was 'overwrought' and 'irritable.'[87] His constant references to *Patton* were unbearable. Other accounts add that Nixon 'was sometimes intoxicated, which slurred his speech and lubricated his belligerence; he was frustrated by his foot-dragging bureaucracy, which threw him into "monumental" rages.'[88] On one such occasion, on 24 April, Nixon had spent the evening watching *The Cincinnati Kid* and drinking martinis with his long-time pal, Miami businessman Charles 'Bebe' Rebozo. Nixon then called Kissinger to discuss plans to attack Fishhook, while 'slurring obscenities.' Nixon suddenly told Kissinger, 'Wait a minute, Bebe has something to say to you.' An unsettled Kissinger then heard Rebozo say, 'The president wants you to know, Henry, that if this doesn't work, it's your ass.'[89]

At this point, it is worth returning to Nixon's observations in his book *Six Crises* about the psychological and physical effects of crises on the leader. Nixon's reference to tensed muscles, fast breathing, tingling nerves, a churning stomach, short temper, and sleepless nights as 'natural and healthy' signs perhaps indicated – as Nixon suggested – that he was 'keyed up' for the battle. However, it is just as likely that they were symptoms of an incapacitated president, overwrought by the weight of his controversial decision. He even found the time to blame his predecessor for the quagmire he now found himself muddling in. It was Johnson's decision to halt the bombing of North Vietnam in 1968,

---

Nevertheless, Kissinger accepted the recommendation of General Abrams, the JCS, and the Defense Department to send U.S. advisors along with ARVN units into Cambodia to assure 'effective use of U.S. tactical air support.' The State Department, on the other hand, expressed concern 'over the possible political reactions to the use of US personnel in Cambodia.' See Memo, Kissinger to Nixon, 'Operations Against North Vietnamese Base in Cambodia,' no date. Folder no. 8, *WSAG Meetings*, MF, Box H-073, NSCIF, NPMP; and Minutes of WSAG meeting, 'Meeting of WSAG Principals on Cambodia,' 23 April 1970. Folder no. 4, *WSAG*, Minutes of Meetings Files (henceforth MMF), Box H-114, NSCIF, MPMP.

[87] Kissinger, *White House Years*, 487–493; Haldeman, *The Haldeman Diaries*, 153–154.

[88] Kimball, *Nixon's Vietnam War*, 204.

[89] Isaacson, *Kissinger*, 262.

Nixon asserted, that had caused the problem in the first place: 'Damn Johnson, if he'd just done the right thing we wouldn't be in this mess now.'[90] Undoubtedly fuelled by Agnew's hard line at the NSC meeting, Nixon was now closer than ever to authorizing the use of American ground forces against all NVA and VC sanctuaries in Cambodia.[91] Delivering a massive blow to the North Vietnamese seemed attractive and inevitable. According to Haldeman, Nixon felt that he could 'get it wound up this year if we keep enough pressure on and don't crumble at home. K agrees.'[92]

However, Kissinger did not readily agree with Nixon's ambitious plan. To a large degree, Kissinger's moderate view in the NSC meeting was mollified by the analysis of his closest advisors on the NSC staff: Winston Lord, Tony Lake, Roger Morris, Larry Lynn, and William Watts. Dubbed by Kissinger the 'bleeding hearts' club, for weeks the group had pressed the case against widening the war into Cambodia. Politically and militarily, the group argued, active engagement of U.S. forces in Cambodia would be disastrous and would yield no benefits to the administration or to the overall war effort in Vietnam. On 2 April, Lord reviewed U.S. options in Cambodia and concluded that 'under no circumstances should we put U.S. troops into Cambodia. The present rules of engagement limiting us to protective reaction along the border should apply in all instances.'[93] A few weeks later, Lord, Morris, and Lake warned that 'any use of US forces in Cambodia...would increase our involvement and prestige in a losing cause, limit diplomatic flexibility, and have severe political consequences in the US.'[94]

Following the NSC meeting and Nixon's decision on Parrot's Beak, Kissinger met with his closest advisors to discuss U.S. options in Cambodia. Once again, Morris and Lord warned Kissinger that 'there would be disastrous domestic dissent...and that the notoriously unreliable intelligence from the region, let alone the larger cause of peace, did not justify a U.S. invasion.'[95] Kissinger's attempts to convince his advisors that their recommendation of shallow cross-border

---

[90] Haldeman, *The Haldeman Diaries*, 153.
[91] Kissinger, *The White House Years*, 492.
[92] Haldeman, *The Haldeman Diaries*, 153–154.
[93] Cited in Hanhimaki, *The Flawed Architect*, 74.
[94] Ibid., 75.
[95] Morris, *Uncertain Greatness*, 174.

penetrations was morally no different from deep ground incursions fell on deaf ears.[96] Out of the five bleeding hearts, only Lord remained in the administration following the invasion. William Watts was first to resign, on 26 April. When asked by Kissinger to coordinate the NSC staff work on the invasion, Watts marched toward Kissinger's office to hand in his resignation letter. Kissinger's deputy, Alexander Haig (an avid supporter of the invasion), confronted Watts: 'You can't refuse. You've just had an order from your commander in chief.' 'Fuck you, Al,' Watts replied, 'I can, and I just quit.'[97] Three days later, Lake and Morris – nicknamed 'The Gold Dust Twins' by their colleagues on the NSC staff because they were Kissinger's 'fair-haired' favourites – followed suit. Several months later, Lynn resigned as well, despite Kissinger's desperate efforts to persuade him to stay, which included a meeting with Nixon in the Oval Office.[98]

However, despite the dissent among his own staff, the more Kissinger mulled over the arguments against the invasion, the more convinced he became that a full-scale invasion was the only option. Vice President Agnew was right: There was no middle ground. A limited operation in one area alone using ARVN forces – Kissinger's original recommendation at the NSC meeting – seemed pointless: 'It would stir up domestic discord, have little effect on the North Vietnamese, and combine the worst elements of all alternatives.'[99] The distraught president of course welcomed Kissinger's new conviction, as he clearly needed his national security advisor on his side – not only to encourage the president and to galvanize his self-image of the tragic, beleaguered leader but also to carry out a task which Nixon was notoriously averse to – confronting the dissenting voices in the administration – namely, Rogers and Laird – and their fellow bureaucrats.

With Kissinger's support, Nixon now steamed ahead with little regard for formalistic, orderly procedures. On the morning of 24 April,

---

[96] For more on this episode, see Isaacson, *Kissinger,* 263–264; Hersh, *The Price of Power,* 187–190; Shawcross, *Sideshow,* 141–142; Hanhimaki, *The Flawed Architect,* 75–76.

[97] Isaacson, *Kissinger,* 276. Kissinger's reaction to the resignation was to throw papers 'around his office in a rage,' and to accuse Watts that 'Your views represent the cowardice of the Eastern Establishment.' Hersh, *The Price of Power,* 191.

[98] Isaacson, *Kissinger,* 276–277.

[99] Ibid., 265.

he met with Kissinger, Moorer, Helms, and his deputy Robert Cushman. Nixon's explanation for the absence of Rogers and Laird, that he 'merely wanted a military and intelligence briefing,' was hardly convincing. Rather, as Kissinger noted, the exclusion of the secretaries of State and Defense was 'a reflection of his extreme irritation at bureaucratic foot-dragging.'[100] When Admiral Moorer asked Nixon what he should report back to Laird, Nixon replied that he was to report nothing. He was attending the meeting 'as the President's military advisor' and not as the Chairman of the JCS.[101] At the meeting, Nixon wished to explore the possibility of attacking Fishhook as well as Parrot's Beak, using ARVN and U.S. forces. All those present supported the attack on Fishhook, and Kissinger later told Laird about the meeting, describing it as a 'military briefing of options, including an American attack on Fishhook.'[102] Indeed, there are evident signs in the Cambodia episode of *groupthink* tendencies within the decision-making framework. Nixon, Kissinger, Haig, and Moorer formed a cohesive, self-supportive group which was blind to alternative options and demonstrated visible signs of high stress from external threat. The result was pressure on dissenters to conform (such as Haig's bust-up with Watts) or simply their exclusion from the decision-making process (keeping Rogers and Laird out of the loop).

Kissinger saw no reason to tell the administration's crisis management group about the meeting either. Convening the WSAG later that morning, Kissinger did not reveal the contents of his meeting with Nixon. Instead, he opened with the usual line: 'There must be no leaks. All the departments will be held responsible.'[103] Admiral Moorer explained that the plan to execute Phase I – the Parrot's Beak operation – was in fact a 'division-plus size operation on two sites. Next is the plan for the COSVN area.' With no mention of his recommendation to Nixon earlier in the morning, Moorer stressed that there was no immediate plan to attack the COSVN, as it would be difficult to launch another major operation simultaneously. Deputy Secretary of Defense Dave Packard remarked that the concentration of forces

[100] Kissinger, *White House Years*, 495.
[101] Shawcross, *Sideshow*, 141.
[102] Kissinger, *White House Years*, 496.
[103] Minutes of WSAG meeting, 'WSAG Meeting (Principals),' 24 April 1970, 10:40 a.m. Folder no. 9, *WSAG Meetings*, MF, Box H-073, NSCIF, NPMP.

near Fishhook was, in fact, 'a feint against COSVN and then [*sic*] they attack Parrot's Beak.' To remove any doubt, Kissinger again reiterated that 'no Americans go into Cambodia.'[104] During the afternoon meeting, the group mainly discussed the military priorities of the operation. However, addressing the aspect of public relations, Kissinger was eager to know 'When will the press know it's a large operation?' and 'When will we begin to get flak?' The group estimated that it would not be possible to keep the press at arms length for more than forty-eight hours. Furthermore, Under Secretary of State Johnson expressed concern that '[Senator] Fulbright will be angry that the Secretary didn't tell him.'[105]

It is hard to ignore the irony behind Johnson's concern. Fearing that Secretary Rogers might keep the Chairman of the Senate Foreign Relations Committee, Senator James Fulbright, in the dark, paled in comparison to the fact that Kissinger and Nixon had kept Secretaries Rogers and Laird, and their respective departments, in the dark about their decision to send U.S. ground troops into Cambodia. Kissinger continued the charade the following day. When William Watts expressed his concern about the involvement of U.S. troops in Cambodia, Kissinger replied, 'Don't worry. I've seen the Old Man and it'll never happen.'[106] However, by 26 April, there was no doubt that it would happen, and soon. Following the meeting with Helms, Moorer, and Cushman, Kissinger persuaded Nixon to hold another NSC meeting. Secretaries Rogers and Laird had been kept out of the loop ever since the NSC meeting four days earlier when Nixon had decided to strike only at Parrot's Beak. Now Kissinger argued that the secretaries should be given the opportunity to express their views: 'Any decision must be discussed with the two Cabinet members – even if the decision has already been made and an order is in the desk drawer. You can't ram it down their throats without their having a chance to give their views.'[107]

Notwithstanding Kissinger's commendable intentions, the meeting was yet another scene in the ongoing pretence. Present at the meeting were Nixon, Kissinger, Admiral Wheeler, Helms, Rogers, and Laird.

[104] Ibid.
[105] Minutes of WSAG meeting, 'WSAG Principals Meeting,' 24 April 1970, 4:20 p.m. Folder no. 4, *WSAG*, MMF, Box H-114, NSCIF, NPMP.
[106] Hersh, *The Price of Power*, 190.
[107] Kissinger, *White House Years*, 497.

Kissinger recalls that Agnew was excluded from the meeting, as Nixon 'was determined to be the strong man of *this* meeting.'[108] The meeting resembled a military briefing of options and, to Nixon's relief, Rogers and Laird said very little and raised no objections. Nixon interpreted their silence as acquiescence, and as soon as the meeting finished, he instructed Kissinger to issue NSDM-57, authorising an attack on Fishhook by U.S. forces. The directive allowed for 'the conduct of ground operations by U.S. forces or by US/GVN [Government of Vietnam] forces into identified North Vietnamese/Viet Cong sanctuaries in Cambodia up to a depth of 30 kilometers...The Washington Special Actions Group is designated as the implementing authority for these steps.'[109]

Once more, the directive brought to the fore the divisions within the administration. The WSAG met the following morning, Monday, 27 April, to discuss the implementation of NSDM-57, when Kissinger was called out of the meeting. Rogers was on the phone, demanding to know whether the directive that he had just received authorized a U.S. ground attack on Fishhook. Kissinger replied that 'there was hardly any other way to interpret it.'[110] Shortly after, Kissinger was called out once more, this time by Laird, who expressed his own reservations. Within the hour, Rogers and Laird met with Nixon, Haldeman, and Kissinger. Haldeman's diary entry shows that Rogers was 'opposed to COSVN decision, taken without consultation. He clearly tried to hang K for inadequate information to P about consequences.' Rogers argued that the operation would 'cost great United States casualties with little gain,' and that the target was 'not significant, not permanent base, not a really clipping blow.' Laird, on the other hand, did not oppose the Fishhook operation in principle but was furious about the provision in NSDM-57 which made the WSAG responsible for the implementation of the operation, and he argued that it should be the responsibility of the secretary of defense.[111] Laird's case was valid. The WSAG was designed to act as a decision-making body, not an implementation

[108] Ibid., 499.
[109] NSDM-57, 'Actions to Protect U.S. Forces in South Vietnam,' 26 April 1970. Folder no. 12, MF, NSCIF, Box H-073, NPMP.
[110] Kissinger, *White House Years*, 500.
[111] Haldeman, *The Haldeman Diaries*, 155.

body. The directive blurred the line (which hardly existed in the Nixon administration anyway) between policy and operations.

Rogers then raised the issue of his scheduled appearance that afternoon before the Senate Foreign Relations Committee to discuss how the United States should respond to Lon Nol's appeal for military aid. Haldeman records that Rogers made it clear that he 'doesn't want to say we're sending United States troops into Cambodia, but he can't say otherwise with NSDM out without lying which he won't do.'[112] Nixon agreed that Rogers should not have to lie to the Senate's most powerful committee and suggested a face-saving solution. He told Kissinger to suspend the execution orders for twenty-four hours, and after Rogers's testimony called for another meeting the following morning.

Rogers had good reasons to be anxious about his testimony on Capitol Hill. Following Nixon's televised address on 30 April, the chairman of the committee, Senator Fulbright, accused Rogers of misleading the committee by saying nothing about the possibility of U.S. troops becoming involved.[113] The criticism came on the heels of an earlier appearance of Rogers on Capitol Hill. On 23 April, he testified before the House Appropriation Subcommittee and failed to disclose the possibility of sending U.S. ground troops into Cambodia. Moreover, Rogers said, 'Our whole incentive is to de-escalate. We recognize that if we escalate and get involved in Cambodia with our ground troops, our whole programme is defeated.' Rogers then emphasised that should the administration consider using American troops, 'we would consult Congress to the fullest extent.'[114] Of course, Rogers made these remarks not knowing that Nixon was by then half-committed to sending U.S. troops to Fishhook. Rogers's explanation that a final decision was only made the following day was hardly convincing. The press was quick to suggest that 'Mr. Rogers cannot have been very close to the president's confidence; and that judging by the line the secretary took on 23 April, his views must in any case have been discounted

---

[112] Ibid.

[113] On the issue of military aid to Cambodia, Fulbright concluded that the members were 'virtually unanimous – and very firmly in agreement – against sending assistance to Cambodia under the circumstances.' Telegram, Freeman to FCO, 'Military Equipment for Cambodia,' 28 April 1970. FCO 15/1187, NA.

[114] Telegram, Freeman to FCO, 'Cambodia: Mr Rogers' Position,' 6 May 1970. FCO 15/1187, NA.

by the president before 24 hours were up.'[115] As John Freeman, the British ambassador in Washington suggested, much of the criticism directed at Rogers was not so much because of his evasiveness but rather because of his 'willingness to let himself be steamrollered by the president and the Pentagon.' That incident demonstrated once again that 'the Department's advice is liable not to count when the chips are down.'[116]

Freeman was remarkably accurate in his observation. When Nixon made his final decision on 28 April, the secretary of state was the last to be informed (with Laird), after Kissinger, Haldeman, and Attorney General John Mitchell. Haldeman recorded that Nixon '[laid] down the law to Rogers and Laird. He's decided to go ahead with the full plan and told them so, with darn good salesmanship.'[117] Nixon also instructed Kissinger to issue another directive, NSDM-58, in lieu of NSDM-57. The essence of the directive remained unchanged, except for the closing provision. In line with Secretary Laird's protest that the WSAG was designated as the 'implementing authority,' the new directive stated that 'The Washington Special Actions Group is charged with coordinating these activities.'[118]

After removing the remaining traces of bureaucratic discontent, Nixon was now preparing himself for the tough days ahead. Bizarrely, however, he found the time to badger Haldeman about the appropriate location for his new pool table. Haldeman was clearly not impressed by the president's effort to deflect the mounting pressure by turning to nitpicking: 'Absolutely astonishing he could get into trivia on brink of biggest step he's taken so far.'[119] A week later, Nixon ordered to remove the White House tennis court, which several cabinet members used occasionally. As Nixon did not play tennis himself, it was evident that his decision was 'a spiteful way to take a jab at the Cabinet' for not supporting him enough on Cambodia.[120] Nixon was nonetheless ready to take a big hit from the media, Congress, and the public for his decision. Haldeman recorded on 28 April that Nixon 'is clearing the decks

[115] Ibid.
[116] Ibid.
[117] Haldeman, *The Haldeman Diaries*, 156.
[118] NSDM-58, 28 April 1970. Folder no. 11, MF, NSCIF, Box H-073, NPMP.
[119] Haldeman, *The Haldeman Diaries*, 157.
[120] Ibid., 161–162.

and gearing up for the whole thing to hit hard, which it may.'[121] Operation Rock Crusher was launched with the ARVN attack on Parrot's Beak on the night of 28 April, and U.S. forces followed two days later at Fishhook (operation Shoemaker). At the same time, Thursday night, 30 April, Nixon addressed the nation.

Nixon's directives signalled a drastic turning point in the performance of the WSAG, which was meeting almost daily in order to coordinate the two operations. Now that a clear presidential decision had finally been made, the meetings turned more purposeful and the coordination between agencies was more efficient. Kissinger recalls that Alexis Johnson produced a 'masterful' comprehensive plan which detailed the tasks of each department and individual in the run-up to the invasion and after it.[122] However, not even the rejuvenated spirit in WSAG meetings could silence the dissenting voices within the bureaucracy. Nixon's speech incensed many in the administration – particularly in the State Department. Perhaps more than the angry reaction to the seemingly reckless decision to widen the war, many were disturbed by the secretive, manipulative way in which the decision had been reached. On 8 May, 250 Foreign Service officers sent a letter in protest to Secretary Rogers, which was later leaked to the press. In the letter, the signatories sought a review of the direction in which U.S. foreign policy was heading. They expressed their 'deepest concern and apprehension over the enlargement of hostilities in South East Asia suggested by American involvement in Cambodia and the recent bombings in North Vietnam.'[123] When Rogers met representatives of the group, he 'got an outburst' about the way in which the decision to send U.S. troops to Cambodia had been reached – in particular, 'the disregard of State Department views [and] eccentric use of established decision-making machinery.'[124]

The WSAG met ten times in the two weeks following Nixon's speech and the commencement of operation Shoemaker. During that period, the group reviewed and recommended courses of action on a range of issues, from logistical support to Lon Nol and the expansion of

[121] Ibid., 156.
[122] Kissinger, *White House Years*, 503.
[123] Memo, Boyd to FCO, 'Cambodia: Morale in the State Department,' 19 May 1970. FCO 15/1187, NA.
[124] Ibid.

operations to other border areas in Cambodia, to press guidance and dealings with Congress. Remarkably, however, there was not a single substantive discussion on COSVN, the elusive North Vietnamese headquarters in Fishhook, which was the very reason for operation Shoemaker in the first place. Kissinger's suggestion that COSVN represented no more than a 'self-inflicted credibility gap irrelevant to the central issue but corrosive of public confidence' is hardly persuasive.[125] Both the president and the U.S. military command in Vietnam described the destruction of the North Vietnamese headquarters in Fishhook as the 'immediate' objective of the operation.[126] The area was described by General Westmoreland as containing 'the main enemy headquarters as well as a large complex of troop and logistics facilities, ammunition storage area, hospitals, POW camps, and command and control headquarters for one division and six regiments. It is a primary staging area for enemy units operating in South Vietnam.'[127]

The main reason for the failure to find the massive COSVN was poor intelligence, as the COSVN proved not to be massive at all, but rather 'a military unit, a group of men who moved about on trucks.'[128] Alarmingly, Nixon ordered the invasion of a neutral country to locate and destroy a target which nobody was sure actually existed – one CIA source conceded that they did not have triangulation.[129] Nevertheless, at the end of the Cambodian operation, the White House claimed that 'it was never our intent to catch COSVN, often described as a floating crap game, a headquarters of 1,000 to 3,000 people, and in mobile configuration.' Furthermore, the official line was now that 'We did not expect to find them when we got there. If we had, it would have been a delightful bonus, but it was not a major objective.'[130] This

---

[125] Kissinger, *White House Years*, 506.
[126] Memo, Westmoreland to Kissinger, 'Plan for Attack on Base Area 352/353,' 23 April 1970. Folder no. 8, *WSAG Meetings*, MF, Box H-073, NSCIF, NPMP.
[127] Ibid.
[128] T. Powers, *The Man Who Kept the Secrets: Richard Helms and the CIA* (New York: Pocket Books, 1981), 279.
[129] Ibid.
[130] American Embassy, Tokyo, 'The Nixon Doctrine and Indochina: A Background Paper on Current U.S. Foreign Policy in Southeast Asia, July 1970.' Document no. 8, Personal Papers, *Papers of William C. Westmoreland*, Box 20, LBJ Library. The editorial note states that this paper 'represents an authoritative view by a representative cross-section of American foreign policy makers at the time of the meeting, early July, 1970.'

statement completely contradicted the stated objectives of the Cambodian operation as they were set by the U.S. military in May 1970: 'Capture enemy supplies and disrupt lines of supply, destroy COSVN headquarters installation and deprive enemy of present sanctuaries.'[131]

In many respects, the COSVN saga epitomizes the two biggest flaws in the decision-making process during the Cambodia crisis: namely, the poor search for information and, perhaps more acutely, the determination to execute decisions despite the fragmentary intelligence. Secretary Laird advised Nixon not to go after COSVN, but he was not shown Nixon's speech until two hours before the president addressed the nation on 30 April. Nixon also ignored a CIA report that suggested that even advanced electronic intelligence means would not be able to triangulate the location of COSVN – the fact was that by then, many of the North Vietnamese command posts had been relocated westward, away from the border areas.[132] Even well into the operation and with thousands of U.S. troops and advisors in Cambodia, reliable information was hard to come by. During a 12 May WSAG meeting, CIA Director Helms lamented about the difficulty of acquiring good intelligence from Cambodia. When Kissinger asked whether the group could get 'an appraisal of the enemy situation in Cambodia,' Helms replied, 'No, we can't get anything solid . . . We have no hard information. We are working hard now to get good information.'[133] Nixon, too, in a rare meeting with the WSAG in June, stressed that 'we need more intelligence from Phnom Penh . . . we [need] to know more of what [is] going on. There would be a problem in having too great a U.S. presence in Phnom Penh, but we should feel our intelligence was adequate, since so much rode on what we got.'[134]

To understand fully Nixon's irritation at the incompetence of the CIA on this matter, one must look at the broader nature of the relationship between Nixon and the agency. Even before his 1968 presidential election, Helms was alarmed by Nixon's antipathy toward the CIA. Like many of Nixon's less amiable traits, this antipathy was

[131] Telegram, Rives to Richardson, no title, 5 May 1970. Folder no. 15, *WSAG Meetings*, MF, Box H-073, NSCIF, NPMP.

[132] Prados, *Keepers of the Keys*, 300.

[133] Minutes of WSAG meeting, 'Cambodia,' 12 May 1970. Folder no. 3, *NSC Subject Files*, Miscellaneous Files of the Nixon Administration, Box 313, NSCIF, NPMP.

[134] Minutes of WSAG meeting, 'Cambodia,' 15 June 1970. Ibid.

fuelled by his dislike of people who he suspected might not be loyal to him, or worse, liberals who he thought might consider themselves socially superior to him. Helms explained in his memoirs: 'Nixon never appeared to have shaken his early impression that the Agency was exclusively staffed by uppity Ivy Leaguers, most of whom lived in Georgetown and spent every evening gossiping about him at cocktail parties.'[135] Even more alarmingly, it seemed that Nixon's personal distrust of the agency translated into a blatant disregard for the intelligence it brought to his attention. Helms recalled that in November 1968, shortly after Nixon's election, Deputy Director for Intelligence Jack Smith reported that 'Nixon did not appear to be reading the President's Daily Brief – the single most important daily intelligence publication. Worse, if he were reading it, he apparently didn't like it.'[136] Another dangerous example of how Nixon's eccentric cognitive make-up (in this case, a sense of an inferiority complex with relation to the intelligence community and the 'east coast liberals') had a detrimental impact on the president's ability to manage the crisis without bias. In a strange way then, the COSVN intelligence fiasco only served to confirm Nixon's negative preconceptions of the CIA.

Apart from the faulty intelligence, another cause of concern for Nixon was the domestic turmoil and the nationwide protest which followed his 30 April speech. Opposition to the president's decision was particularly rife in the campuses and Congress. A week later, the U.S. Senate took the first step to approve an amendment to prevent any future U.S. military operations in Cambodia. The Cooper-Church Amendment was passed on 30 June and coincided with Nixon's announcement of the completion of the withdrawal of U.S. troops from Cambodia.[137] In reaction to the Kent State shooting on 4 May,

---

[135] R. Helms, *A Look over My Shoulder: A Life in the Central Intelligence Agency* (New York: Random House, 2003), 382.

[136] Ibid., 377. Attorney General John Mitchell later explained to Helms that Nixon 'considered the document too far-ranging, and that it covered areas which were of slight interest to the White House.' Mitchell added that Nixon was a lawyer and 'had trouble sorting facts from opinion in the PDB.' Lawyers, Mitchell told Helms, 'liked to have the facts first, with the opinion to follow.' Ibid., 383–384.

[137] For a more comprehensive account of the public reaction to the speech and the domestic turmoil which followed, see, for example, Kissinger, *White House Years*, 509–517; M. Small, *Johnson, Nixon, and the Doves* (New Brunswick, NJ: Rutgers University Press, 1988) 199–210; Kimball, *Nixon's Vietnam War*, 213–223.

Haldeman recorded that Nixon was 'very disturbed. Afraid his decision set it off... really sad to see this added to all his worries about the war. He's out on a tough limb, and knows that.' As for reaction in Congress, Nixon was 'concerned about Senate strategy for Church-Cooper amendment about Cambodia. Wants to be sure that whatever they do is not interpreted as defeat.'[138]

Indeed, the momentous decisions and the domestic unrest they spawned hit Nixon hard. On 14 May, Haldeman observed: 'This whole period of two weeks of tension and crisis, preceded by two weeks of very tough decision making has taken its toll. P[resident] won't admit it, but he is really tired, and is, as some have observed, letting himself slip back to the old ways. He's driving himself way too hard on unnecessary things, and because of this is not getting enough sleep, is uptight, etc.'[139] Nixon's behaviour during that period was anything but ordinary, and perhaps the most bizarre episode came on 18 May, on board Air Force One. Talking to Haldeman, Ehrlichman, and Kissinger, the president expressed his gratitude for the resilient performance of his three gatekeepers in the past few weeks. Then, Nixon announced that they deserved an award and proceeded to present them with the Blue Heart – 'for those who are true blue.' Nixon gave each of them a blue cloth heart made by Bebe Rebozo's wife and said that the honour 'was to be kept very confidential.'[140]

Thus, clearly distraught by the domestic furore, an exhausted Nixon met with the WSAG on 15 June. Conceding that the situation in Cambodia 'looked bleak,' the president went to great lengths to underscore the importance of preventing Cambodia from 'going Communist.' Nixon assured the group that the advantages of keeping Cambodia independent were worth the risks. He concluded that it was his 'intuition that Cambodia could be saved.'[141] However, Nixon's intuition aside, Kissinger's impression was that the president had no concrete idea about the desired U.S. position in Cambodia in the long run. Meeting with British Ambassador John Freeman in June, Kissinger's

---

[138] Haldeman, *The Haldeman Diaries*, 159, 165.
[139] Ibid., 166.
[140] Ibid., 167.
[141] Minutes of WSAG meeting, 'Cambodia,' 15 June 1970.

view was 'uncharacteristically cloudy.' He believed that the president 'has not yet fully thought this through, or perhaps feels that he has insufficient information on which to make a confident assessment of future events in Cambodia.'[142] Recalling the earlier discussion on personalities in the context of crisis decision-making, it is evident that Nixon's handling of the stress associated with making tough decisions was poor and had a debilitating effect on the construction of a coherent and efficient strategy for Cambodia. In many respects, Kissinger's remark captures the essence of decision-making during this crisis: a controversial operation conceived in the mind of a president encouraged by overzealous generals and opposed by senior Cabinet members and NSC staff; a decision backed by incomplete intelligence and made with little consideration of the political costs or, indeed, of the reality the day after the conclusion of the operation.

Performance of the WSAG

As the first major international crisis since the EC-121 incident in April 1969, the Cambodian crisis enabled the administration to test the institutional and procedural mechanisms that Kissinger had put in place to reflect Nixon's hierarchical, formalistic style of management. However, there was nothing formal or orderly about the decision-making process during the Cambodian crisis. Rather, it was a charade of secrecy, back-channelling, exclusion, and evasion, orchestrated from the first day by Nixon and Kissinger. Roger Morris, a member of Kissinger's bleeding hearts club who resigned over the incursion, identified the chief reasons for the faulty crisis management: 'The bizarre, almost manic decisionmaking involved in the invasion belonged chiefly to Nixon; the root logic of the strike was Kissinger's.'[143]

The Foreign Service officers' description of the established decision-making machinery during the crisis as 'eccentric' was not far from the truth. Indeed, a reading of the declassified documents and other published accounts on the crisis makes it almost impossible to construct a picture of coherent, orderly process of decision-making. The manner

---

[142] Telegram, Freeman to FCO, no title, 3 June 1970. PREM 13/3081, NA.
[143] Morris, *Uncertain Greatness*, 175.

in which decisions had been reached hardly resembled the elaborate
model of NSC decision-making meticulously designed by Kissinger
only a year earlier.

The involvement of the WSAG during the crisis ranged from
marginal (up to 28 April) to more significant (during the two weeks
following Nixon's speech). However, while its performance throughout the crisis was far from satisfactory, the group could hardly be held
responsible for the flawed decision-making process, as its performance
was largely a product of Nixon's frantic management of the crisis.
Although the group met regularly during the crisis, its input was routinely ignored by Kissinger and, at least until 28 April, its powers as
the body in charge of coordinating the operation were limited to non-
existent (as demonstrated by Nixon's personal intervention following
the 14 April meeting). Decisions were deliberately taken away from
those who might raise objections – from the 22 April NSC meeting
to 26 April, when Nixon finally decided to 'go for broke,' Secretaries
Laird and Rogers were kept out of the loop. The strong reservations of
Kissinger's very experienced and trusted NSC staff were also ignored.
Instead, the president conferred mostly with DCI Helms and General Abrams in Saigon, who both used intelligence of questionable
quality to justify their recommendations. Indeed, the WSAG was no
more than a victim of Nixon and Kissinger's manipulation of the
bureaucracy.

In the minds of Nixon and Kissinger, the objective of the operation
was apparent from the outset. Soon after the March coup, Nixon
declared that the Lon Nol regime must be upheld and that Cambodia
must not 'go Communist.' This overriding objective had not changed
or even been reconsidered throughout the crisis, despite various efforts
on behalf of the bureaucracy – most notably the bleeding hearts club –
to challenge the logic behind it. Recalling Tetlock's metaphor of the fox
and the hedgehog (see chapter 2), during the Cambodian episode the
simple but powerful priority of the hedgehogs – preventing Cambodia
from going communist, invariably triumphed over the more nuanced
approach to the crisis of the foxes, who paid closer attention to the
domestic, political, and diplomatic ramifications of the operation.

Perhaps more disturbingly than the failure to consider alternative
objectives was the incomplete survey of alternative courses of action to
achieve the stated objective. Kissinger presented three basic alternatives

to the NSC at the fateful meeting on 22 April: (1) do nothing, (2) authorize a limited operation in Fishhook, or (3) go after both areas using U.S. troops. These were predetermined and had not been thoroughly examined at WSAG meetings. Furthermore, Nixon announced his decision at the beginning of the meeting, before a genuine discussion among his top advisors could take place.

One of the inevitable side effects of this disregard of the bureaucracy's views was that WSAG meetings did not run smoothly, as various agencies used the meetings to attempt to stall the implementation of the decision to attack Parrot's Beak. However, these efforts proved irrelevant as Nixon began leaning toward a full-scale operation about a week before his 30 April speech. Kissinger soon followed, and his mind was made up after meeting with his NSC staff on 24 April. 'Once the North Vietnamese forces had spread all over the country,' Kissinger reasons in his memoirs, 'the die had been cast.'[144] In a similar fashion, Nixon and Kissinger prevented a proper discussion of the potential benefits and costs of each alternative. These were dismissed with alarming ease, under the pretext that taking no action would endanger the Vietnamization programme and the lives of U.S. troops in Vietnam, and that military aid on its own would be ineffective. Even the potential consequences of the final decision – to go after all the sanctuaries using U.S. troops – were not seriously debated in the WSAG or, indeed, within the broader context of the NSC. Although Laird, Rogers, and the NSC staff repeatedly warned about the political domestic costs, there was never an orderly discussion about the likely repercussions of the decision. The pros and cons presented by General Westmoreland in his memo to Kissinger on 23 April were not discussed in the NSC. The basic assumption that military gains would outweigh the strength of the domestic outcry was never questioned by Nixon, Helms, Kissinger, and the MACV generals.

The failure to adequately canvass contingencies and their costs was largely due to flawed intelligence or, at the very least, the flawed use of the available intelligence. The search for information was not exhaustive and the CIA and MACV's intelligence estimates which fuelled Nixon's decision were questionable – this point repeatedly resurfaced

[144] Kissinger, *White House Years*, 519–520.

in Helms' memoirs as well as the WSAG minutes. For example, on the matter of the port of Sihanoukville and its alleged use as a major supply source for the North Vietnamese, DCI Helms conceded that the 'intelligence services have never come close to possessing divine insight.' While they knew that NVA and VC forces would 'dodge across the border,' many questions remained unanswered: 'How many troops are in transit, and how much materiel are they toting?'[145] In fact, intelligence was so poor that the Americans were not even aware of some of the operations conducted independently by the ARVN, their primary military ally, in mid-April.[146]

Undoubtedly, the most spectacular failure of intelligence during the operation was the ghostly pursuit of the COSVN. Following the invasion, there had been several references to the incomplete information about the location, size, and nature of many of its targets. U.S. intelligence depicted the COSVN as a Pentagon-like facility, an underground maze with thousands of personnel. It turned out to be no more than a handful of radio operators and equipment in a few trucks.[147] Helms conceded that despite the agency's best efforts, good intelligence was hard to come by: 'We were trying every operational skill in our arsenal to penetrate the policy levels of the government of North Vietnam. I kept a high standard staff personnel in Vietnam, and the best of the Agency operatives around the globe were focused on Hanoi. Nothing worked.'[148]

The operation went ahead despite the looming monsoon season. The estimates of a three- to four-week operation proved wrong, as U.S. forces stayed in Cambodia for two months. Several days into Operation Shoemaker, Lloyd Rives, chargé d'affaires in the U.S. Embassy in Phnom Penh, conceded that 'while some enemy supply and food caches were uncovered, as of 3 May their size did not measure up to advance billing and no main COSVN installations reported discovered by field commanders.' Moreover, 'they also appear to be hedging their predictions regarding size of enemy forces within "sealed-off" areas.'[149]

---

[145] Helms, *A Look over My Shoulder*, 390.
[146] In his telegram to the State Department, Rives referred to a series of ARVN cross-border operations in Cambodia, 'many of which MACV briefers say U.S. learned of after the fact.' Telegram, Rives to Richardson, 5 May 1970.
[147] Powers, *The Man Who Kept the Secrets*, 219.
[148] Helms, *A Look over My Shoulder*, 389.
[149] Telegram, Rives to Richardson, 5 May 1970.

In addition, the intentions of the North Vietnamese in response to the incursion were 'anyone's guess.'[150] Secretary Laird repeatedly told Nixon that no such headquarters existed in Cambodia, but the president preferred the more fantastic version of the MACV.

This dismissal of potentially contradictory information in favour of Nixon's intuition suggests once more that the WSAG's role as an integral unit of the decision-making process was ignored, and that there was no attempt to integrate new or contradictory information, or even consider its merits, partly because there was no orderly process in the first place. Furthermore, there was no genuine effort on behalf of Nixon and Kissinger to accept or even listen to dissonant voices, hence the exclusion of Laird and Rogers following the 22 April NSC meeting. After Nixon's 30 April speech, when WSAG meetings became more efficient, there was apparently no need for a re-examination of previously rejected options. As Nixon ominously told Kissinger after the invasion, 'Henry, we've done it... Remember Lot's wife. Never look back.'[151]

While Nixon did not look back, it is evident that he did not look ahead either. Unsurprisingly, the WSAG did not work out detailed implementation and monitoring plans. Apart from a decision to assign responsibilities to the ARVN following the U.S. withdrawal on 30 June, there is no evidence to suggest that the WSAG discussed what could and should happen in the aftermath of the invasion. Kissinger's admission to British Ambassador Freeman that Nixon 'has not thought this through yet' is alarming, given what was at stake. There was no institutional follow-up to ensure that the North Vietnamese would not return to the border areas. Accordingly, the operation turned out to be a 'one-shot job,' partly due to the rainy season but largely because of the domestic turmoil – both of which should not have come as a surprise to U.S. policy makers.

Jonathan Aitken, one of Nixon's more sympathetic biographers, observed that the Cambodian operation was 'militarily somewhere between a half-success and a half-failure, but... the political price at home was too costly.'[152] Tactically, the operation was not an abject failure. American forces managed to seize large amounts of munitions

[150] Ibid.
[151] Cited in Prados, *Keepers of the Keys*, 301.
[152] J. Aitken, *Nixon: A Life*, 460.

and supplies and to blockade the port of Sihanoukville, an importamt supply route for North Vietnamese forces in Cambodia. A CIA report prepared at the end of the operation estimated that it caused considerable disruption to supply, although the situation of the North Vietnamese there was by no means critical.[153] It was therefore imperative to show some results and, indeed, the administration produced impressive statistics. Daily situation reports showed large numbers of captured weapons and supplies, which no doubt reassured Nixon about the rationale behind his decision.

The Cambodian operation left a weakened and defenceless government in Phnom Penh. Lon Nol felt betrayed by the quick withdrawal. Many Cambodians, now homeless refugees with no hope, joined the Communist Khmer Rouge forces, which soon became a prominent force in the country. Most predictably, only months after the American withdrawal, the North Vietnamese returned to their sanctuaries and increased their influence in southern areas of Cambodia even further. The consequences of the operation were tragically predictable for all to see. When Kissinger met with his NSC staff on 24 April, William Watts warned, almost prophetically, that 'if it was Cambodia this year, it would be Laos next, and the bombing of Haiphong in two.'[154] From the March 1970 coup onwards, there had been an abundance of warning signs advising against the invasion of Cambodia by U.S. ground troops. The writing was on the wall, but Nixon and Kissinger chose not to read it.

[153] The CIA report is discussed at length in Bundy, *A Tangled Web*, 157–158.
[154] Prados, *Keepers of the Keys*, 296.

1. First meeting of the National Security Council, January 1969. Sitting next to Nixon are Secretary of State William Rogers (right) and Secretary of Defense Melvin Laird (left). CIA Director Richard Helms sits at the top of the table, while Joint Chiefs of Staff Chairman Earle Wheeler (left of Laird) keeps a watchful eye on Kissinger. *Source: Richard Nixon Presidential Library and Museum Staff (NLRNS), National Archives at College Park, Maryland (NACP).*

2. President Nixon, National Security Advisor Kissinger, Secretary of Defense Laird, and Chairman of the Joint Chiefs of Staff Earle Wheeler having lunch at the Pentagon, 1969. *Source: Office of Secretary of Defense Historical Office.*

3. Nixon with CIA Director Richard Helms. Helms was concerned about the president's impression of the agency as 'exclusively staffed by uppity Ivy Leaguers, most of whom lived in Georgetown and spent every evening gossiping about him at cocktail parties'. *Source: National Archives and Records Administration.*

4. Nixon with Defense Secretary Laird. Laird feared that the new NSC system would give Kissinger the power to implement policy without consultation or notification of the NSC principals. *Source: NLRNS, NACP.*

NATIONAL SECURITY COUNCIL
WASHINGTON, D.C. 20506

March 21, 1969

~~CONFIDENTIAL~~

National Security Decision Memorandum 8

TO: The Secretary of State
     The Secretary of Defense
     The Director of Central Intelligence

SUBJECT: Crisis Anticipation and Management

   The President has directed that increased emphasis be placed on the anticipation of potential crisis situations that may affect the interests of the United States. The National Security Council structure provides a means for the orderly review of world situations and of our policies, the formulation of possible courses of action to deal with contingency situations and the initiation of actions, when appropriate, to remedy deteriorating situations.

   The President has directed that the National Security Council Interdepartmental Groups shall prepare contingency studies on potential crisis areas for review by the NSC. The studies should include a careful orchestration of political and military actions. It is recognized that not all contingencies can be anticipated and that the specifics of a particular anticipated contingency cannot be accurately predicted. Nevertheless, there are important advantages which might accrue from contingency planning, among which are:

    -- a clearer assessment of U.S. interests and possible need for U.S. action in a particular situation;

    -- an increased likelihood that U.S. actions taken will be timely and will minimize risks or losses;

    -- the possible discovery of actions which might resolve or head off a crisis; and

    -- the familiarization of key officials with factual material and alternative courses of action in event of a crisis.

~~CONFIDENTIAL~~

5. National Security Decision Memorandum 8, which emphasised the importance of orderly procedures of crisis management. *Source: NLRNS, NACP.*

The Review Group shall issue instructions for contingency planning and review contingency studies prepared in the Interdepartmental Groups. The Review Group shall forward contingency studies to the Under Secretaries Committee. When the study is to be submitted to the National Security Council, the Under Secretaries Committee will comment in light of its responsibilities for crisis management.

The Chairmen of the Interdepartmental Groups shall have coordinating authority for the management of crises in their areas when these occur, subject to additional policy and operational guidance provided by higher authority.

The Under Secretaries Committee shall determine the organization and procedures for crisis management.

Henry A. Kissinger

cc: The Chairman, Joint Chiefs of Staff
The Director, United States Information Agency

2

5 (*continued*)

NATIONAL SECURITY COUNCIL
WASHINGTON, D.C. 20506

CONFIDENTIAL   July 3, 1969

National Security Decision Memorandum 19

TO: The Secretary of State
               The Secretary of Defense
               The Director of Central Intelligence

SUBJECT: Washington Special Actions Group

The President has directed that henceforth political-military
contingency plans prepared by NSC Interdepartmental Groups
in accordance with NSDM 8 shall be forwarded to the NSC
Washington Special Actions Group. The Washington Special
Actions Group was created by Presidential decision reported to
you in my memorandum of May 16, 1969.

                                   Henry A. Kissinger

cc: The Chairman, Joint Chiefs of Staff

CONFIDENTIAL

6. National Security Decision Memorandum 19, which introduced the Washington Special Actions Group (WSAG) as the designated interdepartmental
crisis management group. *Source: NLRNS, NACP.*

7. King Hussein of Jordan is greeted by President Nixon and Secretary of State Rogers, April 1969. By then, there were already concerns about the peculiar nature of the Kissinger–State Department relationship. *Source: NLRNS, NACP.*

8. Nixon announcing his decision to send U.S. troops into Cambodia in a televised address to the nation, 30 April 1970. *Source: NLRNS, NACP.*

9. Nixon bowling at the White House bowling alley, 1970. Kissinger described his meeting with Nixon in the bowling alley during the height of the Jordanian Crisis as 'incongruous'. *Source: NLRNS, NACP.*

10. Nixon meeting with President Yayah Kahn of Pakistan, October 1970. White House Chief of Staff 'Bob' Haldeman recalled that the Washington Special Actions Group was 'in open rebellion' against Nixon and Kissinger's decision to 'tilt' in favour of Pakistan in its war with India. *Source: NLRNS, NACP.*

11. The Joint Chiefs of Staff, January 1971. Chairman Admiral Thomas Moorer in the center. Chief of Naval Operations Admiral Elmo Zumwalt (far left) described the National Security studies which came out of Kissinger's office in the run-up to the India-Pakistan war as a 'verbal mudslide'. *Source: Naval Historical Center.*

12. Swearing-in ceremony of George H. W. Bush as U.S. Ambassador to the United Nations, February 1971. Ambassador Bush feared that Kissinger was 'absolutely obsessed' about the State Department's inability to get the job done during the India-Pakistan War. *Source: NLRNS, NACP.*

13. Nixon with Prime Minister Indira Gandhi, November 1971. Kissinger described Nixon's meetings with the Indian Prime Minister in Washington as 'the two most unfortunate meetings Nixon had with any foreign leader'. *Source: NLRNS, NACP.*

14. President Nixon, Henry Kissinger, and Israeli Prime Minister Golda Meir, meeting in the Oval Office, March 1973. *Source: NLRNS, NACP.*

15. Nixon facing the media at the end of the Yom Kippur War, October 1973. *Source: NLRNS, NACP.*

16. Nixon in the Oval Office with (left to right) Kissinger, Vice President Gerald Ford, and Chief of Staff Alexander Haig, October 1973. *Source: NLRNS, NACP.*

4

The Jordanian Crisis, September 1970

> Jordan, a country where you wonder why anybody would ever insure the king. I am sure nobody does.[1]
>
> Off-the-record remark by Nixon, 16 September 1970

The decision-making process during the Jordanian crisis is widely considered to be of the highest quality, compared with the management of any other international crisis during the Nixon administration.[2] While the Cambodian crisis was characterised by disorderly procedures, dissenting bureaucracy, and controversial decisions, the WSAG performed remarkably well throughout the Jordanian Crisis and contributed to a smooth decision-making process which consistently produced the 'best' policy outcomes at each stage of the crisis.

This high-quality crisis management is even more impressive if one examines the Jordanian Crisis in a more global context. The crisis, which lasted nearly three weeks in September 1970, took place during one of the most challenging periods of Nixon's first term. This 'autumn of crises' saw the foreign policy machinery handling almost

---

[1] *FRUS*, Volume I, 251 (doc. 71).
[2] See, for example, W. B. Quandt, *Decade of Decisions: American Policy toward the Arab-Israeli Conflict, 1967–1976* (Berkeley: University of California Press, 1977); Dowty, *Middle East Crisis*; Herek, Janis, and Huth, 'Decision Making during International Crises; Haney, 'The Nixon Administration and Middle East Crises'; Bundy, *A Tangled Web*.

simultaneously major foreign policy crises in Chile (following the presidential election of Socialist candidate Salvador Allende), in Cuba (the construction of a Soviet naval base in the seaport of Cienfuegos), and in Jordan. Furthermore, this autumn of crises took place only months after U.S. troops pulled out of Cambodia following the controversial incursion. The successful management of the Jordanian Crisis suggests that despite the constraints of a foreign policy system working to its full capacity, and the shadow of a divided nation recovering from a traumatic foreign adventure in Cambodia, the theoretical thrust of the NSC system proved highly effective in coping with multiple foreign policy crises. Furthermore, it suggests once more that the structural settings of crisis management are important, because when used properly, they help to deliver favorable results.

The Jordanian Crisis consisted of three distinct phases. The first phase began on 6 September following the hijacking of three western airliners into Jordan by Palestinian terrorists. This was followed by a bloody civil war between the Jordanian Army and Palestinian factions, which prompted a Syrian invasion of Jordan that in turn transformed the conflict into a regional crisis. Hovering above the Jordanian Crisis throughout was the looming prospect of superpower confrontation, which fit rather neatly into Nixon's tendency to downgrade the significance of local or regional developments and instead view events in terms of superpower rivalry. Indeed, the British ambassador in Washington, John Freeman, reported that merely six weeks before the outbreak of the Jordanian Crisis, President Nixon had accepted that 'what was going on in this area involved a confrontation between two major powers, with all the risks that that implied, and he had come to an awareness of the large strategic issues involved.'[3] Unlike during the Cambodian Crisis, however, the president actively sought advice and information from the bureaucracy and relied more heavily on formal NSC procedures. In this context, the WSAG proved a highly effective body in coordinating and managing the crisis.

This chapter suggests that the ability of the foreign policy system to produce the 'best' policy outcomes based on a formalistic process

---

[3] Ambassador Freeman, Memo for the record, 27 July 1970. PREM 15/673, NA.

of decision-making is very real. There is little doubt that when Nixon used the system according to its theoretical design, the WSAG was more effective as a decision unit and enjoyed a more dominant role throughout the crisis. One immediate reason for the successful management of the Jordanian Crisis is the relative lack of interest and commitment by Nixon and Kissinger to the Middle East during the first year of the administration. This was evident by the fact that the first diplomatic initiatives in the region were handled by the State Department and not by the White House. Thus, while the Cambodian operation was interpreted by Nixon in the broader context of the Vietnam War, which of course preoccupied him from the first day in office, Middle East politics – at least initially – did not generate particularly intense emotions in the White House, which may well have had an effect on the decision-making process during the crisis in Jordan.

This chapter begins by placing the Jordanian Crisis in the broader context of U.S. Middle East policy during the first two years of the Nixon administration. This initial policy was remarkably even-handed and provided the State Department with considerable leverage in the region. After tracing the roots of the Jordanian Crisis, the chapter then outlines the crisis decision-making process during the period. It then provides a more detailed analysis of the performance of the WSAG at the heart of the policy-making process. The analysis demonstrates that despite constraints of time and incomplete intelligence, the Jordanian Crisis was managed better than any other crisis during the Nixon administration.

The Middle East Policy of the Nixon Administration

The Middle East was not considered a top priority during the first year of the Nixon administration. Nixon outlined his foreign policy priorities to his three gatekeepers in March 1970. The president accepted that hitherto, the administration's greatest weakness was 'in spreading my time too thin – not emphasizing priorities enough.' Accordingly, he asked Haldeman, Ehrlichman, and Kissinger to ensure that in the field of foreign policy, only issues concerning East-West relations, the Soviet Union, China, Eastern Europe, and NATO be brought to his immediate attention. Middle East affairs were mentioned only at the next level outside the big five issues.[4] The immediate implication of Nixon's priorities was the delegation of Middle East policy formulation and analysis to the State Department. Indeed, British Ambassador Freeman reported in the aftermath of the Jordanian Crisis in October 1970 that 'The Arab/Israel dispute was for a long time handled by the State Department without much intervention (or even close interest) on the part of the White House.'[5] Notwithstanding the limited nature of White House interest in the region, Nixon was well aware of its potential to push the superpowers toward direct confrontation. Yitzhak Rabin, the Israeli Ambassador in Washington between 1968 and 1973, recalled that early on, Nixon referred to the Middle East as a 'powder keg' that was 'liable to explode and set off a world-wide conflagration.'[6]

As noted in the previous chapter, the firm conviction that U.S.-Soviet relations underscored local politics was not unique to the Middle East and displayed itself in U.S. foreign policy towards other regions as well. This realist, power-driven, bipolar fixation is a frequent subject of criticism of U.S. foreign policy during the Nixon-Kissinger years. Various observers have suggested that the failure to give due weight to complex local and regional developments in the analysis of Cold War politics consistently undermined the administration's policies, and the Middle East was a prime example of this failing.[7] As Hersh eloquently observed, the overriding misperception of U.S. policy in the Middle East during this period 'lay in the White House's inability to understand that the Russians were not behind every sand dune in the Middle East.'[8]

The White House's lack of interest in the region led to a policy that was initially decidedly even-handed. However, the State Department's mandate to negotiate the terms of a future Arab-Israeli agreement was perceived in Israel as nothing more than pro-Arab policy. Israel had

---

[4] *FRUS*, Volume I, 204 (doc. 61).

[5] Memo, Freeman to Greenhill, 'The White House and the State Department,' 28 October 1970. PREM 15/2231, NA.

[6] Y. Rabin, *The Rabin Memoirs* (Berkeley: University of California Press, 1996), 143.

[7] See, for example, W. B. Quandt, *Peace Process: American Diplomacy and the Arab-Israeli Conflict since 1967* (Washington, DC: Brookings Institution, 2001, rev. ed.), and *Decade of Decisions*; Bundy, *A Tangled Web*; A. Dowty, *Middle East Crisis*.

[8] Hersh, *The Price of Power*, 234.

enjoyed a favourable status in Lyndon Johnson's White House, but the first year of the Nixon administration signalled a dramatic shift in American Middle East diplomacy. Joseph Sisco, Assistant Secretary of State for Near Eastern and South Asian Affairs, explained this shift in policy to Ambassador Rabin:

Our interests in the Middle East do not center on Israel alone... Our moral and practical commitment to Israel is by no means toward everything Israel wants or does... If our friendship with Israel is the only thing the United States is left with in the Middle East, that will be a catastrophic setback for American policy.[9]

Sisco's comment reflected the views held by some sections of the bureaucracy about the prospects of stability in the Arab-Israeli conflict. Particularly prevalent in the State Department, this view suggested that only by diplomatic manoeuvres could stability be attained, and that this policy could best be achieved by putting pressure on Israel to withdraw from territories seized in the 1967 Six-Day War. The main implication for U.S. policy according to this view was that Israel should no longer be perceived as a strategic asset in the region but rather as an impediment to strengthening relations with the Arab world.[10]

Nixon and Kissinger held a different view – one that meshed closely with their dogmatic outlook of superpower competition and the priority they assigned to global considerations of balance of power over local or regional requisites. This approach was closely tied to Kissinger's pursuit of linkage with the Soviet Union; namely, that progress in one area was predicated on progress on a broader range of U.S.-Soviet affairs.[11] Conversely, Nixon and Kissinger feared that Soviet advantages in one region would increase Moscow's prestige in other areas. In contrast to the State Department's view, the policy implication here was that a strong Israel was a strategic asset to the United States in its efforts to counter Soviet challenges for dominance in the Middle East. Success in negotiations, then, could only come once the Arab states realised that the military option was no longer tenable as a means to regain territory lost in the 1967 Six-Day War.

---

[9] Rabin, *The Rabin Memoirs*, 149.
[10] Quandt, *Decade of Decisions*, 120.
[11] For Kissinger's ideas on linkage, see *White House Years*, 123–129.

The Jordanian Crisis of September 1970 proved to be a watershed for U.S. Middle East policy, not least in terms of the growing U.S. military and economic assistance to Israel and a greater role for Henry Kissinger in the region. As British Ambassador Freeman explained in the aftermath of the crisis:

> Sometime during the summer, the President (or his advisers) began to question the [State] Department's unsupervised handling of a situation which was growing increasingly dangerous and was increasingly affecting US-USSR relations. The White House moved in. Important decisions concerning Arab/Israel [*sic*] are now taken in the White House, and the State Department is fairly closely tied by presidential rulings. The department is nevertheless still much involved in decision-making, since it is recognised as having a wealth of expertise in this area which is not equalled in the White House. Sisco is still a key-figure. But he is no longer a free-booter. He must now get clearance, not only from Rogers ... but from Kissinger or the President.[12]

Washington's even-handed policy in the Middle East produced two diplomatic initiatives in the first eighteen months of the administration. The first Rogers Plan came in December 1969 and called for a comprehensive settlement of the Arab-Israeli conflict based on United Nations Security Council Resolution 242, which called for an Israeli withdrawal from territories occupied in the Six-Day War in exchange for Arab recognition of the Israeli state and the mutual termination of territorial claims and belligerency to be negotiated under the auspices of Swedish Ambassador to the United Nations, Dr. Gunnar Jarring.[13] The plan never took off and came to an abrupt end only weeks after it was launched. The Israeli government felt that Rogers did not fully understand the nature of the Arab-Israeli conflict and criticised him for relying too heavily on the verbal promises of Arab leaders.[14] The Soviets refused to support the initiative since they saw it as an American attempt to separate them from their Arab clients during negotiations.[15]

Notwithstanding the refusal of the parties to accept the plan, an important factor in the failure of the plan was the growing tension between the White House and the State Department over the Middle

---

12 Freeman to Greenhill, 'The White House and the State Department.'
13 A. Shlaim, *The Iron Wall: Israel and the Arab World* (London: Penguin, 2001), 260.
14 G. Meir, *My Life* (Jerusalem: Steimatzky's Agency, 1975), 321; A. Eban, *An Autobiography* (Tel Aviv: Sifriat Maariv, 1978), 457–458.
15 Bundy, *A Tangled Web*, 128–129.

East. Nixon refused to back up Rogers and sided with Kissinger, who argued that the plan was too ambitious to be accepted.[16] The failure of the Rogers Plan strengthened Kissinger's position within the administration, as his earlier reservations about the plan proved accurate. It was a step further in the growing isolation of the secretary of state, which inevitably led to great confusion in Moscow. Ambassador Anatoly Dobrynin recalled that Foreign Secretary Andrei Gromyko told him after visiting Washington, 'First I spoke to the secretary of state, and then to Kissinger and the president, and they had a completely different position from Rogers . . . who am I going to write [sic] in Washington when I get home? Rogers or Kissinger?'[17] Gromyko's puzzlement provides a telling testimony to the emerging pattern in the conduct of U.S. foreign policy throughout the world, not just the Middle East.[18]

The second Rogers Plan came in response to the growing tension between Israeli and Egyptian forces along the Suez Canal during the summer of 1970. This time publicly supported by Nixon, the plan called for a ninety-day cease-fire and commitments by Egypt, Israel, and Jordan to accept United Nations Resolution 242, and to return to the negotiation table with Dr. Jarring.[19] The cease-fire came into effect on 7 August 1970. However, the following day it was violated, when Israeli intelligence spotted movement of Egyptian artillery within a 50-km standstill zone, in clear violation of the cease-fire terms. Israeli protest turned into anger when the State Department dismissed the reports as inconclusive. As more information arrived in Washington to support the Israeli claims, the White House responded by sending a forceful message to Cairo and to Moscow. A dismissive reply from Egypt prompted Nixon to reevaluate the administration's policy in the region. With Kissinger's encouragement, Nixon decided the time had come to counter Soviet attempts to tilt the balance of power in the region in favour of Egypt.[20] On 1 September, he met with

---

[16] Nixon, *RN*, 479.
[17] A. Dobrynin, *In Confidence: Moscow's Ambassador to America's Six Cold War Presidents* (New York: Times Books, 1995), 205–206.
[18] Hoff, *Nixon Reconsidered*, 257.
[19] Kissinger, *White House Years*, 576–579.
[20] Quandt, *Decade of Decisions*, 107–108; S. Brown, *The Faces of Power: Constancy and Change in United States Foreign Policy from Truman to Reagan* (New York: Columbia University Press, 1983), 391–392.

Rogers, Kissinger, and Sisco to review Middle East policy. The effects of the new policy were evident within days, when the administration announced that Israel was to receive at least eighteen F-4 Phantom jets. Nixon also announced his unconditional support for Israel and his commitment to maintain her qualitative superiority in the region. The following day, the Senate approved the Military Procurement Authorization Act, which allowed Israel to receive almost unlimited military aid in order to offset Soviet military aid to the Arabs.[21]

In the long run, the new Middle East policy proved just as if not more flawed than the first. It led to American and Israeli complacency and overconfidence with respect to Israel's military superiority in the region. Nixon and Kissinger believed that as long as this advantage was maintained, the Arabs would not dare to escalate the situation and risk another humiliating defeat like in 1967. However, this complacency eventually led to the failure to anticipate the outbreak of the Yom Kippur War, as will be discussed in chapter 6. Nevertheless, in the autumn of 1970, Nixon – and especially Kissinger – felt that 'it was crucial to take a harder line against violations of the cease-fire and to bring their responsibilities home to the Soviets.'[22] The Jordanian Crisis presented Nixon and Kissinger with the perfect opportunity to demonstrate their new Middle East policy. Although somewhat domestic and regional in nature, the Jordanian Crisis was used ultimately to display the president's resilience against the Soviets and their clients in the Middle East.

The Unfolding of the Jordanian Crisis[23]

King Hussein of Jordan was by far the most pro-American leader in the Arab world and the most moderate in his views of the conflict with Israel.[24] This made him the target of Palestinian radicals who tried their

---

[21] Bundy, *A Tangled Web*, 185; Thornton, *The Nixon-Kissinger Years*, 55.

[22] Kissinger, *White House Years*, 589.

[23] There are some minor discrepancies in the literature about the dates of some of the decisions and actions taken by various actors during the crisis, perhaps due to the difference in time zones between Washington and the Middle East. Dowty alludes to this point in *Middle East Crisis*, 147 (fn. 1). In cases of such inconsistency, this chapter will follow the timeline of events as they appear in the archival material, followed by the Kissinger memoirs if necessary.

[24] For consistency in U.S. attitudes towards Hussein, see S. Kaplan, 'United States Aid and Regime Maintenance in Jordan, 1957–1973,' *Public Policy*, 23:2 (Spring 1975), 189–217.

best to topple his regime. Hussein had survived several assassination attempts, including two in the first week of September 1970 alone. Analysed against the background of the Arab-Israeli conflict, the crisis in Jordan was hardly a sudden or accidental event. Following the 1967 Six-Day War, various Palestinian factions had risen to prominence, seeking to use Jordan as an operational base. By the summer of 1970, Palestinian guerrillas (*fedayeen*) were virtually running a state within a state, and clashes with the Jordanian Army were commonplace.[25]

On 6 September 1970, members of the Popular Front for the Liberation of Palestine (PFLP) hijacked three commercial airliners. Pan Am Flight 93 from Amsterdam was redirected to Cairo and was blown up after the passengers had descended. TWA Flight 741 from Frankfurt and Swissair Flight 100 from Zurich landed at Dawson's Field, a abandoned desert strip in northern Jordan. The hijacking of El Al Flight 219 from Amsetrdam was foiled by Israeli air marshals but three days later, a fourth plane, BOAC Flight 775 from Bahrain, was hijacked and flown into Dawson's Field. Setting an initial deadline of seventy-two hours, the hijackers demanded the release of thousands of Palestinian guerrillas held in Israeli and European jails in exchange for the release of nearly 500 passengers.[26] The PFLP sought to sabotage the cease-fire along the Suez Canal and to push other Palestinian groups to rise against the king's regime. At the same time, Iraqi and Syrian forces were ready to assist the Palestinians in their cause – there were already nearly 20,000 Iraqi troops in eastern Jordan which had remained there since the 1967 Six-Day War, and Syrian forces were positioned along the Jordanian border.[27] Hussein's prospects looked dim. Failure to act swiftly and decisively would spell the end of his regime and probably his life. On the other hand, if he did act forcefully against the fedayeen, Syria and Iraq were likely to take advantage of the chaos and join the fighting in order to topple him. The king finally opted for the second option and, on 15 September, he declared martial law in the country, which was soon engulfed in a bloody civil war, as Palestinian refugees joined the fighting with the fedayeen against the Jordanian Army. The situation deteriorated further on 19 September when Syrian tanks invaded Jordan from the north. The Soviets were

[25] Bundy, *A Tangled Web*, 183–184.
[26] Quandt, *Peace Process*, 76–77; Dowty, *Middle East Crisis*, 139–140.
[27] Bundy, *A Tangled Web*, 185.

quick to warn against outside intervention and supported President Nasser of Egypt's call for a cease-fire. Fearing his military would not be able to stop the advancing Syrian armored forces, the king made a dramatic appeal to Washington for help. As American intelligence and military capabilities in the region were limited, Israel was brought into the picture, and contingency plans were prepared for Israeli air strikes, as well as a ground operation against the invading Syrian forces.[28]

The following day, the northern city of Irbid fell to Syrian forces and on 21 September, the crisis reached its pinnacle, when Israeli ground forces were fully mobilised. Moscow denounced any form of external intervention in Jordan and called upon Washington to restrain the Israeli government; however, this was not necessary as the Jordanian air force managed to stop the Syrian tanks in the north and the following day saw the Syrian forces retreat back to the border. The Israeli forces were called off and, on 23 September, the king's army regained control of Jordan. In the following days, the fedayeen accepted the terms of the cease-fire and by 29 September, the remaining hostages were released. The Jordanian Crisis was over.[29]

Crisis Decision-Making

For Washington, the primary concern throughout the crisis was to prevent another Arab-Israeli war. At no stage was the Jordanian Crisis treated or understood solely as a Jordanian crisis *per se*. Although the causes of the civil war in Jordan were domestic in nature, Nixon and Kissinger feared that things might get out of control and that the civil war could potentially lead to a confrontation with the Soviets. As soon as news of the hostilities in Jordan reached Kissinger, he advised Nixon: 'It looks like the Soviets are pushing the Syrians and the Syrians are pushing the Palestinians. The Palestinians don't need much pushing.'[30]

Kissinger's remark is not surprising given the predominant perception in the White House that Soviets were testing American resilience worldwide. The simultaneous crises in Cienfuegos and Chile during

[28] Quandt, *Decade of Decisions*, 110–115.
[29] Dowty, *Middle East Crisis*, 172–174.
[30] Nixon, *RN*, 483.

the autumn of 1970 had led Kissinger to believe that 'they all represented – or seemed to us to represent – different facets of global Communist challenge.'[31] The crisis in Jordan seemed the perfect opportunity for Nixon to demonstrate his new hard-line policy in the region.
Still, it was difficult to find evidence of direct Soviet culpability. They
were certainly not behind the hijacking or, indeed, behind the Syrian
offensive into Jordan which followed. Nevertheless, Kissinger accused
Moscow of 'getting too greedy by not helping to rein in their clients.'[32]
Kissinger's conviction that Moscow was acting behind the scenes
is telling, given that there was little evidence to suggest that at the
time.[33]

The survival of the king's regime was seen as key to stability in the
region given the strong rapport Hussein had enjoyed with successive
administrations in the White House and his moderate views on the
Arab-Israeli conflict. At the same time, Kissinger acknowledged that
intervening by force on behalf of Hussein would seriously jeopardise
the king's status in the Arab world. Importantly, however, Washington
had to assist Jordan because of the potential implications for the entire
region should the crisis broaden. Kissinger believed that in that event,
another Arab-Israeli war would be highly likely.[34] Kissinger communicated these concerns to the WSAG early on and throughout the crisis.
The group convened no less than fourteen times until the abatement
of the crisis on 24 September.[35] Generally present at meetings were
Kissinger, U. Alexis Johnson and Joseph Sisco from the State Department, David Packard from the Defense Department, Admiral Thomas
Moorer, and Richard Helms. Lower-ranking officials such as NSC
staff members Harold Saunders and Richard Kennedy, Sisco's Deputy
Rodger Davies, and Warren Nutter (Assistant Secretary of Defense for
International Security Affairs) were also occasionally present. Towards
the end of the crisis, the NSC had met a few times; however, as Dowty

---

[31] Kissinger, *White House Years*, 594.

[32] Ibid., 609.

[33] Secretary Rogers was not as quick as Kissinger to see a direct link between Moscow
and the Syrian actions and proposed a joint superpower initiative to bring about a
cease-fire. Kalb and Kalb, *Kissinger*, 201–202; Hersh, *The Price of Power*, 238.

[34] Kissinger, *White House Years*, 596.

[35] Despite the release of several documents concerning the workings of the WSAG
during the crisis, a large number of documents remains classified.

correctly observed, these meetings were largely a matter of formality and no concrete decisions were taken in that forum.[36] While the WSAG worked intensively and relentlessly during the crisis, intimate discussions between Nixon and Kissinger increased in frequency towards the end of the crisis, when the prospect of superpower confrontation became more real. This suggests that even when the advisory system worked well, Nixon and Kissinger still found it necessary to work occasionally outside formal structures, as testified by Helmut Sonnenfeldt's recollection in chapter 2.

Perhaps more than any other crisis examined in this book, the Jordanian episode was characterised by the fast pace of events and the limited sources of information available to policy makers. This partly explains why the WSAG met so frequently during the crisis, almost on a daily basis and sometimes twice a day. The implications of these constraints on the decision-making process were summarised exactly by Kissinger himself:

> During fast-moving events those at the center of decisions are overwhelmed by floods of reports compounded of conjecture, knowledge, hope, and worry. These must then be sieved through their own preconceptions. Only rarely does a coherent picture emerge; in a sense coherence must be imposed on events by the decision-maker, who seizes the challenge and turns it into opportunity by assessing correctly both the circumstances and his margin for creative action. . . . Decisions must be made very rapidly; physical endurance is tested as much as perception because an enormous amount of time must be spent making certain that each of the key figures at home and abroad acts on the basis of the main information and purpose.[37]

The management of the Jordanian crisis began months before the situation deteriorated into a crisis – an indication that careful attention to developments and adequate preparation of contingency plans were key to a smooth decision-making process once the crisis was in full flow. The White House was well aware of the potential threat of the fedayeen to the survival of Hussein, and several WSAG meetings on Jordan had taken place over the summer of 1970 with this regard. Following an assassination attempt on the king in June and his failure to crack down on the fedayeen, the assessment of the NSC staff was bleak:

[36] Dowty, *Middle East Crisis*, 148.
[37] Kissinger, *White House Years*, 617.

'[T]he authority and prestige of the Hashemite regime will continue to decline ... Greater fedayeen freedom of action will inevitably result in more serious breaches of the cease-fire in the Jordan Valley ... Hussein faces an uncertain political future.'[38]

These WSAG meetings ensured that the administration was not surprised by subsequent events. Following the attempt on Hussein's life on 9 June, the group met to consider contingencies, including evacuation of U.S. citizens and military options. After discussing at length the implications of using U.S. troops in Jordan, Kissinger concluded that intervention would be required only if American citizens were in imminent danger and if Hussein asked for protection from outside intervention, most likely against the Iraqis and Syrians. Admiral Moorer was ordered to define objectives and draw up scenarios for possible military action.[39] The situation in Jordan triggered another WSAG meeting, on 22 June, held to review the status of contingency planning for military-supported evacuation from Arab nations and for possible military intervention in response to requests for assistance from friendly Arab governments threatened by outside or indigenous forces. The organisational objective of that review was to provide the NSC with 'a complete analysis of alternatives and implications' in the event of the NSC being faced with a decision on whether to take military action to meet a crisis in one or more Arab countries. In a similar fashion to the previous meeting, great emphasis was placed on 'setting forth the pros and cons of military intervention at the invitation of a friendly Arab government.'[40]

The June meetings proved beneficial once the group started to convene more frequently during the September crisis. Events in Jordan did not catch the WSAG by surprise, and the group was quick to respond to unfolding events, such as the outbreak of civil war and the Syrian invasion. Early on in the crisis, Nixon had asked that plans be prepared for three contingencies: a punitive attack in Jordan if the plane was destroyed and passengers were killed, a military evacuation if the security situation in Amman had broken down, and a plan for U.S.

---

[38] Ibid., 597.
[39] Minutes of WSAG meeting, 'Jordan,' 11 June 1970. Folder no. 4, *WSAG Meetings*, MMF, Box H-114, NSCIF, MPMP.
[40] Minutes of WSAG meeting, 'Middle East,' 22 June 1970. Ibid.

military support for Hussein should he decide to go to war with the fedayeen.[41]

Nixon's initial reaction to the hijacking was almost visceral, in concurrence with Israel's known policy of not negotiating with terrorists or yielding to their demands. He put forward the need to evacuate U.S. citizens from Jordan and to coordinate through the Red Cross a coherent negotiation policy with the British, Swiss, Israeli, and West German governments for the release of the hostages. The hijackers aimed to negotiate separately with each government, which made the American task of pursuing a united front extremely difficult, as the European governments were more lenient and asked the Americans to urge the Israelis to soften their position.[42] On 9 September, three days after the hijacking, Kissinger reported to Nixon that the Red Cross representative in Amman believed the situation to be 'extremely serious' and that it might end in tragedy. There was 'perhaps one chance in two we will get everyone out.' At the same time, and somewhat contradictory to his first somber assessment, the representative was positive that 'no one will be killed tomorrow afternoon unless by accident.'[43] This incongruous report started a pattern of incomplete and contradictory intelligence assessments which made the task of policy making significantly harder. It is not surprising that in the later stages of the crisis, Nixon and Kissinger preferred to rely on their intuition rather than the sketchy intelligence at their disposal.

Notwithstanding these difficulties, the evaluation of alternative courses of action was performed on a regular basis. In the first days of the crisis, the Defense Department prepared an extensive study of political-military options and the steps to follow them. The study, which was submitted on 9 September, examined the assumption that the hostages were still alive and also looked at alternative scenarios and courses of action available: If the fedayeen blew up the aircraft with passengers aboard, the United States could (1) take action with

---

[41] Memo, Kennedy and Saunders to Kissinger, 'WSAG Meeting on Hijacking Contingencies,' 9 September 1970. Folder no. 12, *WSAG Meetings*, MF, Box H-077, NSCIF, NPMP.

[42] Kissinger, *White House Years*, 601; Quandt, *Decade of Decisions*, 112; H. Brandon, *The Retreat of American Power* (New York: Doubleday, 1973), 129–133.

[43] Memo, Kissinger to Nixon, 'Hijacking Status,' 9 September 1970. Folder no. 12, *WSAG Meetings*, MF, Box H-077, NSCIF, NPMP.

other major powers to cut civil air links with countries who harboured terrorists (the study specified Cuba, Syria, and Algeria as potential targets); (2) organise an international punitive expedition against the PFLP; (3) undertake a swift unilateral punitive mission; (4) undertake efforts to evacuate all U.S. citizens in Amman, by force if necessary (plans for this action were already laid out in June); or (5) demand that the government of Jordan act against the fedayeen (either by diplomatic means or coercive measures). Two more possible scenarios included a full-scale Jordanian–fedayeen confrontation and the release of the hostages without an agreement with the PFLP.[44]

Following WSAG deliberations, Nixon ordered the movement of the Sixth Fleet eastward in the Mediterranean, the deployment of six C-130 aircraft (for possible evacuation of Americans citizens) and F-4 Fighter Jets to Turkey, and the placing of the 82nd Airborne Division on semi-alert. These actions were not announced publicly, but it was anticipated that they would not go unnoticed in Moscow.[45] Considerable emphasis was also placed on evaluating the potential benefits and costs of military action, even though it was considered an unattractive option because of limited intelligence and logistical constraints. Nevertheless, questions such as 'Should U.S. intervention be threatened publicly, either directly or by letting preparations leak?' and 'What preparatory military moves can be made without upsetting the Red Cross negotiations?' were raised at meetings during the early stages of the crisis.

The chaotic situation in Jordan and the lack of direct communication with the PFLP made the task of analysis and recommendation more difficult, especially when the hijackers moved some of the passengers to various locations in Amman and blew up the aircraft. This was a key reason for the decision to postpone any military action (although contingencies were developed regardless) and to follow the more moderate policy of coordinating positions with the other governments with the help of the Red Cross and to continue developing plans for the evacuation of U.S. citizens.[46] Nevertheless, when new information did arrive, it was successfully integrated into the process and new

---

[44] Ibid.
[45] Kissinger, *White House Years*, 604–605.
[46] Dowty, *Middle East Crisis*, 143.

objectives and contingencies were evaluated, with close attention to likely costs and benefits. On 10 September, Sisco informed the group that the hijackers had modified their demands and were now willing to release all women and children (including Israeli nationals) in return for the release of seven Palestinian guerrillas from British, German, and Swiss prisons. The remaining hostages would be released in exchange for the fedayeen held in Israel. Accordingly, two new contingencies were debated at the WSAG meeting: possible Israeli intervention and possible Soviet intervention. Kissinger stressed the importance of being attentive, even to seemingly unlikely developments: 'Having a contingency plan doesn't mean we would do it. I don't want the President to tell us to do something without our knowing: 1) what we must do for Israel and 2) what measures we should take to prevent Soviet intervention.'[47] To some extent, the two new contingencies were Kissinger's way of seeing off two challenges posed by the bureaucracy. The first was the State Department's reluctance to support Israeli intervention because of the obvious political implications. The second concerned the Pentagon's reservations about a large-scale U.S. military operation due to the lack of credible deterrent against Soviet intervention in the region.[48]

By 11 September, it seemed that the actions undertaken over previous days had achieved the desired effect. While no concessions to their demands were made, by the end of the day, the fedayeen released a group of eighty-eight hostages.[49] The following day, the Palestinians blew up the aircraft and the hostages were transferred to various unknown locations in Amman.[50] Although the hijackers failed to secure a single concession from the western governments, some strains

---

[47] Minutes of Senior WSAG Meeting, 'Middle East,' 10 September 1970. Folder no. 2, MMF, Box H-114, NSCIF, NPMP.

[48] Admiral Elmo Zumwalt, Chief of Naval Operations during the crisis, recalled that when Johnson and Sisco asked the JCS whether 'it was possible to establish in the Middle East a "credible deterrent" . . . to military intervention by the Soviets . . . the only answer we could give them after much discussion was "not really."' See E. Zumwalt, *On Watch: A Memoir* (Arlington, VA: Admiral Zumwalt & Associates, 1973), 296.

[49] The same day, Nixon announced a programme to counter airplane hijacking. Nixon, 'Statement Announcing a Program to Deal with Airplane Hijacking,' 11 September 1970. *PPPUS 1970*, 742–743.

[50] Kissinger, *White House Years*, 607.

in the united front began to appear when the Germans showed willingness to negotiate separately with the hijackers in order to release German nationals. Still, by 14 September, mostly as a result of the outraged reactions in the West to the hijacking, most of the passengers were released, leaving only fifty-four, who were held on account of their alleged connections to Israel.[51]

The issue of the hostages was pushed aside in the next few days as there were growing signs that Hussein had reached a decision to go to war with the fedayeen. Although the State Department's assessment was that the situation in Amman had 'quieted down,' Nixon and Kissinger anticipated a dramatic showdown between the king and the fedayeen.[52] There were some signs of irritation within the Jordanian army over Hussein's reluctance to crash the fedayeen, and it seemed that the king would have to make a decisive move in order to save his regime. Nixon and Kissinger's more pessimistic assessment proved accurate. On 15 September, Hussein decided to use military force against the fedayeen, and a new phase in the crisis – a bloody civil war – quickly ensued.

When the WSAG learnt of the king's decision, new scenarios were developed in the event of a request for external (including Israeli) assistance. Again, the group went to great length to ensure that nearly every possible course of action was considered in advance. The recommendation of the WSAG working group was that Israeli intervention should be limited to air strikes against Iraqi forces, as ground invasion was likely to prompt Egyptian retaliation.[53]

The prevalent assumption was that a declaration of war on Palestinian factions would bring about clashes with the indigenous Palestinian population, which in turn could draw in the Syrians and the Iraqis. In that event, the actions of Egyptian President Nasser were hard to predict. The same applied to the Soviet Union, patron of the radical regimes of Syria and Egypt. To that extent, new scenarios were once again developed, with careful calculation of likely benefits and costs of each action. Once fighting between the king's army

---

[51] Bundy, *A Tangled Web*, 184.
[52] Minutes of Senior WSAG Meeting, 'Middle East,' 10 September 1970. See also Dowty, *Middle East Crisis*, 143–144.
[53] Memo, Saunders and Kennedy to Kissinger, 'WSAG Meeting on Jordan,' 15 September 1970. Folder no. 10, *WSAG Meetings*, MF, Box H-077, NSCIF, NPMP.

and the fedayeen began, the general assessment in the administration was that the qualitatively and quantitatively superior Jordanian Army would triumph. Attention was therefore directed toward the prospects of outside intervention. The imminent issue following the king's crackdown on the fedayeen was possible Syrian and Iraqi intervention. Kissinger's NSC staff researched three key questions: timing, the role of Israel, and the nature of measures that should be taken against Syria and Iraq. Although it was estimated that the Jordanian army could defeat the fedayeen and Iraqi forces simultaneously, the timing of an American decision to intervene, if necessary, was crucial. The arguments in favour of a late decision were that it would be wise to wait for Jordanian confirmation that they could not stop the Iraqi or Syrian forces on their own. An early decision, on the other hand, had the potential advantage of deterring Iraqi or Syrian intervention in the first place, although a premature move could also trigger an Egyptian or even Soviet intervention.[54]

Although contingencies for Iraqi as well as Syrian interventions were drawn, the consensus in Washington was that Iraqi intervention was far more realistic, as there were already 17,000 Iraqi troops in Jordan. Even when Hussein himself argued to the contrary, the American ambassador in Amman, Dean Brown, 'shrugged this off.' Kissinger conceded that 'no one else in the government took [the prospect of Syrian intervention] seriously.'[55] Still, the fact that contingencies for Syrian intervention were nevertheless discussed suggests that the WSAG was aiming to cover every possible course of action. As for the role of Israel, the basic question was whether the United States should move quickly to deter Israeli air intervention. This point exemplifies again the careful examination of costs and benefits of possible courses of action. Eight arguments for support for Israeli intervention were brought forward, while no less than ten points emphasised the drawbacks of such action.[56] Finally, the issue of nonmilitary measures

---

[54] Memo, Kennedy and Saunders to Kissinger, 'Air Strikes Against Iraqi or Syrian Forces Intervening in Jordan,' 17 September 1970. Folder no. 7, *WSAG Meetings*, MF, Box H-077, NSCIF, NPMP.

[55] Kissinger, *White House Years*, 612.

[56] Kennedy and Saunders to Kissinger, 'Air Strikes Against Iraqi or Syrian Forces Intervening in Jordan.'

to deter Iraq and Syria was debated. The NSC staff suggested that some diplomatic moves would be useful, such as a Jordanian request that Moscow would restrain Iraq and Syria, or to enlist the diplomatic and military support of Egypt's President Nasser.[57]

The outbreak of civil war in Jordan led to an increase in U.S. military measures, although at this stage they were still tantamount to no more than the deployment of more naval forces in the Mediterranean.[58] Nixon followed the developments from Chicago, where he met editors and broadcasters from the Midwest. Having been updated on recent events in Jordan and after approving the naval manoeuvres, Nixon was by apparently unnerved the pressure of the moment and at an off-the-record meeting with the editors of the *Chicago Sun-Times*, he let off steam, knowing that the details of the meeting would be leaked. The news headlines that evening carried a tough message from Nixon: 'We will intervene if the situation is such that our intervention will make a difference.'[59] Nixon then sent an even clearer signal to the Soviets and their clients in the region, warning that the United States was prepared 'to intervene directly in the Jordanian war should Syria and Iraq enter the conflict and tip the balance against government forces loyal to Hussein.'[60] The direct, confrontational tone in Nixon's remarks was all too familiar, echoing the tenor used in his 'madman theory.' As one observer remarked, 'This was vintage Nixon – be tough; keep your opponents off balance; remain mysterious and unpredictable. With luck, no one will then test to see if you are bluffing.'[61]

Kissinger believed that Nixon's remarks, although risky, were overall helpful. Not only did they demonstrate American resilience, they also strengthened the resolve of King Hussein, whose army slowly but successfully fought off pockets of Palestinian resistance inside Amman. Outside of the capital, however, the estimate was that the struggle 'may turn out to be more protracted and the results less clear-cut' than previous assessments. Kissinger believed that Hussein would try to crush

[57] Intelligence reports suggested that Nasser had 'no interest in Iraqi, Syrian or radical fedayeen dominance in Jordan.' Ibid.
[58] See the details of the naval deployment in Kissinger, *White House Years*, 614.
[59] Quoted in ibid., 615.
[60] Quoted in Quandt, *Decade of Decisions*, 114.
[61] Ibid.

the fedayeen, but that he might also attempt to reach a compromise with the fedayeen if he felt that he had regained much of his status and authority.[62]

Nevertheless, the progress of the Jordanian army, combined with the passivity of the Syrian and Iraqi forces, led to some degree of optimism in Washington. This buoyant mood was further supported by a reassuring message from Moscow. The tone of the letter from Moscow was appeasing, urging the governments of Jordan, Iraq, Syria, and Egypt to bring an end to the war. The Soviet assurance that they were 'searching for ways of bringing our viewpoint also to the attention of the leadership of the Palestinian movement' was interpreted by Kissinger as proof that the Soviets were distancing themselves from the Palestinian factions and from the hijacking in particular.[63] Nevertheless, during a WSAG meeting on 19 September, Kissinger and Under Secretary Johnson agreed that there was 'no need to rush a reply . . . the less said now the better, as long as the military situation is OK.'[64]

While the administration had good reasons to be pleased with the tone of Moscow's communication, the sketchy intelligence reports continued to be a cause of concern. Throughout the crisis, information on developments in the area relied for the most part on Israeli sources (most notably Ambassador Rabin), as American intelligence capacity in the area was limited. Rabin boasted in his memoirs that he 'now became the major source of intelligence on the conflict.'[65] Whatever sources of information were available before the outbreak of the civil war, they were no longer available when the U.S. embassy in Amman had been cut off. As a result, Ambassador Dean Brown often had to look out for Hussein in an armoured car which, as Kissinger noted, 'did not make for rapid communication.'[66] The British reported that the American ambassador was only able to emerge from his residence, which came under heavy fire, 'after several days, in a tank (with guns

[62] Memo, Kissinger to Nixon, 'The Situation in Jordan,' 18 September 1970. Folder no. 6, MF, Box H-077, NSCIF, NPMP.

[63] Kissinger, *White House Years*, 616.

[64] Minutes of Senior WSAG Meeting, 'Middle East,' 19 September 1970. Folder no. 2, *WSAG*, MMF, Box H-114, NSCIF, NPMP.

[65] Rabin, *The Rabin Memoirs*, 188.

[66] Kissinger, The White House Years, 618.

firing).'[67] Accordingly, King Hussein opted to use the British Embassy (which was closer to the king's residence) to send messages to Washington, a practice which, according to Kissinger, 'inevitably produced a delay in transmissions' as the British wanted to add their own interpretations and suggestions that Washington take 'a more measured pace.'[68]

The partial reliance on foreign intelligence also meant that policy makers in Washington found it difficult to digest the news of the Syrian intervention on 19 September. Only one day before the invasion, Kissinger reported to Nixon that the Israelis believed that there would be 'no Iraqi intervention nor do they think there will be intervention by Egypt or Syria, barring unexpected moves.'[69] Even when British reports about the invasion arrived in Washington, little significance was attached to them, partly because the source was a British official in Cairo, to which the British government itself did not attach too much significance. Kissinger acknowledged that despite the incoming reports, policy makers in Washington 'believed that Hussein would have found a way to notify us had he been deeply concerned.'[70] Thus, perhaps more worrying than the objective difficulty in gathering reliable information was the reluctance to follow up new information in favour of sticking with existing working assumptions. Nevertheless, when more reports arrived to confirm the initial message from Cairo, Kissinger acted swiftly to re-evaluate the situation and to work out new contingencies.

Jordanian reports about the Syrian invasion arrived the following day, 20 September. The king requested U.S. air strikes but rejected Israeli ground intervention. He also asked that the U.S. and Britain prepare for a co-coordinated ground intervention. The assessment of the NSC staff was that air strikes alone would probably not suffice to drive the Syrians out of Jordan and that 'stiff ground action' might be necessary.[71] Viewing developments in the familiar context of superpower

---

[67] Report, British Embassy, Amman to FCO, no title, 9 November 1970. FCO 17/1059, NA.
[68] Kissinger, *White House Years*, 618.
[69] Memo, Kissinger to Nixon, 'The Situation in Jordan.'
[70] Kissinger, *White House Years*, 618.
[71] Memo, Saunders and Kennedy to Kissinger, 'Background Perspective for WSAG,' 21 September 1970. Folder no. 2, *WSAG Meetings*, MF, Box H-077, NSCIF, NPMP.

rivalry, Kissinger had no doubt that the Syrian challenge had to be met, explaining that 'if we failed to act, the Middle East crisis would deepen as radicals and their Soviet sponsors seized the initiative. If we succeeded, the Arab moderates would receive a new lease of life.'[72] The same day, the WSAG met in order to make a final recommendation to Nixon about the possible use of U.S. or Israeli forces in Jordan. Debating again the costs and benefits of American intervention, the group decided that without heavy equipment and with Israel as the only possible overland supply route, U.S. forces could be best employed in the background to counter a potential Soviet intervention.

Furthermore, incomplete intelligence meant that the U.S. could not respond quickly and adequately to Hussein's request for immediate air strikes. The group concluded that a 'massive blow' against Syria was the only remedy if the situation in Jordan got out of control – a mission for which the Israeli army was best suited.[73] To that extent, the following recommendations were approved: increasing the alert status of the Airborne Brigade in Germany, putting the 82nd Airborne Division on full alert, and flying a reconnaissance plane from a carrier to Tel-Aviv to pick up targeting information. Undoubtedly, these actions were directed primarily at the Soviets rather than the Syrians. Expecting Soviet intelligence to pick up the signals, Kissinger aimed to heighten the perception that 'American or Israeli intervention is threatening.'[74] Bizarrely, Kissinger had to convey the WSAG recommendations to Nixon in the basement of the Executive Office Building, as the president had decided to go bowling. Kissinger recalls in his memoirs: 'Nixon calmly listened to our report and approved the recommendations while incongruously holding a bowling ball in one hand.'[75]

Despite the decisive actions recommended by the WSAG, imperfect intelligence meant once again that the group had to rely on Israeli sources, which inevitably slowed the decision-making process. As the situation in Jordan continued to deteriorate – the northern town of Irbid was now under Syrian control and elements of the Jordanian

---

[72] Kissinger, *White House Years*, 618–619.
[73] Ibid., 620.
[74] Ibid., 622.
[75] Ibid.

forces had lost contact with each other – the king once again asked Washington for air strikes. Constrained by insufficient intelligence and logistical difficulties, Kissinger then contacted Israeli Ambassador Rabin and informed him of the king's message. Rabin suggested that Israel fly a reconnaissance plane to assess the situation on the battle-field. Bringing Israel into the picture further complicated an already dif-ficult situation. Nevertheless, constrained by time, and after consulting their respective leaders, Kissinger and Rabin reached an understanding. Israeli forces would be mobilised, and should the reconnaissance flight confirm the gravity of the situation in Jordan, then the United States would look 'favorably' upon an Israeli air strike. If required, Israeli ground forces were prepared to attack the Syrians near Irbid and retreat once the operation had successfully ended. In return, Israel asked to be compensated for damaged or lost equipment and to be provided with American protection from Egyptian or Soviet intervention.[76] Later on, the State Department objected to this understanding, mainly because it did not approve of the Israeli ground operation. Secretary Rogers favoured a slow and measured escalation, while Kissinger convinced Nixon that such action would merely make the situation increasingly unmanageable.[77]

This point illustrates the significant gap in perceptions and attitudes towards crisis management between Kissinger and Rogers. Kissinger was very critical of passivity in crises and believed that 'for maxi-mum effectiveness one's actions must be sustained; they must appear relentless, inexorable; hesitation or gradualism invites an attempt to test one's resolution by matching the commitment.'[78] Rogers, on the other hand, was reluctant to confront the Soviets and dismissed the military options. Kissinger too wished to avoid direct confrontation but believed that the way to achieve that goal was by creating 'rapidly a calculus of risks they would be unwilling to confront, rather than let them slide into the temptation to match our gradual moves.'[79] Still, the constraints of time and limited intelligence required deci-sive decision-making. Accordingly, the NSC met on the morning of

[76] Rabin, *The Rabin Memoirs*, 187–188.
[77] Kissinger, *White House Years*, 626.
[78] Ibid.
[79] Ibid.

21 September, primarily to discuss how to respond to Israeli assessments that air strikes might not be enough and the possibility of mobilisation of Israeli ground forces. Nixon supported Kissinger's view that
decisive action was needed, in contrast to the slow and measured
escalation proposed by Secretary Rogers. He agreed to Israeli ground
action, although Hussein was to be consulted before a final decision
was made.[80]

Some good news finally arrived the next day, 22 September, when
the WSAG heard that Jordanian forces had managed to regain the
initiative on the battlefield, while the Iraqi forces remained inactive
on the border. The group met to examine a list of possible U.S. military actions to deter Soviet intervention. The options ranged from
low-key measures which carried minor costs (such as improved readiness), through larger-scale operations (reinforcement of U.S. forces
in Europe and the Middle East), to full-scale interdiction of Soviet
forces. As illustrated previously, the evaluation of alternative courses
of action and the potential benefits and costs related to them was
performed very well. In this case, potential costs such as personnel
turbulence, negotiations for base access and overflights, political risks,
and augmentations to the defense budget were considered.[81] With the
situation in Jordan stabilising, the group took the following measures:
diplomatically, updating the king on developments in Washington and
keeping channels to Israel open; militarily, preparing a package of
materials destined to Jordan, reviewing contingency plans in case the
Soviets countered Israeli attacks against Syria, and increasing intelligence watch and general readiness. The latter included shifting more
military equipment and aircraft to Europe and putting elements of the
Airborne Brigade in Germany and the 82nd Airborne Division at Fort
Bragg on higher alert.[82]

With these measures taken, and given the developments on the
battlefield, Kissinger felt that all possible courses of action had been
evaluated. Presented with the full spectrum of contingencies, it was

[80] Ibid., 622.
[81] Memo, Robinson to Kissinger, 'U.S. Military Actions to Deter Soviet Intervention
in the Middle East,' 22 September 1970. Folder no. 7, *WSAG Meetings*, MF, Box
H-076, NSCIF, NPMP.
[82] Memo, Kissinger to Nixon, 'WSAG Actions – Jordan,' 22 September 1970. Folder
no. 1, CF – Middle East, Box 615, NSCF, NPMP.

now up to Nixon to make the final decision – exactly how the process ought to work according to the original design of the NSC system:

Basically, as I told the president, we had reached the point where we had done all that was possible; our contingency planning was essentially completed for whatever option he chose. The maximum pressures available had been assembled; the final decision would depend on how others assessed them and responded.[83]

Later that day, Kissinger met Ambassador Rabin in the White House to reaffirm their understanding on possible intervention by Israeli forces. It was agreed that after coordinating positions with Jordan through Washington, Israel would launch air strikes against Syrian forces in Jordan (operations in Syria were considered too risky politically and militarily). If the air strikes alone were insufficient, Israel would then initiate ground operations as well.[84]

By the following day, 23 September, it appeared that Israeli intervention would not be required after all.[85] Jordanian forces were holding their own against the fedayeen as well as the Syrians. Zaid Rifai, the king's confidant, reported to Washington that, provided that the Syrians did not move up reinforcements and Iraqi forces remained inactive, the Jordanians could 'handle the situation' themselves.[86] Still, Kissinger believed that it was imperative that the Syrians withdraw their forces and not dig in. He thus argued that it was crucial to keep applying pressure on Damascus and Moscow: 'I thought it wisest to strengthen the balance of incentives until we knew in fact that the Syrian forces had withdrawn. Letting up now would surely leak and convey the wrong signal at a critical moment.'[87] Within hours, Kissinger

[83] Kissinger, *White House Years*, 628.
[84] Memorandum of Conversation (henceforth Memcon), Rabin, Argov, Kissinger, and Haig, 22 September 1970. Folder no. 3, CF – Middle East, HAK Office Files, Box 134, NSCF, NPMP; Memo, Haig to Kissinger, 'Conversation with Ambassador Rabin,' 22 September 1970. Ibid.
[85] Contrary to most accounts, Alexander Haig's memoirs suggest otherwise. Haig maintains that decisive Israeli air strikes against Syrian forces took place on 21 and 22 of September, to the extent that they were 'breaking the back of the Syrian invasion.' A. M. Haig (with C. McCarry), *Inner Circles: How America Changed the World, A Memoir* (New York: Warner Books, 1992), 251.
[86] Memo, Kissinger to Nixon, 'The Situation in Jordan,' 23 September 1970. Folder no. 7, *WSAG Meetings*, MF, Box H-076, NSCIF, NPMP.
[87] Kissinger, *White House Years*, 630.

received conclusive reports that the Syrians were pulling their forces out of Jordan. The Syrian withdrawal was followed by a quick capitulation of the Palestinian guerrillas and, by 29 September, the remaining hostages were released, following an Arab summit conference and declaration of a cease-fire. The Jordanian Crisis was over, and the key to its successful resolution – indeed, to the successful conclusion of any crisis, as far as Kissinger was concerned – was timing:

> Paradoxically, perhaps the most critical moment occurs when the opponent appears ready to settle; then it is the natural temptation to relax and perhaps to ease the process by a gesture of goodwill. This is almost always a mistake; the time for conciliation is *after* the crisis is surmounted and a settlement or modus vivendi has in fact been reached. Then moderation can be ascribed to generosity and goodwill; before, it may abort the hopeful prospects by raising last-minute doubts as to whether the cost of settlement need in fact be paid.[88]

With the successful resolution of the Jordanian Crisis, the WSAG became less central in the process, and subsequent meetings were convened as combined Senior Review Group (SRG) and WSAG meetings. Although the membership of these groups was in practice similar, the institutional signalling was important as it suggested the abatement of crisis. Furthermore, it was now the job of the SRG, which acted as the ultimate coordinating body between the various interdepartmental groups and the NSC, to oversee future actions concerning Jordan and the Middle East. Additionally, the State Department regained a more substantive role in policy formulation.

Shortly after Kissinger's return from a visit to Europe in early October, the WSAG met to conclude the Jordanian episode with a look to the future.[89] During the meeting on 9 October, the group considered the balance of power in Jordan after the crisis and developed new contingencies based on recent events. Not only did the group pay close attention to monitoring the situation in the aftermath of the crisis, it did not eschew the task of assessing and integrating new information into the planning of new contingencies. Importantly, the group acknowledged that a shift in power relations in Jordan had occurred.

[88] Ibid., 629.
[89] On 27 September, Nixon started a ten-day trip to Europe, with visits to Italy, Yugoslavia, Spain, the UK, and Ireland, as well as the Sixth Fleet in the Mediterranean.

In preparation for the meeting, the NSC staff suggested that despite the king's victory, they 'can no longer ignore that there may be two separate sovereignties in Jordan.'[90] Furthermore, they suggested that it might be necessary to accommodate the Palestinians in future peace negotiations: 'Now we must reconsider the question of whether we back Hussein 100% or couple our backing with some effort to open the door for the Palestinian option – whether and how to try to involve responsible Palestinians in peace negotiations.'[91] Again, this view suggests willingness to reconsider previously rejected assumptions in light of new developments. The main objective of the meeting was to evaluate the balance of authority between the king and the Palestinian organisations in Jordan in the wake of the crisis.[92] To that end, the CIA had prepared an analysis of the situation which suggested that Hussein and his army 'appear to be ahead, at least for the short term. They have made a dent in the Fedayeen capability to take over the Government, but not necessarily in their capability for terrorist or guerrilla activities.' In essence, the view was that in the short term, Hussein was 'in a better position than he was before the troubles.'[93]

Another WSAG meeting followed on 15 October, this time with a broader perspective in mind. The aim of the meeting was to assess the implications of recent events not only for Jordan but also for the Arab-Israeli conflict and the prospects of future peace negotiations. In assessing the situation, the group took into account two factors which had the potential to upset future negotiations. These were the death of President Nasser of Egypt in late September and the pending conclusion of the ninety-day cease-fire along the Suez Canal which was announced in early August as part of the second Rogers Plan. The group recommended that the State Department begin work on a

---

[90] Kennedy and Saunders to Haig, 'The Next WSAG/SRG Meeting,' 2 October 1970. Folder no. 4, *WSAG Meetings*, MF, Box H-076, NSCIF, NPMP.

[91] Ibid.

[92] Ibid.

[93] Combined SRG and WSAG Meeting, 'Jordan,' 9 October 1970. Folder no. 1, MMF, Box H-114, NSCIF, NPMP. Another matter for discussion was the re-evaluation of potential contingencies and their estimated costs and benefits. The prospects of renewal of the civil war, consolidation of the guerrilla position, and Iraqi or renewed Syrian intervention were also considered. Finally, the group discussed at length future military assistance for Jordan in light of the recent events and the changing nature of threat to the king.

new formula for resuming the Arab-Israeli negotiations. Second, and perhaps more important, the group recommended that NSC staff, in consultation with the State Department, prepare a paper on the Palestinian problem and its possible solutions, and the implications for Jordan and King Hussein.[94] This point suggests that the group was quick to adapt to the new realities of the Middle East. An important consequence of the Jordanian Crisis was the rise of the Palestinian question, and although no tangible actions were taken on the issue in Washington in following years (largely because of Israeli intransigence), it was evident that the Palestinian question would have to be addressed in the long run.

Performance of the WSAG

In line with the hierarchical organisation of the NSC system, the process of WSAG meetings was well defined and clear to all the participants. Kissinger set the agenda of the meeting (based on background papers prepared by his NSC staff), asked the important questions, and received the relevant answers during discussions. The minutes of WSAG meetings do not show dissent or conflict between the advisors. Nixon never 'reached down' for information and relied on the information and advice provided by the WSAG and Kissinger. The records show that following WSAG meetings, Kissinger would send a memo to Nixon summarising the recommendations or actions taken. In essence, decision-making during the Jordanian Crisis confirmed the theoretical attributes of Alexander George's formalistic model of presidential management of the advisory system, which aimed to protect the president's time and to provide him with a wide range of processed options.

Nevertheless, informal and close consultations between Nixon and Kissinger still took place, particularly during the last stages of the crisis when the stakes were particularly high and reliable information was harder to come by. However, the frequency and magnitude of these informal meetings between the two pale in comparison to the Cambodian experience, suggesting that Nixon and Kissinger found little

---

[94] Minutes of combined SRG and WSAG Meeting, 'Middle East,' 15 October 1970. Ibid.

reason to personalise the process. By letting the advisory system do its work – and do it well, despite managing simultaneously crises in Chile and Cienfuegos – the routinisation of crisis management produced the desired results without the need for constant personal intervention, exclusion of cabinet members, or other evasive tactics.

The performance of the WSAG during the crisis shows that there was great awareness and ability to implement the formalistic, hierarchic procedures put in place by Nixon and Kissinger. Although these procedures can be criticised for inducing certain cognitive rigidity into the process, they ensured that little was left to chance or to improvisation. For the most part, the group's performance was very methodical and proved effective in providing the president with the information and advice he was seeking during the crisis. Nevertheless, one area with which the group struggled repeatedly was in the search for accurate and timely information, which often resulted in the making of recommendations based on second-hand information and foreign intelligence.

The overriding objective throughout the period, as it transpired during the various phases of the crisis, was the preservation of King Hussein and his regime. Other objectives, such as the evacuation of U.S. citizens from Jordan and the release of the hostages, also guided the decision-making process. However, following the outbreak of civil war, the preservation of the king was perceived as the primary objective because of the potential implications that his fall would have on the region, including another Arab-Israeli war and possibly a direct confrontation between the superpowers. With the invasion of Syrian forces, efforts were made to persuade Moscow to apply pressure on Syria to withdraw its forces. Throughout the crisis, there were no signs of conflict or dissent within the bureaucracy about these objectives. In short, 'the administration appeared united, purposeful, and clear-headed about its goals.'[95]

In pursuing these objectives, the decision-makers were fairly constrained in their search for information. Handicapped by incomplete information, the group often relied on Israeli intelligence and British

---

[95] W. B. Quandt, 'Lebanon, 1958, and Jordan, 1970,' in B. M. Blechman and S. Kaplan (eds.), *Force without War: U.S. Armed Forces as a Political Instrument* (Washington, DC: Brookings Institution, 1978), 268.

assessments, which for the most part could not be interpreted as un-
biased. When the U.S. embassy was cut off, Washington became increasingly reliant on Israeli intelligence – to the extent that following
the Syrian invasion, Ambassador Rabin briefed Kissinger twice daily.[96]
That Iraq and Syria did not have diplomatic relations with the United
States made the task of assessing their moves more difficult. Thus, CIA
analysis in WSAG meetings was based less on hard data than on speculations. This intelligence handicap explains why most reports assessed
that the Iraqis were more likely to intervene than the Syrians – the presence of nearly 20,000 Iraqi troops in Jordan seemed more threatening
than the build-up of Syrian forces along the border. The latter point,
coupled with Kissinger's interpretation of the events, partly explains
why the issue of deterring Soviet intervention was prominent in several
WSAG discussions following the Syrian invasion. Incomplete intelligence constrained not only military decisions but also political ones –
namely, the intentions behind the Syrian decision to intervene or the
state of mind in the PFLP.

The need to reconsider basic assumptions based on the integration of new information into the process was relatively slight, partly
because, as far as Nixon and Kissinger were concerned, the decisive
actions already taken had proved effective. The working assumption
of Soviet involvement behind the Syrian intervention was never questioned, despite the little evidence to support it. There was little chance
for contradictory information to surface during the crisis, owing to the
group's reliance on Israeli intelligence reports. The lack of diplomatic
relations with Syria, Iraq, or the PFLP precluded the use of a varied
pool of information. Nevertheless, when contradictory information did
surface – such as the report from the Cairo official regarding the Syrian
invasion – Kissinger and the WSAG chose to ignore it and preferred
to wait for Jordanian confirmation, believing that if something dramatic as that had actually happened, King Hussein would have found
a way to contact them. This decision suggests a certain degree of cognitive rigidity. On the other hand, the decision not to follow up on the
Cairo report can be understood in terms of cautiousness in the face of

---

[96] Dowty, *Middle East Crisis*, 183.

uncertainty. As Secretary of Defense Laird suggested: 'If there's one thing we'd learned, it's that you never believe the first story, and only one-half of the fourth story during a crisis.'[97]

Although information was limited, the group constantly assessed and developed alternative courses of action. This was evident in the first days of the crisis, when the group developed plans to evacuate U.S. citizens, despite the limited intelligence. These contingencies were fairly elaborated and were updated frequently as subsequent reports arrived from Jordan. Following the outbreak of civil war in Jordan, and certainly after the Syrian intervention, the emphasis shifted to the consideration of military measures (e.g., air strikes against Iraqi/Syrian forces, advancement of U.S. forces in the Mediterranean). Only minor nonmilitary actions were taken, such as communicating with Moscow, briefing the French government, or enlisting the support of the Shah of Iran.[98]

Alternative courses of action were assessed in tandem with the evaluation of potential benefits and costs of each action. This was evident in the planning of evacuation of U.S. citizens, the use of military and nonmilitary measures to assist Hussein, the use of American or Israeli forces against Syria, and the nature of Israeli assistance. Although on the issue of negotiating for the release of the hostages with the PFLP, the need to coordinate a unified front with four other governments further complicated the process, nevertheless a comprehensive assessment of options was carried out.

The group paid close attention to the implementation and monitoring of decisions, and frequent updates on the movement of U.S. forces in the Mediterranean were produced. The deployment of the Sixth Fleet and placement of U.S. forces in Fort Bragg and in Germany on high alert was intended to allow a quick response should U.S. intervention in Jordan be called for. Similarly, several C-130 transport aircraft were advanced to Turkey to help with the evacuation of U.S. citizens. The minutes of WSAG meetings suggest that all these decisions were not randomly made. Often, they followed elaborate

---

[97] Cited in Hersh, *The Price of Power*, 243.
[98] Minutes of WSAG meeting, 'Jordan,' 21 September 1970, Folder no. 2, *WSAG Meetings*, MF, Box H-077, NSCIF, NPMP.

discussions which addressed seemingly minute details concerning the implementation of the group's recommendations – such as the number of companies needed to secure the airfield in Amman or the type of equipment required and the flight time from Germany of U.S. troops to accomplish that mission. The need to monitor decisions and ensure their implementation increased following the Syrian invasion. To that extent, the close cooperation with Ambassador Rabin proved important to the successful implementation of decisions in the last stages of the crisis.

Nixon and Kissinger had many reasons to be pleased with the management of the crisis and its outcome. The hostages were released without any concessions being made, the Syrians and the fedayeen were defeated, relations with Israel and Jordan were strengthened, and Arab bitterness towards Moscow grew stronger, as Soviet support during the crisis proved inept. Importantly, however, there were no discussions in the aftermath of the crisis to examine the extent to which the results of the crisis were directly affected by actions taken by the administration. Stated differently, can a causal link be drawn between the successful management of the crisis and its favourable outcome to U.S. interests? As discussed in chapter 1, the link between the quality of the decision-making process and the outcome of a crisis is rather untenable. This institutional failure to produce concrete analysis about the quality of the decision-making process during the Jordanian Crisis is alluded to by Quandt, who suggests that 'Apparently successful policies are spared the type of critical scrutiny reserved for failures.'[99] Reiter's analysis of analogical reasoning (cited in chapter 1) reiterates this point by concluding that, often, 'continuity of policy follows success, while innovation follows failure.'[100]

Although at times Nixon and Kissinger were too quick to view the crisis as a matter primarily of superpower concern, in sum the decision-making process was impressive. The president and his national security advisor set clear guidelines and objectives to follow. They kept their options open and were flexible enough to adapt quickly to new developments. Nonetheless, despite the successful resolution of the crisis,

[99] Quandt, *Decade of Decisions*, 120.
[100] Reiter, 'Learning, Realism, and Alliances,' 490.

the new, tougher U.S. Middle East policy devised in September 1970 would ultimately prove disastrous. As will be shown in chapter 6, within three years, its dramatic long-term implications would affect not only the Middle East but U.S.-Europe relations and the world's economy as well.

5

The India-Pakistan War, December 1971

What I'm concerned about, what I'm really worried about, is whether or not I was too easy on the goddamn woman when she was here . . . This woman suckered us. But let me tell you she's going to pay. She is going to pay.[1]

Nixon to Kissinger, after his meeting with Indian Prime Minister Indira Gandhi, 6 December 1971

Perhaps more than any other crisis examined in this book, the management of the 1971 India-Pakistan War epitomised the extent to which the decision-making process was constrained by Nixon and Kissinger's style of foreign policy making. Moreover, often during the crisis it seemed that Kissinger's own design of the advisory system acted as the ultimate constraint on Nixon's efforts to run U.S. foreign policy with as little bureaucratic meddling as possible. The impact of this pattern was manifested in three areas, which as has already been established, were the dominant features of the making of U.S. foreign policy during the Nixon-Kissinger years: first, the two men's disregard of the bureaucracy's advice, particularly that of the State Department; second, their predisposition to view what was in essence a regional crisis in terms of a realist, power-centred triangular politics, thus unnecessarily bringing China and the Soviet Union into the equation; and third,

[1] *FRUS*, Volume XI: South Asia Crisis, 1971, 662 (doc. 235).

the issue of excessive secrecy, which was brought to the fore following the dramatic disclosure of WSAG minutes by a syndicated columnist.

U.S. policy during the conflict in the subcontinent, which lasted from March to December 1971, is commonly known as 'The Tilt' – referring to Nixon's decision to ignore the advice of the bureaucracy and the reports from the ground, and to tilt in favour of Pakistan in its third war with India in a generation. The war between India and Pakistan in December 1971 followed months of civil war in East Pakistan and a ruthless regime of terror by the Pakistani leader, General Yahya Khan. The civil war coincided with a devastating cyclone in East Pakistan, which led to an influx of millions of refugees into India. The tension along the eastern border between India and East Pakistan gradually escalated and a third war between the two countries ensued.

Nixon's directive to the bureaucracy that U.S. policy should tilt toward Pakistan was revealed to the public by the journalist Jack Anderson at the end of the war. In mid-December 1971, excerpts from four WSAG meetings began to appear in his syndicated columns in the *Washington Post* and the *New York Times*. In early January 1972, Kissinger complained that the quotations were 'out of context,' whereupon Anderson released to the press what became known as 'The Anderson Papers' – the full texts of WSAG minutes of meetings from December 3, 4, 6, and 8. Anderson's lists were significant not only because they provided a fascinating account of the decision-making process and Kissinger's control of the bureaucracy but more important because they proved that the administration pursued a policy in South Asia which favoured Pakistan, despite Washington's official denials.[2] This remarkable episode illuminated an inherent weakness in Nixon's approach to policy making. Perhaps more than in any other modern presidency, a key requisite to the success of the Nixon-Kissinger foreign policy operation hinged on the careful manipulation

---

[2] Anderson's source was Navy Yeoman Charles Radford, who was assigned to liaise between the Joint Chiefs of Staff and the White House. His identity was exposed during a White House investigation of the Anderson leaks. It turned out that Radford was at the heart of a spy network operated by the Joint Chiefs to obtain classified information from Kissinger's office and other people in the NSC. Beginning in 1970, Radford copied more than 5,000 NSC documents. See Prados, *Keepers of the Keys*, 315–317; Small, *The Presidency of Richard Nixon*, 54–55; F. Emery, *Watergate: The Corruption of American Politics and the Fall of Richard Nixon* (New York: Times Books, 1994), 83–85.

of the bureaucracy, the public, and Congress by resorting to secrecy and evasion. However, keeping the Washington media at arm's length proved an almost impossible task. Helmut Sonnenfeldt recalls that this was the case even before he joined Kissinger's NSC staff. He laments that while serving in the State Department during the Kennedy administration, 'I found the journalists knew a hell of a lot more than I did.'[3]

The dramatic revelations of the Anderson Papers at the end of the crisis are important in explaining why the management of the India-Pakistan crisis proved to be one of the most controversial foreign policy episodes of the Nixon administration. Beyond the immediate reason – Nixon and Kissinger's personification of the decision-making process and their blatant lies about their priorities during the crisis – equally alarming was the motivation behind those lies. As the first section of this chapter will demonstrate, U.S. foreign policy in the run up to the India-Pakistan War was shaped by two factors. First, President Nixon's sense of debt to the Pakistani leader, General Yahya, for his role in opening a back channel to Beijing compared with his awful relations with the Indian Prime Minister Indira Gandhi. Indeed, this chapter provides perhaps the most vivid example of the importance of personal characteristics and cognitive schemes in the making of foreign policy. Second, policy choices were ultimately constrained by Nixon and Kissinger's proclivity to interpret developments in the subcontinent as a U.S-Sino-Soviet conflict by proxy. This tendency to downgrade in importance local and regional factors was discussed earlier and, as Hanhimaki suggests, it proved crucial in Kissinger's interpretation of unfolding events during the crisis: 'Kissinger, apparently, saw only one reality: India was a friend of the Soviet Union; Pakistan a friend of China's. The United States needed to side with Pakistan in order to safeguard the opening to China... Sadly, all of this amounted to a false reading of South Asian realities in 1971.'[4] Thus, in a July 1971

---

[3] Interview with Sonnenfeldt.

[4] Hanhimaki, *The Flawed Architect*, 155. Hanhimaki's assessment of the tilt policy is more sympathetic than traditional accounts. He downplays the long-term damage caused by the policy and argues that while the policy was indeed disastrous, we cannot ignore the inherent logic behind the decision to accommodate Pakistan, as in the eyes of Kissinger, it provided the crucial key in the evolution of triangular diplomacy. *The Flawed Architect*, 155–156. For more traditional accounts, see Bundy, *A Tangled Web*,

meeting with Joseph Farland, U.S. ambassador to Pakistan, Nixon expressed his concern over the emerging crisis in South Asia – not merely because of the human tragedy 'but also because it could disrupt our steady course in our policy toward China.' At the end of the meeting, Nixon asked the ambassador to 'convey again to Yahya his appreciation for Pakistan's contribution to the China initiative. As for Pakistan's present difficulties, the President wanted it made clear to Yahya that we would not add to his burdens.'[5] Kissinger reiterated this position the following month in a meeting with the Chinese ambassador in Paris, stating that the U.S. government 'would do nothing to embarrass Pakistan publicly.'[6] Similarly, Nixon and Kissinger feared that U.S. support for secession and self-determination in East Pakistan would clash with their overriding strategic interest in placating the government in Beijing, whose policies over Taiwan and Tibet could not be ignored.[7] This theme is further elaborated in the second part of the chapter, which examines the decision-making process during the crisis. In particular, it demonstrates how Nixon and Kissinger repeatedly circumvented the system they created, either by not heeding the bureaucracy's advice or by taking decisions without prior consultation with their advisors. Finally, in analysing the performance of the WSAG during the crisis, the observation most pertinent to the theme of this book is that while the group convened rather frequently during the crisis, it was not given the tools to adequately perform its most basic tasks. In a fashion similar to the Cambodian crisis, rather than acting as the key decisional unit in the decision-making process, the WSAG became a victim of Nixon and Kissinger's tactics of secrecy, lies, and manipulation.

269–292; R. L. Garthoff, *Détente and Confrontation: American-Soviet Relations from Nixon to Reagan* (Washington, DC, Brookings Institution, 1994, rev. ed.), 295–322; Morris, *Uncertain Greatness*, 222–228; C. Van Hollen, 'The Tilt Policy Revisited: The Nixon-Kissinger Geopolitics and South Asia,' *Asian Survey* 20:4 (April 1980), 339–361.

[5] Memo for the President's file, 'President's Meeting with Ambassador Farland,' 28 July 1971. The National Security Archive website, George Washington University (henceforth NSA website), http://www.gwu.edu/~nsarchiv/NSAEBB/NSAEBB79/BEBB18.pdf.

[6] Memo, Kissinger to Nixon, 'My August 16 Meeting with the Chinese Ambassador in Paris,' 16 August 1971. NSA website, http://www.gwu.edu/~nsarchiv/NSAEBB/NSAEBB79/BEBB23.pdf.

[7] *FRUS*, Volume XI, 345–347 (doc. 127).

This account is thoroughly supported by recently declassified material, most notably the State Department's Foreign Relations of the United States series (*FRUS*) series. The volume dealing with the South Asian crisis was published in 2005 and provides telling evidence about the workings of the Nixon administration during the crisis. It reveals that Nixon and Kissinger habitually referred to Mrs. Gandhi as 'that bitch,' downplayed reports of Pakistani genocide, and even suggested that China come to Pakistan's help in its war with India.[8] Within this context, it is hard to eschew the conclusion that in the process of policy making, the status of the WSAG had changed dramatically from its original design. At least during the India-Pakistan War in 1971, it had moved from a central apparatus of decision-making to a bureaucratic battleground and a regular impediment to policy making.

U.S. Foreign Policy and the Emergence of the India-Pakistan Conflict

The war between India and Pakistan in December 1971 was the inevitable result of a civil war in East Pakistan which broke out the previous March, but its historical roots date back to 1947, when the Indian subcontinent gained its independence from Britain and was partitioned along religious lines. Mostly Hindu, India was bordered on the west and east by Pakistan, which was composed of two entities – West Pakistan and East Pakistan. Despite the apparent religious homogeneity, a cultural, economic, and eventually political rift emerged between the two Pakistani entities separated by a thousand miles of Indian territory. As home to the political, industrial, and economic centres, West Pakistan had always been the dominant partner, despite the fact that 60 percent of the population resided in East Pakistan.[9] Meanwhile, power relations between India and Pakistan began to shift heavily in favour of the former after the 1965 Pakistani defeat in the war over

---

[8] For a recent review, see G. Warner, 'Nixon, Kissinger and the Breakup of Pakistan, 1971,' *International Affairs*, 81:5 (October 2005), 1097–1118.

[9] R. J. Leng, *Bargaining and Learning in Recurring Crises: The Soviet-American, Egyptian-Israeli and Indo-Pakistani Rivalries* (Ann Arbor: University of Michigan Press, 2000), 239.

Kashmir. Indo-Soviet cooperation increased as the Soviets saw India as an important counterbalance to China. Pakistan, at the same time, received substantial military support from China, while the United States pursued a policy of embargo of military equipment on both India and Pakistan, which was imposed after the 1965 war.[10]

The first signs of crisis appeared in November 1970, when a devastating cyclone hit East Pakistan, killing more than 200,000 people and leaving millions homeless. Only weeks later, elections in Pakistan saw the Awami League from the East winning an absolute majority in the National Assembly. Yahya Khan, the Pakistani president who came to power in March 1969 after a military coup, responded forcefully to the Awami League's call for self-rule in East Pakistan and, in late March 1971, announced that the opening of the new National Assembly would be postponed indefinitely. Sheikh Mujib Rahman, leader of the Awami League, was arrested and sent to prison in West Pakistan, together with other members of his party. The next few days saw a systematic campaign of ruthless repression, which by some estimates claimed 15,000 lives in East Pakistan in the first three days and a million by the end of the year.[11] The Pakistani civil war, combined with the devastating effects of the cyclone, saw some ten million Bengali refugees fleeing East Pakistan into the bordering Indian state of West Bengal. The brutal handling of the uprising by the Pakistani government set off a world outcry, yet there was no official statement by the American administration condemning the actions of Yahya's regime. The reasons behind Nixon's decision to remain on the sidelines were not immediately clear to outside observers. During the first months of the fighting, no one but Nixon and Kissinger knew about the crucial role played by Yahya in mediating secret talks between Washington and Peking. Washington's official policy was in line with every other

[10] Between 1965 and 1970, the Soviets delivered to India $730 million worth of goods, compared with $133 million worth of supplies delivered to Pakistan. American contributions to both countries reached $70 million in nonlethal goods. See Thornton, *The Nixon-Kissinger Years*, 109–110.

[11] *Time*, 6 December 1971, 10-14; *The New Republic*, 17 April 1971, 9–10. For an account of the events leading to the civil war, see H. Feldman, *The End and the Beginning: Pakistan 1969–1971* (Oxford: Oxford University Press, 1975), 76–126; R. Jackson, *South Asian Crisis: India-Pakistan-Bangla Desh* (London: Chatto & Windus, 1975), 9–32.

nation observing the conflict, that of noninvolvement. Nevertheless, the White House's refusal to condemn Islamabad's actions seemed to many both puzzling and suspicious.[12]

Despite substantial foreign aid, the influx of refugees placed a heavy burden on an already overpopulated India and increased her stakes in the outcome of the Pakistani crisis. As far as the Indian government was concerned, the secession of East Pakistan and the formation of an independent Bangladesh would substantially weaken her bitter rival West Pakistan, which had already fought India immediately after independence in 1947 and again in 1965. Accordingly, Prime Minister Indira Gandhi sent forces to the border with East Pakistan, hoping to achieve two objectives: slow the influx of Bengali refugees, and encourage the creation of an independent state in East Pakistan to further cement India's predominance in South Asia.[13] On 9 August, an already explosive situation reached new levels of volatility when India signed a treaty of 'peace, friendship and cooperation' with the Soviet Union, which obliged each side to assist the other in the event of threat to national security, and stated that neither country would support a third party against the other.[14]

During the summer of 1971, Indian-sponsored guerrillas (the *Mukti Bahini*) began to infiltrate into East Pakistan and carried out various sabotage missions. As tension in the region grew, both India and Pakistan began deploying their forces closer to the border, and by early November, there were already minor skirmishes along the eastern front and an all-out war seemed inevitable. In the weeks leading up to the war, the White House had made several futile attempts to persuade Moscow to act jointly in order to prevent further deterioration of the situation. Notwithstanding Moscow's refusal to cooperate, neither the Soviets nor the Chinese wanted to be drawn into the conflict and risk the possibility of direct confrontation. By late 1971, Washington and Moscow were committed to the SALT talks and the spirit of détente. At the same time, the world had learned about Kissinger's first official

---

[12] Bundy, *A Tangled Web*, 271.
[13] Thornton, *The Nixon-Kissinger Years*, 110–111; D. K. Hall, 'The Laotian War of 1962 and the Indo-Pakistani War of 1971,' in B. M. Blechman and S. Kaplan (eds.), *Force without War: U.S. Armed Forces as a Political Instrument* (Washington, DC: Brookings Institution, 1978), 176–177.
[14] Bundy, *A Tangled Web*, 273; Kissinger, *White House Years*, 866–867.

visit to Peking in an effort to thaw Chinese-American relations. As Leng correctly observed, 'None of these parties wanted a war in South Asia to upset these delicate diplomatic efforts.'[15]

In early November 1971, Mrs. Gandhi visited several western capitals, ending her trip with two meetings with Nixon in Washington. Kissinger later remembered these occasions to be 'without doubt the two most unfortunate meetings Nixon had with any foreign leader.'[16] Nixon's historical aversion to India dated back to his days as Eisenhower's Vice President in the 1950s, when the American administration did not appreciate the Indian government's nonalignment policy in the height of the Cold War. Nixon also felt that the receptions he received from the political elite as well as the press on his visits to India were rather lukewarm, partly because of the popular support for Senator John F. Kennedy during the 1960 presidential campaign. Furthermore, Mrs. Gandhi had never made an effort to conceal her downright dislike of Nixon and on more than one occasion criticised him personally or ignored his gestures. On his part, Nixon habitually referred to the Indian leader in derogatory terms.[17] Recalling Janis's discussion of egocentric psychological make-up (chapter 1), it is easy to see how these early personal ill feelings later contributed to Nixon's distorted and rather emotionally constructed image of India and its leader during its war with Pakistan. In other words, India was Nixon's default choice as the 'bad guys,' almost regardless of what had happened on the ground. Most important Nixon's antipathy towards India stood in stark contrast to his good relations with the political elites in Pakistan. Ever since the 1962 war between India and China, Nixon viewed Pakistan as an important instrument in advancing relations between Washington and Beijing. Despite Pakistan's important role in the U.S.-led Baghdad Pact and SEATO (South East Asia Treaty Organisation), the Chinese saw Pakistan as a useful partner, and from 1962, Beijing had courted Pakistan as an ally on its southern border and importantly as a counterweight to India.[18] Accordingly, in a meeting with President Yahya Kahn in April 1969, Nixon asked his counterpart

---

[15] Leng, *Bargaining and Learning in Recurring Crises*, 242.
[16] Kissinger, *White House Years*, 878.
[17] Van Hollen, 'The Tilt Policy Revisited,' 341; Hall, 'The Laotian War,' 179–180.
[18] See G. W. Choudhury, 'Reflections on Sino-Pakistan Relations,' *Pacific Community*, 7:2 (January 1976), 248–270.

to act as courier in the secret negotiations between the two powers.[19] Yahya's role was crucial to the success of Kissinger's subsequent secret visits to Beijing, which ultimately led to Nixon's historic trip to China in May 1972. Understandably, the secret opening to China left Nixon with feelings of gratitude and indebtedness to the Pakistani leader.[20] As early as October 1970, Nixon assured Yahya that 'nobody occupied the White House who is friendlier to Pakistan.'[21] As a token of his appreciation of Yahya's efforts, Nixon authorised a 'one-off' $50 million aid package to assist Pakistan, in clear violation of the arms embargo which had been in place since 1965.[22]

In light of this history, then, there was little surprise that the Nixon-Gandhi meetings in November 1971 produced nothing but further discomfort and resentment on both sides. In his memoirs, Kissinger vividly summarises the atmosphere:

Mrs. Gandhi began by expressing admiration for Nixon's handling of Vietnam and the China initiative, in the manner of a professor praising a slightly backward student... Nixon reacted with the glassy-eyed politeness which told those who knew him that his resentments were being kept in check only by his reluctance to engage in face-to-face disagreement.[23]

Nixon and Kissinger met in the Oval Office the following day to discuss the meeting. Kissinger praised Nixon's performance and concluded that 'while she was a bitch, we got what we wanted, too... She will not be able to go home and say that the United States didn't give her a warm reception and therefore in despair she's got to go to war.' Nixon shared Kissinger's impression: 'We really slobbered over the old witch.' The two agreed that in the next meeting, Nixon's

---

[19] At the meeting, Nixon told Yahya that the U.S. 'should not be party to any arrangements designed to isolate China'; he asked his counterpart to 'convey his feeling to the Chinese at the highest level.' See *FRUS*, Volume I, (doc. 33).

[20] Hersh, *The Price of Power*, 444–447; Ambrose, *Nixon*, 482. At the same time, the State Department was trying to improve relations with India to counter Chinese influence in the region. Leng, *Bargaining and Learning in Recurring Crises*, 241.

[21] Choundhury, 'Reflections on Sino-Pakistan Relations,' 266.

[22] D. Kux, *India and the United States: Estranged Democracies, 1941–1991* (Washington, DC: National Defense University Press, 1993), 181–183. See the memo from Secretary Rogers to President Nixon on 13 October, following the completion of the plan in R. Khan, *The American Papers: Secret and Confidential India-Pakistan-Bangladesh Documents, 1965–1973* (Oxford: Oxford University Press, 2000), 429.

[23] Kissinger, *White House Years*, 878–879.

approach should be 'a shade cooler.'[24] According to Jack Anderson, the columnist who published the secret WSAG minutes in December 1971, Nixon was not alone in bearing a grudge against India. Kissinger too demonstrated an alarming degree of 'anti-India zeal,' which troubled some members of his NSC staff. Anderson quoted sources as saying that 'sometimes Kissinger acted like a wild man . . . His animus toward India seemed irrational.'[25] After the Nixon-Gandhi meeting in November, for example, Kissinger observed that '[the] Indians are bastards anyway . . . They are starting a war there.'[26]

On 21 November, reports arrived in Washington about further escalation along the India-Pakistan border, but the intelligence community was divided over the nature of the clashes or the identity of the aggressor. The Americans had no independent information to confirm the reports that arrived from Pakistan. More than ever before, Nixon and Kissinger found it impossible to impose their pro-Pakistani policy on the bureaucracy. Coming under heavy criticism from Congress and the media for the failure to voice his outrage over Pakistani aggression in the early days of the crisis, Nixon simply could not manage to impose on the bureaucracy the required discipline to execute his decisions.

Crisis Decision-Making

By the time of the India-Pakistan War in 1971, conflicting views between the White House and the bureaucracy were hardly a novelty. Still, this crisis presented an almost unprecedented case of dissent, as Kissinger himself lamented in his memoirs: 'On no issue – except perhaps Cambodia – was the split between the White House and the departments so profound as on the India-Pakistan crisis in the summer of 1971. On no other problem was there such flagrant disregard of unambiguous Presidential directives.'[27]

With Nixon's aversion to face a dissenting bureaucracy, it was down to Kissinger to discipline his unruly colleagues in the WSAG and the departments more generally. George H. W. Bush, U.S. ambassador to

---

[24] *FRUS*, Volume XI, 499 (doc. 180).
[25] J. Anderson with G. Clifford, *The Anderson Papers* (New York: Random House, 1973), 210.
[26] *FRUS*, Volume XI, 499 (doc. 180).
[27] Kissinger, *White House Years*, 863–864.

the United Nations during the crisis, was particularly anxious about Kissinger's animosity toward the State Department during the crisis: 'The State Department to him is an increasing obsession. He is absolutely obsessed by the idea that they are incompetent and can't get the job done. It comes out all the time . . . The situation is getting increasingly intolerable.' Referring to the impact of Kissinger's behavior on the overall foreign policy system, Bush observed:

I worry about the system, about this two State Departments thing. I have no knowledge as to how thoroughly staffed out the Kissinger operation is. I understand the staff is big, but I don't know how those things work. Henry is very excitable, very emotional almost. He has a great sense of humor and sometimes is tremendously relaxed and buoyant. Often, however, he hits the ceiling and raises hell . . . Kissinger is absolutely brutal on these guys, insisting that they don't know anything and asking why they are screwing up policy etc.[28]

Bush's observation goes a long way in explaining the roots of the flawed decision-making process during the crisis. Too often it resembled a duel between Nixon and Kissinger on one side and the State Department on the other. In no other forum was this tension more evident than in WSAG meetings. The leak and subsequent publication of minutes from several WSAG meetings further compounded the difficulties the White House was having in justifying its policy. Nixon and Kissinger were evidently concerned by the dissenting voices in the WSAG, which, as Bob Haldeman suggested, were 'in open rebellion against Henry and P[resident]'s position.'[29] In other words, there are visible signs here of the most common symptoms of bureaucratic politics. Competition and dissent among advisors in the context of WSAG meetings were largely the result of departmental priorities. But this bureaucratic dissent, however acute, can only go so far in explaining the many faults in the making and executing of U.S. policy during the crisis. The decision-making process during the India-Pakistan War was flawed from the outset. More than any other factor, it was Nixon and Kissinger's insistence on accommodating Pakistan that had the most damaging effect on the process. From an institutional perspective, much like the Cambodian crisis, the India-Pakistan War tested

[28] Summary of meeting by Ambassador George H. W. Bush, 10 December 1971. NSA website, http://www.gwu.edu/~nsarchiv/NSAEBB/NSAEBB79/BEBB32.pdf.
[29] Haldeman, *The Haldeman Diaries*, 381.

the fundamentals of the foreign policy machinery. The hierarchical, orderly procedures failed to produce the desired outcome in terms of U.S. national interests, not least because of bureaucratic foot-dragging when it came to implementing the president's orders.

Much like in previous crises, the NSC in its function as a forum for the president and his top advisors to mull over policy did not perform effectively. Nixon convened the NSC only twice, on an ad hoc basis in July and December but, as Christopher Van Hollen, deputy assistant secretary of state for Near Eastern and South Asian Affairs, lamented, those discussions 'did not deserve the label "NSC meetings."'[30] For the most part, Nixon preferred to consult with Kissinger, who himself failed to provide the necessary policy guidance at the interdepartmental meetings. Usually attending the WSAG meetings during the crisis were U. Alexis Johnson and Joseph Sisco (under secretary of state for political affairs and assistant secretary of state for Near Eastern and South Asian affairs, respectively), Warren Nutter (assistant secretary of defense for international security affairs), and Maurice Williams from the Agency for International Development.

The WSAG first met on 26 March 1971 to consider the emerging crisis in Pakistan. Its initial actions followed the theoretically 'rational' process of decision-making – namely, evaluating U.S. objectives, judging between alternatives, and recommending courses of action. However, as the tension along the India-Pakistan border intensified, by late November the group's recommendations were no longer taken into account by Kissinger and Nixon, who preferred to maintain their tilt policy. More than any other constraining factor, it was their fear that Beijing might view the United States as a weak power that had a detrimental impact on the decision-making process. Meeting during the first week of fighting in December 1971, Kissinger expressed his concern that if Pakistan was dismembered by India, the Chinese might conclude that the United States was 'just too weak' to have prevented the humiliation of an ally and would then look elsewhere to break their encirclement. He concluded, 'So I think this, unfortunately, has turned into a big watershed.'[31]

Still, in the early days of the crisis, Kissinger was certainly responsive to the developments in East Pakistan. The rapid pace of events

[30] Van Hollen, 'The Tilt Policy Revisited,' 345 (fn. 15).
[31] *FRUS*, Volume XI, 705 (doc. 251).

prompted him on 16 February to direct the bureaucracy to prepare contingencies outlining possible U.S. actions in the event of East Pakistani secession (NSSM-118).[32] The directive was first of many over a period of a year and had placed heavy burden on the bureaucracy. As discussed in chapter 2, this was often Kissinger's way of keeping the departments busy so that he and Nixon could run U.S. foreign policy with fewer obstructions. Admiral Elmo Zumwalt, chief of naval operations during the India-Pakistan crisis, recalled that in a period of just over a year, Kissinger had ordered no less than five studies on various aspects of the emerging crisis in South Asia, the benefit of which was doubtful: 'This piling of study upon study resulted in what I can only call a verbal mudslide.'[33]

Bizarrely, Kissinger alerted the bureaucracy about the delicacy of the emerging situation in the subcontinent three weeks before the outbreak of the civil war in Pakistan, thus providing a first hint about Nixon's preferred direction for U.S. policy. During a SRG meeting on 6 March 1971, U. Alexis Johnson expressed the view of the State Department that the interests of the United States, the Soviets, and India were best served by the preservation of a united Pakistan. The developing crisis, Johnson argued, did not have direct bearing on superpower or Indian-American relations. At this point, Kissinger alerted the group to Nixon's special relationship with President Yahya. He then insisted that even if the U.S. ambassador in Pakistan were to put pressure on Yahya, this would make no difference. Given the 'highly emotional' atmosphere, Kissinger concluded, 'I can't imagine that they give a damn what we think.' Kissinger's subtle warning worked well and the group failed to propose a concrete policy of action, other than a recommendation to consult with the British and to guide the U.S. consulate in Dacca to say nothing.[34]

A few weeks later, on 26 March, following the military crackdown in East Pakistan, the WSAG met again – a first indication that the administration perceived the situation as tantamount to an emerging crisis. The group was in consensus that the inevitable result of recent

---

[32] NSSM-118, Kissinger to Secretary of State, Secretary of Defense, and DCI, 'Contingency Study on Pakistan – Addendum to NSSM 109.' 16 February 1971. In Khan, *The American Papers*, 489.

[33] Zumwalt, *On Watch*, 362.

[34] *FRUS*, Volume XI, 15 (doc. 6).

events would be 'civil war resulting eventually in independence or for independence fairly quickly.'[35] Kissinger also convinced the group to follow the president's line, that it would be better to remain inactive. He observed that '[this] seems to be a straightforward operational problem' and concluded, as if to make a point, that there were 'no major interdepartmental differences.'[36] However, this nominal collegial atmosphere gradually turned sour, as American diplomatic missions in India and Pakistan began reporting on Yahya's campaign of terror in the East. There were emerging voices of concern and puzzlement over Nixon's decision to remain mute, despite the call from the bureaucracy and the NSC staff to reconsider the public posture. In late March, Samuel Hoskinson from the NSC staff reported to Kissinger that the latest developments 'would seem to raise new policy issues for us . . . Is the present U.S. posture of simply ignoring the atrocities in East Pakistan still advisable or should we now be expressing our shock at least privately to the West Pakistanis?'[37] Similarly, Kenneth Keating, U.S. ambassador in New Delhi, expressed his concern over the administration's public posture. In his meeting with Kissinger in June, the ambassador said that he recognised Nixon's 'special relationship with President Yahya – although he did not understand it.' Kissinger concurred and, without revealing too much, confirmed that 'the President has a special feeling for President Yahya. One cannot make policy on that basis, but it is a fact of life.'[38] When the news of Pakistan's important role in thawing Sino-American relations became public in the summer of 1971, the bureaucracy was even more relentless in trying to influence policy, despite Nixon's clear orders not to apply pressure on Yahya. The State Department was particularly concerned by the incarceration of the democratically elected leader from East Pakistan, Mujib Rahman. Thus, on 22 November, Kissinger complained to Nixon: 'Now, we've got a case of almost total insubordination from the State Department, they want to go to Yahya and ask him to release Mujib.'[39]

---

[35] Ibid., 26 (doc. 11).
[36] Ibid., 27, 28.
[37] Ibid., 34 (doc. 13).
[38] Ibid., 164 (doc. 64).
[39] Conversation No. 622-1. 22 November 1971, 3:15 p.m.–3:58 p.m., Oval Office. White House Tapes, Miller Center of Public Affairs.

The influx of refugees into India, combined with the atrocious manner in which the regime of Yahya Kahn dealt with the political situation in East Pakistan, made the public, as well as Congress and the bureaucracy, sympathetic to India's difficult position. The unfolding tragedy quickly raised human rights concerns in U.S. missions in Pakistan and India. Archer Blood, the Consul General in Dacca, went as far as outright condemning the public policy of the Nixon administration in the face of the atrocities. In a telegram to Washington titled 'selective genocide,' Blood reported on 28 March:

Here in Dacca we are mute and horrified witnesses to a reign of a terror by the Pak military. Evidence continues to mount that the MLA [Martial Law Administration] authorities have a list of Awami League supporters whom they are systematically eliminating by seeking them out in their homes and shooting them down...

Full horror of Pak military atrocities will come to light sooner or later. I, therefore, question continued advisability of present [United States Government] posture of pretending to believe [Government of Pakistan's] false assertions and denying, for understood reasons, that this office is communicating detailed account of events in East Pakistan. We should be expressing our shock, at least privately to [Government of Pakistan], at this wave of terror directed against their own countrymen by Pak military.[40]

Blood's strong demarche did not have the desired effect on the White House, and ten days later the resilient diplomat sent an even more critical 'dissent cable' which openly criticised U.S. policy. Importantly, attached to this cable were the signatures of more than two dozen Foreign Service officers in Dacca who expressed dissent over the administration's public posture. Suggesting that the U.S. government had demonstrated 'moral bankruptcy,' Blood charged that

with the conviction that U.S. policy related to recent developments in East Pakistan serves neither our moral interests broadly defined nor our national interests narrowly defined, numerous officers... consider it their duty to register strong dissent with fundamental aspects of this policy. Our government has failed to denounce the suppression of democracy. Our government has failed to denounce atrocities. Our government has failed to take forceful measures to protect its citizens while at the same time bending over backwards to placate

---

[40] Telegram, Blood to Secretary of State, 'Selective Genocide,' 28 March 1971. NSA website, http://www.gwu.edu/~nsarchiv/NSAEBB/NSAEBB79/BEBB1.pdf.

the West Pak [*sic*] dominated government and to lessen likely and deservedly negative international public relations impact against them.[41]

The second cable proved more successful than the first in making waves in Washington, although Blood had no reason to be content with the reaction in the White House. A few months later, he was summoned back to Washington and was reprimanded for his highly publicised and critical cables. He was transferred from his post and placed into virtual exile within the State Department.[42]

Blood was not alone in voicing strong discontent in relation to his government policies. Sharing his strong views on the situation was Ambassador Keating in New Delhi. Like Blood, Keating was concerned about the horrific news from East Pakistan – not least because of the U.S. administration's failure to protest and distance itself from Yahya's murderous regime:

[*sic*] Am deeply shocked at massacre by Pakistani military in East Pakistan, appalled at possibility the atrocities are being committed with American equipment, and greatly concerned at United States vulnerability to damaging allegations of association with reign of military terror.

I believe [United States Government]: (A) should promptly, publicly and prominently deplore this brutality, (B) should privately lay it on line with [Government of Pakistan] and so advise [Government of India], and (C) should announce unilateral abrogation of one-time exception military supply agreement [to Pakistan].

It [*sic*] most important these actions be taken now, prior to inevitable and imminent emergence of horrible truths and prior to Communist initiatives to exploit situation. This is time when principles make best politics.[43]

Remarkably, in the face of this criticism, not only did the Pakistani government acknowledge the killings, it also praised the Nixon administration for its public inaction during the first days of the crisis. Meeting with Joseph Sisco from the State Department, the Pakistani ambassador in Washington, Agha Hilali, asked that 'due allowance be made for behavior of Pak officials and others during what had

[41] *FRUS*, Volume XI, 1971, 45 (doc. 19).
[42] Anderson, *The Anderson Papers*, 215.
[43] Telegram, Keating to Secretary of State, 'Selective Genocide,' 29 March 1971. NSA website, http://www.gwu.edu/~nsarchiv/NSAEBB/NSAEBB79/BEBB1.pdf.

amounted to civil war for a few days' and then added that 'great tragedy had befallen Pakistan and army had to kill people in order to keep country together.' The ambassador did not forget to thank the U.S. administration for its insipid public posture during the crisis. Hilali 'expressed appreciation [of the] restraint of [United States Government] to date and said [he] could not have expected more of [the State] Department.' He also asked Sisco to pass to President Nixon the 'appreciation of President Yahya for [United States Government] posture to date on East Pakistan.'[44] While not denying the acts of the Pakistani military, the ambassador nevertheless protested the 'misrepresentation' of the situation in East Pakistan, particularly in the U.S. Congress and media, including Ambassador Keating's report from New Delhi about 'massacre' in East Pakistan. The government of Pakistan, Hilali stressed, 'was not ashamed of the situation.'[45]

President Nixon was not ashamed either about the public posture he adopted early on in the crisis. This was a posture based not on principles, as Ambassador Keating had hoped, but rather on realist geopolitical calculations of great power diplomacy. Kissinger too, of course, concentrated on the bigger, strategic picture and was rather dismissive of Blood's reports on the unfolding human tragedy: 'That Consul in Dacca doesn't have the strongest nerves,' he told Nixon.[46] Kissinger was evidently more concerned with maintaining good relations with Yahya than about the genocide unfolding in East Pakistan. Meeting with the SRG on 9 April, Kissinger was relentless in forcing his views on the group and opposing any attempts by the bureaucracy to link the delivery of humanitarian aid to Pakistan to a promise from Yahya that the food would reach the most needed areas in the East. Moreover, Kissinger opposed assisting the Pakistani government through the international community and insisted that the aid package, which was originally put together following the cyclone in November 1970, be sent to Yahya irrespective of the situation in East Pakistan.

---

44 Telegram, Department of State, 'USG Expression of Concern on East Pakistan,' 6 April 1971. NSA website, http://www.gwu.edu/~nsarchiv/NSAEBB/NSAEBB79/ BEBB7.pdf.

45 Ibid.

46 Kissinger made this remark during a telephone conversation with Nixon on 30 March. *FRUS*, Volume XI, 37 (doc. 15).

Once more, the issue quickly turned into a bureaucratic squabble, this time between Kissinger and Assistant Secretary of State Sisco. The latter emphasised the humanitarian concerns while Kissinger preferred to see the geopolitical angle of the situation. Sisco warned that working outside the international system would appear to support Yahya in relation to the East Pakistan crisis. Kissinger was quick to point out that the issue was more complicated than the technical aspect of food provision: 'If the President decides to work through the existing government, with some humanitarian wrinkles, any failure to carry out our agreement, or to impose conditions that make it impossible to carry out, would represent a major shift in policy. This is not a technical question of how the food should be distributed. The position of the East Pakistanis as "rebels" is practically official.'[47] This exchange illustrates Quandt's assertion in chapter 2 that Kissinger sometimes used interdepartmental meetings to dictate his views rather than to encourage an open debate.

In late April 1971, Kissinger presented Nixon with three policy options regarding the situation in Pakistan. Kissinger began by explaining the significance of Nixon's decision on this matter. 'I do not normally bother you with tactical judgments,' he explained, but in the case of the present situation in Pakistan, 'policy depends on the posture adopted toward several major problems.' He then presented Nixon with three alternative courses of action: unqualified backing for West Pakistan, neutrality which in effect leans toward the East, and an effort to help Yahya achieve a negotiated settlement. Kissinger recommended that Nixon adopt the third option, as it 'would have the advantage of making the most of the relationship with Yahya, while engaging in a serious effort to move the situation toward conditions less damaging to US and Pakistani interests.' Nixon accepted Kissinger's analysis and approved the third policy option. At the end of the memo, he added: 'To all hands: *Don't* squeeze Yahya at this time.'[48] Accordingly, on 10 May, Nixon promised Pakistani officials that the U.S. government 'would not do anything to complicate the situation for

[47] Ibid., 60–61 (doc. 23).
[48] Memo, Kissinger to Nixon, 'Policy Options Toward Pakistan,' 28 April 1971. NSA website, http://www.gwu.edu/~nsarchiv/NSAEBB/NSAEBB79/BEBB9.pdf (emphasis in original text).

President Yahya or to embarrass him.'[49] Kissinger relayed this message to the bureaucracy when he convened the WSAG on 26 May. Discussing the shipment of military supply to Pakistan in the face of an intransigent Congress, Kissinger observed that he was not aware of a White House commitment to inform Congress about future shipments, but deputy assistant secretary of state Van Hollen promptly replied, 'We sent a memorandum to you.' Nonetheless, once again, Kissinger stressed to the group that the overriding objective of current U.S. policy was maintaining good relations with Pakistan: 'The President is eager to avoid any break with Yahya.'[50]

A necessary element of Nixon and Kissinger's grand design in South Asia was deceiving the Indian government about the administration's regional priorities. Meeting with Indian officials in New Delhi in July – only days before his secret trip to Beijing – Kissinger blatantly lied and assured his hosts that 'under any conceivable circumstances the U.S. would back India against any Chinese pressures... India was a potential world power, as well as being the region's only functional democracy, while Pakistan was a regional power. Our priorities would reflect these facts.'[51] Less than two weeks later and after Kissinger's return from Beijing, Harold Saunders from the NSC staff raised concern over possible criticism in Congress that 'Pakistan has earned continuing military assistance because of its role in facilitating your trip to Peking.' Kissinger directed that the State Department refrain from making this link in public and then added at the bottom of the page: 'But it is of course clear that we have some special relationship to Pakistan.'[52] Kissinger's orders to avoid linking U.S. policy on Pakistan with its China policy were pointless, as the media became increasingly critical over the administration's posture in South Asia. In response, on 7 December, Kissinger held a background briefing at the White House. Attempting to explain how the South Asian crisis had been handled since March, Kissinger reiterated that the administration

---

[49] *FRUS*, Volume XI, 115 (doc. 44).
[50] Ibid., 155 (doc. 60).
[51] Ibid., 164 (doc. 64).
[52] Memo, Saunders to Kissinger, 'Military Assistance to Pakistan and the Trip to Peking,' 19 July 1971. NSA website, http://www.gwu.edu/~nsarchiv/NSAEBB/NSAEBB79/BEBB17.pdf.

was 'not anti-Indian. This is totally inaccurate.'[53] The following day, Ambassador Keating in New Delhi expressed his concern that some of the 'facts' Kissinger was referring to in his briefing did not 'coincide with my knowledge of the events of the past eight months.' Referring in particular to Kissinger's remarks that Washington was always in favour of an autonomy for East Pakistan, Keating concluded, 'On the basis of what I do know, I do not believe [*sic*] of those elements... either add to our position or, perhaps more importantly, to our credibility.'[54]

As mentioned earlier, Nixon rarely used the NSC forum as a decision-making body, and his meeting with his top advisors on 16 July was no exception. True to form, Nixon did not ask his cabinet members for their views but instead stressed that the purpose of the meeting was to 'get the South Asian situation into perspective.' He opened the discussion with a familiar mantra: 'It is imperative that the Pakistanis, if possible, not be embarrassed at this point.' As for the Indians, they were 'a slippery, treacherous people.' Nixon acknowledged his bias on the matter and warned that the Indians would not receive a 'dime of aid, if they mess around in East Pakistan.'[55] The discussion was dominated by Kissinger, with only minor contributions by the other participants. There was no debate over substance and no decisions were made. While the NSC forum continued to be no more than a virtual medium, the formal NSC process continued to provide policy options for the president. In mid-August, the NSC staff prepared a contingency paper on possible Indian-Pakistani hostilities. The study suggested three possible courses of action in the event of hostilities: assuming a relatively passive international role, providing military assistance to either India or Pakistan, or intervening politically in order to achieve a settlement. Meeting on 17 August, the WSAG agreed to adopt the third option as the most suitable strategy for the

---

[53] Background Briefing (India-Pakistan) with Henry Kissinger,' 7 December 1971, the White House. NSA website, http://www.gwu.edu/~nsarchiv/NSAEBB/NSAEBB79/BEBB30.pdf.

[54] Telegram, Keating to Secretary of State, 'U.S. Public Position on Road to War,' 8 December 1971. NSA website, http://www.gwu.edu/~nsarchiv/NSAEBB/NSAEBB79/BEBB31.pdf.

[55] *FRUS*, Volume XI, 264–265 (doc. 103).

United States in the event of hostilities. Nevertheless, Sisco pointed out
that U.S. leverage in the subcontinent remained marginal, with little
ability to influence events: 'In this contingency paper there are a lot
of unilateral steps indicated. I think we ought to realize that in case
of war there is very little that we can do unilaterally. We will have
to rely on what parallel interests the US, the USSR, and China may
have in localyzing the war.' This analysis resurfaced during the second
week of fighting in December. In both cases, Kissinger was reluctant
to accept it. On this occasion, he told Sisco, 'We can figure that out,'
but Sisco was not convinced: 'By ourselves we have a limited capacity
to influence the situation.'[56]

In the three months leading up to the war (September to November
1971), the WSAG convened only on a monthly basis to monitor the
situation. The main issues discussed concerned the humanitarian effort
to stop the flow of refugees into India, the provision of aid packages,
and the suspension of U.S. economic aid to India.[57] The group also
considered diplomatic options in the event of war, most notably the
use of the UN Security Council – although Kissinger and the bureaucracy were in agreement that a UN resolution 'doesn't do a damn
thing.'[58] After months of infrequent meetings, the WSAG began meeting on an almost daily basis following the military escalation along
the eastern border Indo-Pakistani during the last week of November.
The group was somewhat in the dark about the nature of the escalation and the identity of the aggressor. The CIA relied on press reports
in Pakistan, which made the task of policy making understandably
difficult. There was no doubt, however, that India enjoyed absolute
superiority in all military aspects and that in the event of war, Pakistan
would be defeated. Meeting three times between 22 and 24 November, the group concentrated primarily on drafting a Security Council

---

[56] Ibid., 342 (doc. 126).
[57] Although the group discussed the prospect of cutting off aid to India at some length,
the actual amount of U.S. aid was negligible and was not expected to have a serious
effect on the Indian economy. A Pentagon report from November 1971 suggested that
direct grant aid to India had been suspended since 1965, and there was no more than
$20 million in approved military sales to India in the pipeline. The State Department
supported this estimate and added that $38 million in approved economic assistance
remained to be delivered to India. See *FRUS*, Volume XI, 554 (fn. 5, 6) (doc. 198).
[58] The group met on 8 September, 7 October, and 12 November. Minutes of those
meetings are available in *FRUS*, Volume XI, docs. 144, 159, and 183, respectively.

resolution and taking further diplomatic steps to reduce the growing tension. These included using U.S. missions in India and Pakistan to express the administration's concern and to urge restraint on both parties.

Much like during previous crises, incomplete intelligence continued to be an acute problem in WSAG meetings. The CIA could not provide additional information beyond what was established in the press – that some Indian units had crossed the border into East Pakistan. General Cushman, deputy director of the CIA, conceded that the main problem was that 'we don't have anyone on the ground where the fighting is.'[59] Although the group acknowledged that there was not enough evidence to suggest that the Indian army (as opposed to Indian insurgents) had launched a military campaign against Pakistan, Kissinger was eager to punish India. However, the bureaucracy was rather more reticent, arguing repeatedly that there was not much that Washington could do. Kissinger stressed that 'The President, the Secretary of State and I have told the Indians that there will be consequences if they start a war.' Deputy Secretary of Defense Packard reiterated a familiar problem: 'But what can we do? I don't see that we have any effective leverage on India.' Kissinger replied, 'We can cut off aid. We can move diplomatically.' However, Packard quickly brought Kissinger down to earth: 'Fine – we should, but with what likelihood of success? We don't know.'[60] Once again, the bureaucracy resisted Kissinger's attempts to drive U.S. policy in a direction that could prove counterproductive.

The next two meetings, on 29 November and 1 December, saw more technical discussions about cutting off aid to India and the likely scenarios involving a Security Council resolution. However, these discussions became academic when on 3 December a war between India and Pakistan began in earnest. Again, the CIA concluded the following day that it was impossible to determine with certainty which side initiated the hostilities. However, it was later established that Pakistan launched a series of air and ground offensives from the west against targets in India, which were quickly followed by Indian retaliation. The Indian military was quantitatively and qualitatively superior, and in talks with Moscow, Indian officials had targeted a time frame of ten

[59] Ibid., 553 (doc. 198).
[60] Ibid.

days to liberate East Pakistan. Kissinger himself thought that Yahya's decision to go war was 'suicidal.'[61]

In subsequent WSAG meetings during the first week of fighting, State Department representatives called for noninvolvement (in line with the public posture of the international community), based on the assumption that the independence of East Pakistan was both desirable and inevitable. They concluded that the probability of direct Soviet or Chinese involvement in fighting was minimal but, predictably, Nixon and Kissinger disagreed with the analysis and sought to tilt U.S. policy in favour of Pakistan. Nixon recalled in his memoirs that 'it was important to discourage both Indian aggression and Soviet adventurism, and I agreed with Kissinger's recommendation that we should demonstrate our displeasure with India and our support for Pakistan.'[62]

Accordingly, Nixon directed that the administration's official policy should depict India as the aggressor and that the Indian government should be deterred from launching an offensive against West Pakistan as well. Kissinger communicated Nixon's order to Secretary Rogers first: 'He is raising cain again. I am getting the hell. He wants to tilt in favour of Pakistan.' Rogers listened but raised his own objections, on the basis that the facts had not yet been established: 'I just hesitate putting out a statement condemning India . . . Should we take a judicial role ourselves and decide who is guilty? I think it should be better placed at the Security Council.'[63] Determined to implement the president's order and in the face of an unruly and dissenting bureaucracy, Kissinger repeated the theme in the first WSAG meeting following the outbreak of the war, on 3 December: 'I've been catching unshirted hell every half-hour from the President who says we're not tough enough. He believes State is pressing us to be tough and I'm resisting. He really doesn't believe we're carrying out his wishes. He wants to tilt toward Pakistan, and he believes that every briefing or statement is going the other way.'[64]

---

[61] Jack Anderson, 'U.S. Task Force Didn't Frighten India,' *Washington Post*, 21 December 1971; Bundy, *A Tangled Web*, 277; Hanhimaki, *The Flawed Architect*, 179.

[62] Nixon, *RN*, 526.

[63] *FRUS*, Volume XI, 595 (doc. 217).

[64] Ibid., 597 (doc. 218). Also provided in slight variation in M. Nicholas and P. Oldenburg, *Bangladesh: The Birth of a Nation: A Handbook of Background Information and Documentary Sources* (Madras: M. Seshachalam and Company, 1972), 115.

Kissinger's warning to the bureaucracy on the first day of the war indicated how removed he and Nixon were from the realities of the conflict, not least because the incomplete information in the first days of the fighting made it impossible to establish the identity of the aggressor. CIA Director Helms conceded that 'there are conflicting reports from both sides and the only common ground is the Pak attacks on the Amristar, Pathankat and Srinagar airports.' Admiral Moorer added that 'the present pattern is puzzling... The Pak attack is not credible... We do not seem to have sufficient facts on this yet.' Struggling to fit facts to policy, Kissinger pressed Moorer: 'Is it possible that the Indians attacked first and the Paks simply did what they could before dark in response?'[65] Even two days later, Secretary Rogers warned Nixon that it was impossible to assess the severity of the situation on the ground: 'It's very hard to tell because we don't have any independent sources with information... and they [India and Pakistan] both lie and both claim victory.'[66]

Nixon was clearly not concerned about the lack of facts to support his cause. As had been the case in the previous nine months, his determination to tilt in favour of Pakistan regardless of the causes of war or its consequences rendered the information and advice generated by the bureaucracy inconsequential. Following the WSAG meeting on 3 December, Kissinger recommended to Nixon that economic aid to India in the form of $90 million worth of unsigned letters should be frozen. Nixon agreed and decided to go further: 'I think we should go slow on giving visas to Americans going there... We don't want to have to evacuate some jerks and businessmen trying to make investments.'[67] Later, after ordering Kissinger again to cut off aid to India, the president exclaimed: 'I really feel – oh, I know all the arguments that [*sic*] well then we're choosing up sides, we're not neutral. Of course, we're not neutral. Neither are the Indians. They're always neutral against us.'[68]

Kissinger's relentless efforts to sway a resilient bureaucracy continued during the next WSAG meeting on 4 December. The main

---

[65] Quoted in Anderson, *The Anderson Papers*, 219–220.
[66] Conversation No. 16-6. 5 December 1971, 7:56 p.m.–8:03 p.m., White House Telephone. White House Tapes, Miller Center of Public Affairs.
[67] *FRUS*, Volume XI, 608–609 (doc. 221).
[68] Ibid., 619 (doc. 223).

hurdle at the meeting concerned the language of a public statement about the situation in the subcontinent. Once more, Kissinger wanted it to tilt towards Pakistan, whereas the bureaucracy preferred a more balanced approach. As on previous occasions, Kissinger resorted to explicit threats: 'I'm under instruction from the President to tilt our statements toward Pakistan. Now, either the bureaucracy will put out the kind of statements the President wants or they will be issued from the White House.'[69]

During the first week of the fighting, Nixon and Kissinger hardened their position even further. Early on, Yahya appealed to Washington for urgent military supply. Constrained by the 1965 arms embargo, Kissinger suggested to Nixon that they might be able to assist Pakistan through third parties, such as Iran and Jordan. Completely dismissing the legal constraints on such action, Kissinger explained that 'if we tell the Iranians we will make it up to them we can do it.' Nixon agreed, emphasising the advantage in such approach: 'If it is leaking we can have it denied . . . I like the idea. The main thing is to keep India from crumbling them up.' The sale went ahead.[70] Another idea that Nixon liked (and frequently toyed with, as noted in chapter 3) was sending signals to Moscow that on certain issues he was irrational and crazy enough to risk superpower relations, particularly during times of crisis. Following the WSAG meeting on 4 December, Nixon directed his ambassador to the UN, George Bush, to call for an immediate cease-fire and a withdrawal of forces to the pre-war borders. This

---

[69] Ibid., 622 (doc. 224).

[70] *FRUS*, Volume XI, 610 (fn. 3); Telcon, Nixon and Kissinger, 4 December 1971, 10:50 a.m. NSA website, http://www.gwu.edu/~nsarchiv/NSAEBB/NSAEBB79/BEBB28. pdf. Three days later, Harold Saunders informed Kissinger that the sale of arms to Pakistan through a third country was not possible. Discussing the possibility of transferring F-104 aircrafts through Jordan, Saunders suggested that the U.S. government 'by law cannot authorize it unless we were to change our own policy and provide equipment directly.' Memo, Saunders to Kissinger, 'Jordanian Transfer of F-104s to Pakistan,' 7 December 1971. NSA website, http://www.gwu.edu/~nsarchiv/NSAEBB/NSAEBB79/BEBB29.pdf (emphasis in original text). Despite the legal advice, the transfer of arms to Pakistan via third parties went ahead. Meeting the Chinese Ambassador to the UN a few days later, Alexander Haig reported that Jordan, Saudi Arabia, Iran, and Turkey had sent various aircrafts, arms, and ammunition to Pakistan. As for the role of the U.S. administration in the illegal transfer of arms to Pakistan, Haig said, 'We, of course, are doing all we can to facilitate this.' Memcon, Huand Hua, T'ang Wen-sheng, Shih Yen-hua, Alexander Haig, Winston Lord. 12 December 1971. NSA website, http://www.gwu.edu/~nsarchiv/NSAEBB/NSAEBB79/BEBB36.pdf.

call clearly favoured Pakistan, as Indian forces were already sweeping through East Pakistan. Expecting the Soviets to veto the resolution, Nixon was eager to flex his muscles but was stopped in his tracks by Kissinger, who believed that this was not the time to raise the stakes with Moscow. Disregarding Kissinger's advice that U.S. options were 'limited' on the diplomatic front, Nixon charged: 'Now in the event we are going to end up by saying to the Russians [*sic*] you proved to be so untrustworthy we can't deal with you on any issues. Let's use that card now . . . Let's do it.' Kissinger cautioned Nixon that 'this is premature' as the Soviets might still be able to secure a cease-fire in the UN. If they didn't, he asked Nixon, 'What do we do then?' The president's reply was typically vehement: 'Cut off the Middle East talks, pour arms into Israel, discontinue our talks on SALT and the Economic Security Council can go [*sic*] the public and tell them what the danger is . . . I would go further. We have to stop our talks on trade, don't let Smith have any further things on the Middle East and stop seeing Dobrynin under any circumstances . . . Another thing I would beef up the Defense Budget plans then.'[71]

By the time the WSAG met again, on 6 December, the CIA had established that the weight of evidence suggested that Pakistan was the aggressor and that its forces initiated the hostilities on 3 December with a series of air strikes in India.[72] Still, it did not lead to any change in policy or attitude towards India. Kissinger explained to the group that Nixon wanted 'to show certain coolness toward the Indians . . . In general, the President wants to appear a little cool.'[73] To do so, Nixon convened the NSC for the second and last time during the crisis. In a similar fashion to the July meeting, the discussion did not produce any concrete policy guidelines, although the atmosphere was more collegial – no doubt due to the fact that Nixon had invited a crew from the NBC network to film part of the meeting which was to be included in a TV Christmas special program, 'A Day in the Life of the President,' which was aired a few weeks later.

A much more significant meeting took place a few hours later, between Nixon and Kissinger. The two agreed to 'cool it' not only with India but with the Soviet Union as well – although they were

[71] Telcon, Nixon and Kissinger, 4 December 1971, 10:50 a.m. Ibid.
[72] *FRUS*, Volume XI, 622 (fn. 7).
[73] Ibid., 662 (doc. 235).

aware of the fact that the war 'threatens the whole climate of confidence' between the superpowers.[74] As the two men predicted, the Soviets vetoed the American resolution in the UN on two successive attempts. Following the deadlock in the Security Council, Ambassador Bush took the matter to the General Assembly, where he labelled India the 'major aggressor.' An Argentinean resolution similar to the American one finally passed on 8 December with an overwhelming 104 to 11 majority, opposed only by the Soviet block and India. Though Pakistan accepted the resolution, the Indian rejection prompted the United States to return the matter to the Security Council and to send a strong warning to Moscow to act 'constructively' along the U.S. lines, which called for cease-fire and withdrawal of forces.[75] This decision was prompted by a mysterious CIA report which Kissinger received that day. According to the report, Mrs. Gandhi told her cabinet on 6 December that she was determined to establish the independent state of Bangladesh, to liberate the southern part of Kashmir, and to destroy Pakistan's air and armoured forces. Kissinger claimed that the administration 'had never had any reason to doubt' the reliability of the report.'[76] The source of the report was later identified as Morarji Desai, a member of the Indian Parliament, who was close to the late Prime Minister Nehru and was a vocal critic of Mrs. Gandhi. In 1969, Gandhi fired him from his post as deputy prime minister, but he stayed in her cabinet.[77]

Alarmed by the report, Kissinger convened the WSAG on 8 December, hoping to agree on the next 'turn of the screw' in case India decided to attack West Pakistan. He asked the group whether the United States could protest the Indian blockade of Pakistani ports: 'Can we allow a U.S. ally to go down completely while we participate in a blockade? Can we allow the Indians to scare us off, believing that if U.S. supplies are needed they will not be provided?' When Alexis Johnson from the State Department replied that the United States had no legal case since blockading was a legitimate act between nations at war, Kissinger retorted,

---

[74] Ibid., 675, 676 (document 239).

[75] Bundy, *A Tangled Web*, 277; Memcon, Huand Hua, T'ang Wen-sheng, Shih Yen-hua, Alexander Haig, Winston Lord. 12 December 1971.

[76] Kissinger, *White House Years*, 901–902.

[77] See Hersh, *The Price of Power*, 450, 453. See the CIA report in *FRUS*, Volume XI, 686–687 (doc. 246).

We're not trying to be all that even-handed. The President has told all of you what he wants – do any of you have any doubts as to what he wants? He doesn't want to be completely even-handed. He's trying to get across to the Indians that they are running a major risk in their relations with the US. If every time we do something to the Indians, we have to do the same thing to Pakistan, we will be participating in the rape of Pakistan, given the difference in their strengths. This blockade protest is a tactical decision that doesn't bother me one way or the other. Am I misrepresenting what the President has said? You have all heard him. He said to look for things we can do to get the message across to India.[78]

When the fall of East Pakistan and the creation of an independent Bangladesh seemed inevitable, Nixon and Kissinger had turned their efforts to preventing the complete disintegration of the Pakistani state. Heeding Kissinger's advice about the administration's limited options, Nixon conceded: 'We don't really have any choice. We can't allow a friend of ours and China's to get screwed in a conflict with a friend of Russia's.'[79] Nixon and Kissinger were content with the CIA report even though it was not backed by additional evidence to suggest that India was about to invade West Pakistan. Signalling the shift in attention from the Indo-Pakistani crisis to superpower politics, Kissinger later explained in his memoirs: 'Our only card left was to raise the risks for the Soviets to a level where Moscow would see larger interests jeopardized.'[80] To that extent, Nixon and Kissinger were even willing to call on the Chinese to send forces to the border in order to deter the Indians and their Soviets sponsors. Following the WSAG meeting on 8 December, the two met with Attorney General John Mitchell in the Oval Office. Kissinger conceded that 'we're in trouble' and went on to suggest that 'we could give a note to the Chinese and say if you are ever going to move, this is the time.' Nixon agreed and Mitchell added, 'All they have to do is put their forces on the border.' However, unlike his fervid president, Kissinger was aware of the danger in such a move – a corresponding mobilisation of forces by the Soviets: 'I must warn you, Mr. President, if our bluff is called, we'll be in trouble.' Nixon had none of that: 'No more goddamn meetings to decide this,' referring to the scheduled WSAG meeting for the next day. Still, the president agreed with Kissinger that the United States did not have sufficient leverage

---

[78] Ibid., 698 (doc. 248); Anderson, *The Anderson Papers*, 228.
[79] Nixon, *RN*, 527.
[80] Kissinger, *White House Years*, 903.

in the subcontinent (which he credited to his predecessor in the White House) and concluded: 'We can't do this without the Chinese helping us . . . As I look at this thing, the Chinese have got to move to that damn border. The Indians have got to get a little scared.'[81]

This episode, and Nixon's blatant disregard of the 'goddamn' inter-departmental meetings, is telling not least because it demonstrates his determination to carry on without consulting the bureaucracy. Most important, this remark encapsulates the inherent irony within the Nixon-Kissinger foreign policy operation. The very system that was designed to produce efficient decision-making process and the 'best' policy outcome was now a major impediment to the president's efforts to run U.S. foreign policy based on his intuitive understanding of world politics.

The strong denials of Mrs. Gandhi and Ambassador Singh in the UN that India had no plans to attack West Pakistan did not satisfy Nixon. As the deadlock in the Security Council continued, Nixon was determined to flex his muscles in an effort to deter the Indians (and by extension, the Soviets) from taking further military action in West Pakistan.[82] Meeting on 9 December, the WSAG continued to discuss the possible implications of an Indian attack on West Pakistan. Kissinger also expressed Nixon's desire to send an aircraft carrier to the Bay of Bengal, seemingly in order to evacuate American citizens from the area. Within days, the mission of this naval task force would prove to be the most bizarre decision taken by Nixon during the crisis. While the most important decisions in this period were largely the result of private conversations between Nixon and Kissinger, the two were still concerned about their inability to impose discipline on the bureaucracy. To that effect, on 9 December, Nixon met with the senior members of the WSAG (Kissinger, Irwin, Packard, Helms, and Moorer). The purpose of the meeting, as Kissinger explained to Nixon, was 'to instill the necessary discipline within the bureaucracy and the forum of the Washington Special Actions Group to insure compliance with your policies on South Asia . . . Inform the group that you have

---

[81] *FRUS*, Volume XI, 703 (doc. 251).

[82] The Indian Ambassador declared that 'India has no territorial ambitions in Bangladesh or in West Pakistan,' failing to mention the disputed territory of Kashmir. Jackson, *South Asian Crisis*, 129.

convened them on short notice to insure that your policies are clearly understood with respect to the situation in South Asia.'[83] Nixon's personal appearance seemed to have the desired effect, as during the group's meeting the following day there were no signs of discord but instead a general consensus about the next step in U.S. policy, which followed Nixon's guidance to call for a cease-fire in West Pakistan.[84] This is a telling episode which points to the benefits of a more collegial advisory system where direct presidential engagement can help in motivating the advisory group and channel individual efforts to focus on the problem at hand. Alas, Nixon's aversion to large group meetings and his reluctance to reach down for information meant that his chosen style of management suited more hierarchical-formalistic procedures of decision-making. Rather oddly, then, it was only when Nixon acted out of character and personally interacted with the bureaucracy through the WSAG forum that he finally managed to achieve some order and purpose in the decision-making process. However, this was too little and too late to any consequence on the overall tilt strategy or on bear U.S. diplomatic and military manoeuvres during the final days of the crisis.

Having failed to secure a Soviet acquiescence to the American initiative in the United Nations, on 12 December, the WSAG recommended a unilateral move in the United Nations. Ambassador George Bush introduced the American resolution before the Security Council later in the day, which called for an immediate cease-fire, the withdrawal by India and Pakistan of their armed forces from each other's territory, and facilitating the safe return of the refugees to their homes. However, once again, a Soviet veto brought the resolution down.[85] Alongside the diplomatic efforts, Nixon actively sought to wield American military power to prevent the disintegration of the Pakistani state. His order to assemble a naval task force on 10 December was an important instrument in advancing his goals; however, just like most of Nixon's previous decisions during the crisis, this one too was ill conceived, cloaked in secrecy, and ultimately failed to bolster American influence in the subcontinent. Nixon took the decision to assemble the flotilla

---

[83] *FRUS*, Volume XI, 727 (doc. 258).
[84] Ibid., 735–739 (doc. 263).
[85] Ibid., 789–791 (doc. 285).

without consulting Defense Secretary Laird or the Joint Chiefs of Staff and instead directly ordered Admiral Elmo Zumwalt, Chief of Naval Operations, to assemble an eight-ship task force from the Seventh Fleet, which was positioned off the coast of Vietnam at the time, and to send it to Singapore.[86] In fact, Nixon had made his mind up two days earlier, on 8 December, when he contemplated asking the Chinese for help. By introducing American naval power to the area, Nixon and Kissinger were hoping to prevent 'a Soviet stooge, supported by Soviet arms' from defeating an ally.[87] Zumwalt and Admiral Moorer were naturally concerned when Nixon did not specify the mission of the task force.

On 12 December, the task force was ordered to enter the Indian Ocean but within an hour the order was rescinded. The next day, the flotilla was ordered again to enter the Indian Ocean during daylight, so its movement could be easily detected by the Indians and the Soviets.[88] Nixon and Kissinger had no illusions about what was at stake. Meeting that day, 13 December, in the Oval Office, Kissinger egged on Nixon: 'You're putting your chips into the pot again. But my view is that if we do nothing, there is a certainty of disaster. This way there is a high possibility of one, but at least we're coming off like men.' Nixon concurred and concluded that the Chinese, Soviets, and Indians needed to be shown that the 'man in the White House' was tough.[89] Once more, Nixon's self-image as 'tough' suggests the importance of cognitive-emotive schemes as a psychological mechanism to deal with the high levels of stress and uncertainty which leaders may experience during crises.

Officially, Washington argued that the flotilla – named Task Force 74 – was sent to evacuate American citizens from Dacca in East Pakistan. However, the Indian government claimed that the idea that such a powerful task force – which included the world's largest nuclear aircraft carrier (the USS *Enterprise*), the amphibious assault

---

[86] Laird was later informed and supported the President's decision. See Bundy, *A Tangled Web*, 279.

[87] *FRUS*, Volume XI, 705 (doc. 252). Later on, Nixon and Kissinger learned that the Chinese decided to refrain from military moves and instead called for a cease-fire and mutual troop withdrawal.

[88] Zumwalt, *On Watch*, 367.

[89] *FRUS*, Volume XI, 779 (doc. 281).

ship *Tripoli* with a Marine battalion, assault helicopters, and a nuclear attack submarine – was assembled and sent purely to evacuate fewer than fifty civilians seemed incredible.[90] Furthermore, by the time the task force had entered the Indian Ocean, all American civilians had already been evacuated from Dacca. It was also highly unlikely that the task force was intended to break the Indian blockade of East Pakistan, since it would risk direct confrontation with the Soviet naval contingent already present in the Bay. The Indians concluded that the American task force was sent to divert their attention away from the fighting and that the best response was therefore to simply ignore the American manoeuvre.[91] In his memoirs, Kissinger acknowledges that the naval deployment was made 'ostensibly for the evacuation of Americans but in reality to give emphasis to our warnings against an attack on West Pakistan.'[92] In any case, the merit in such action was questionable given that the American task force was considerably outnumbered by its Soviet counterpart.[93] Admiral Zumwalt described accurately the futility behind the mission, given the lack of U.S. military leverage in the Indian Ocean: 'The United States "tilted" toward Pakistan, but tilt as we would, we could not affect the war's outcome, even after we had sent Task Force 74.'[94] But Nixon and Kissinger saw it differently. Meeting in the Oval Office on 15 December, they discussed the naval mission's worth. Kissinger observed: 'That carrier move is good,' and Nixon agreed: 'Why hell yes ... the point about the carrier move, we just say ... we got to be there for the purpose of their moving there. Look these people are savages.'[95] When the task force approached the coast of Sri Lanka on 16 December, the third India-Pakistan War was already over. The fall of Dacca and the unconditional surrender of the outnumbered Pakistani forces in the East were followed the next day by a mutual declaration of cease-fire along the Western border. In the next six months, the independent state of

[90] J. McConnell and A. Kelley, 'Super-Power Naval Diplomacy: Lessons of the Indo-Pakistani Crisis 1971,' *Survival* 15:6 (November/December 1973), 289; Jack Anderson, 'U.S., Soviet Vessels in Bay of Bengal,' *Washington Post*, 14 December 1971.

[91] P. Chopra, *India's Second Liberation* (Delhi: Vikas Publishing House, 1973), 198–204.

[92] Kissinger, *White House Years*, 905.

[93] Zumwalt, *On Watch*, 367–368.

[94] Ibid., 360.

[95] *FRUS*, Volume XI, 825 (doc. 309).

Bangladesh was recognised by the Soviet Union, Britain, France, and ultimately by the United States, in April 1972.

Performance of the WSAG

The schedule of WSAG meetings reflects the administration's growing concern over the crisis, which peaked during the first week of December with five meetings, and eight meetings altogether between December 3 and 16. However, the profusion of meetings during this period does not suggest that the WSAG had been used effectively in the crisis decision-making process. The most important decisions (the Tilt policy, cutting off of aid to India, Task Force 74) were not adequately debated in this forum. As noted earlier, Kissinger often convened the interdepartmental groups (the WSAG and the SRG in this crisis) with two objectives in mind. First, to instill the necessary discipline in the bureaucracy and to ensure it operated in accordance with Nixon's priorities (as was evident in the 9 December meeting, for example). Second, to involve the bureaucracy in the process, as it was ultimately charged with executing the decisions made at the White House.

The minutes of WSAG meetings precisely depict the mood of the administration during the crisis, which in effect seemed worse than the group's experience in previous crises. Two immediate conclusions about the performance of the group stand out: First, long-term policy planning was abandoned in favour of ad hoc meetings which rendered the input of the WSAG inconsequential. Once the war began in earnest, the only concrete guideline that Nixon produced was to tilt in favour of Pakistan. The WSAG had failed consistently – or was rather consistently thwarted by Kissinger – to produce a serious discussion about the likely costs and benefits of such policy. Moreover, notwithstanding some vocal concerns by the State Department representatives, the group did not consider alternative courses of action. Nor did it outline the desirable objectives of the American policy, apart from preventing the disintegration of the Pakistani state during the second week of the fighting. Finally, apart from Nixon and Kissinger's unflinching determination to support Pakistan, the group's work was constrained by conflicting reports from the ground and the lack of reliable intelligence. However, even the steadfast reports from the American missions in New Delhi and Dacca failed to bring a change in U.S. policy during the early months of the conflict.

Second, it is also evident that throughout the crisis, the United States was struggling to assume the role of a major actor. Nixon and Kissinger – as well as India and the Soviet Union – knew that the United States had no real leverage in the subcontinent, militarily or politically. Mrs. Gandhi went to war despite Washington's warnings, American resolutions in the Security Council were repeatedly defeated, and the ill-conceived mission of Task Force 74 in the last days of the war only served to illuminate the extent of American impotence. During a WSAG meeting on 8 December, Dave Packard from the Defense Department accurately summarised the realities of the situation by suggesting that it might be better to do nothing, given that American initiatives so far have been ineffective: 'If you don't win, don't get involved. If we were to attempt something it would have to be with a certainty that it would affect the outcome. Let's not get in if we know we are going to lose.'[96] Packard's point went unnoticed. Two days later, Nixon ordered the naval task force into the Bay of Bengal.

The failure of the WSAG to perform its tasks is, of course, not a sign of incompetence on behalf of its members. Any attempt to survey objectives or alternative courses of action other than those designed to serve the interests of the emerging Sino-American alliance were bound to be rejected by Kissinger, who chaired the meetings and controlled the agenda. Similarly, the costs of such policy were almost robotically discounted. Nixon and Kissinger showed no hesitation in endangering relations with India, the largest democracy in the world, and the spirit of détente with the Soviet Union, in favour of the likely benefits of saving Yahya's regime, and, by extension, thawing relations with China.

During its last meeting during the war, on 16 December, the WSAG performed in a way which was more close to its theoretical design. In the short meeting at the end of the war, the group discussed the implications of the recent crisis for future U.S. policy in the region. Kissinger convened the meeting (entitled 'where do we go from here') in order to assign to the bureaucracy the tasks of preparing five study papers on

---

[96] 'Report on Washington Special Action Group Meeting, December 8, 1971' (Appendix 10). In Nicholas and Oldenburg, *Bangladesh: The Birth of a Nation*, 130.

U.S. foreign policy priorities after the war. These covered the issues of humanitarian and economic assistance, relations with Bangladesh, the territorial status of Kashmir, and military supply policy.[97] However, this meeting was hardly a positive conclusion to a dismal process. To a large extent, 'where do we go from here' meetings are not about substantial policy making but rather involve the technical assignment of study papers to the bureaucracy. It is evident that while Kissinger trusted the group to perform its tasks, he preferred to rely on his and Nixon's intuitive understanding of great power politics during the height of crises – particularly when the group provided information and advice which seemed contradictory to Nixon and Kissinger's grand design of *realpolitik and* triangular diplomacy.

One constraining parameter on the WSAG's performance which was not a result of the tilt policy was the alarmingly poor quality of intelligence with which the group had to work. The decision-making process was plagued by contradictory or incomplete intelligence reports from the early days of the crisis and more acutely from late November with the first skirmishes along the eastern border. Bob Haldeman recorded in his diary on 22 November that for most of the day, the administration had no concrete information about recent developments: 'Henry burst in at noon to say that the radio and TV [*sic*] reports that India has attacked Pakistan. He has no confirmation. By 9:00 tonight he still didn't have any confirmation. Our vast intelligence network doesn't seem to be able to tell us when a couple of major nations are at war, which is a little alarming, to say the least.'[98] Just as worrying was Nixon and Kissinger's blind conviction that India was about to attack West Pakistan, despite the lack of hard evidence. A single intelligence report was based on a source in the Indian cabinet who was a consistent vocal opponent of Mrs. Gandhi. If an Indian attack on West Pakistan was indeed imminent, as Nixon believed, then surely reconnaissance flights or satellite images could have shown the mobilisation of Indian forces toward the western border. However, as far as the available records suggest, no such data were produced or used. Rather, as Bundy observes, it was more likely that an Indian attack in the west was merely a contingency plan discussed in Gandhi's

97 Volume XI, 842–843 (doc. 318).
98 Haldeman, *The Haldeman Diaries*, 377.

cabinet rather than a concrete decision to mobilise the Indian Army for a full-scale engagement in the west in order to eliminate Pakistan's air and ground forces.[99]

Despite its frequent meetings, therefore, the WSAG was unable to perform its most basic function: managing the crisis. A series of flawed decisions – from the quiet public posture during the genocide in East Pakistan in the first days of the crisis, through to the decision to tilt in favour of Pakistan, and the inane mission of Task Force 74 at the end of the war – were taken by Nixon and Kissinger without adequate consultation with the group which they had positioned at the heart of the NSC crisis decision-making process. The WSAG performed badly during the crisis, but ultimately it could only operate within the limited boundaries set by the president. This observation is consistent with the analysis of the Cambodian crisis eighteen months earlier. While the Jordanian case tells a different story, it is impossible to trace a pattern of institutional learning here from previous crises. Nixon and Kissinger repeated the mistakes they made during the Cambodian operation with their mismanagement of the advisory system, and the results were equally dismal. Nixon and Kissinger's approach to the crisis was similar to the one adopted during the 1970 Jordanian Crisis in assuming that a regional war was tantamount to a conflict between Washington and Moscow. They both intuitively downgraded the local causes of the war and overestimated the role of the superpowers in it.

In his memoirs, Nixon observed that the war was brought to an end due to 'diplomatic signals and behind-the-scenes pressures.'[100] Indeed, Nixon tried to exercise influence over Moscow to restrain India, but his efforts were futile. The Soviets vetoed two American-sponsored resolutions in the UN and then ignored an American initiative for a joint call for a cease-fire. Similarly, Nixon's idea to persuade the Chinese to mobilise their forces along the Indian border was ill conceived. Even the desperate measure of sending the naval task force to the region did not bother India. Mrs. Gandhi's decision to accept the Pakistani call for a cease-fire on 17 December was not the result of U.S. military resilience but rather the weighing of the political advantages of

---

[99] Bundy, *A Tangled Web*, 285.
[100] Nixon, *RN*, 530.

ending the war. As far as Gandhi was concerned, it was irrational
to attack West Pakistan. By negotiating a cease-fire, Gandhi proved
Washington wrong and saved her country from diplomatic isolation
in the UN. Gandhi knew very well that any territorial gains were not
worth damaging India's reputation, and her assessment was supported
by Moscow.[101]

The ill-fated decision to send a task force to the Indian Ocean was
symptomatic of a flawed decision-making process that started as early
as March 1971, and ended with the cease-fire at the end of the war
in mid-December 1971. In his memoirs, Kissinger observes that the
India-Pakistan crisis was 'perhaps the most complex issue of Nixon's
first term.'[102] This assertion is not erroneous, though the conclusion
that it was Nixon and Kissinger's tilt policy that had made the situation
so complex in the first place is unavoidable.

---

[101] Hall, 'The Laotian War,' 212–213; Bundy, *A Tangled Web*, 285–286.
[102] Kissinger, *White House Years*, 913.

6

The Yom Kippur War, October 1973

> This has been the best-run crisis since you have been in the White House.[1]
>
> Kissinger to Nixon, 17 October 1973

The making of U.S. foreign policy during the Yom Kippur War in October 1973 was distinctly different from the other cases examined in this book. More than any other international crisis during the Nixon years, this one was invariably influenced by domestic politics. The fourth Arab-Israeli war that began on 6 October and lasted for nearly three weeks coincided with a series of domestic crises in Washington which directly impinged on the president's ability to fully commit himself to foreign policy making. On 10 October, Vice President Spiro Agnew resigned and pled *nolo contendere* to charges of tax evasion and bribery. Two days later, the U.S. Court of Appeals ordered Nixon to release a series of White House tapes to Archibald Cox, the Watergate special prosecutor. On 20 October (while Kissinger was in Moscow negotiating a cease-fire to end the war), the infamous 'Saturday Night Massacre' saw the resignations of Attorney General Elliot Richardson and his Deputy William Ruckelshaus,

---

[1] Memcon, 'WSAG Principals: Middle East War,' 17 October 1973, 4:00 p.m. Folder no. 6, *WSAG Meetings*, MF, Box H-092, NSCIF, NPMP.

which were then followed by Nixon's dismissal of Special Prosecutor Cox.[2]

In his memoirs, Nixon referred to the debilitating effect of the domestic turmoil on his ability to run U.S. foreign policy and prevent the Soviets from capitalising on the crisis in the Middle East. It was important, Nixon rationalised after finally turning in the White House tapes to the courts, 'to relieve the domestic crisis in order to reduce the temptation the Soviets would feel to take advantage of our internal turmoil by exploiting the international crisis in the Middle East.'[3] In a similar fashion, Alexander Haig was adamant that Moscow was bent on extracting advantage from Nixon's domestic crisis: 'I know of no knowledgeable person who does not believe that one of the important reasons the Kremlin put the crisis in motion was its calculation that the President of the United States was so distracted and disabled by his domestic problems that he would be unable to react with adequate force and dispatch.'[4] The view from the Kremlin, however, was different. Foreign Minister Gromyko referred to the Watergate affair in his memoirs as 'a minor episode, and an internal one at that.' In effect, he surmised, the affair boiled down 'to nothing more than a symptom of social decline.'[5] Ambassador Dobrynin too believed that Moscow 'could not (or would not) understand how the president of the United States could be prosecuted for what it viewed as such a "small matter."'[6] Rather than exploiting the domestic crisis in order to take advantage in the Middle East, the Kremlin firmly believed that the real source behind Watergate 'was some conspiracy by anti-Soviet and pro-Zionist groups trying to scuttle Nixon's policy of good relations with Moscow.'[7]

Henry Kissinger was the immediate beneficiary of Nixon's predicament. The new round of hostilities in the Middle East saw Kissinger reaching his zenith as the chief architect and executer of U.S. foreign policy. First, Nixon's increasing preoccupation with the unremitting

---

[2] L. Colodny and R. Getlin, *Silent Coup: The Removal of Richard Nixon* (London: Victor Gollancz, 1991), 337–359; *Time*, 29 October 1973, 48–53.
[3] Nixon, *RN*, 937.
[4] Haig, *Inner Circles*, 409–410.
[5] A. Gromyko, *Memories* (London: Hutchinson, 1989), 278.
[6] Dobrynin, *In Confidence*, 310.
[7] Ibid.

revelations of the Watergate affair and its implications (two of his gatekeepers, Bob Haldeman and John Ehrlichman, resigned in April 1973 following their involvement in the Watergate cover-up) created a vacuum at the top of the pyramid which was willingly filled by Kissinger. Second, in late September 1973, only two weeks before the outbreak of the October War, Kissinger was sworn in as the new Secretary of State. After four years of being marginalised by Nixon and Kissinger on the most important policy issues, Secretary Rogers finally resigned in August 1973, and Kissinger now found himself in a position which gave him unprecedented control over foreign policy. In his memoirs, Kissinger blames Nixon's poor management style for bringing his rivalry with Rogers to an intolerable pitch so early on in the administration. By giving priority to his national security advisor in foreign policy without cementing his decision with decisive and unambiguous support, Nixon created a situation which by 1971, Kissinger acknowledged, made it impossible for the two men to work together.[8] Now, as the national security advisor (a position he retained until 1975), Kissinger continued to set priorities and to control the flow of information and advice to the White House. As the secretary of state, he was recognised formally as the president's top foreign policy advisor, and his de facto position as a statesman was now officially cemented. On 16 October 1973, in the midst of the war, Kissinger learned that he was to be awarded the Nobel Peace Prize for his efforts to end the Vietnam War. Albeit tentative, Kissinger's success in the Vietnam negotiations, combined with his historic visits to China and Moscow in the previous two years, had made him the most famous man in world politics, a 'Super K.' Set against the demise of President Nixon, Secretary Kissinger was now viewed as the most powerful man in Washington.

Ironically, Kissinger's ascendancy had an adverse effect on the formal process of decision-making. His dual position in the administration made formal NSC procedures even more cumbersome, as he now reviewed and recommended policies to the president as the national security advisor as well as the secretary of state. This created an absurd situation of bureaucratic politics in which one person argued

---

[8] H. Kissinger, *Years of Upheaval* (Boston: Little, Brown, 1982), 419.

at the same time for different policy preferences while representing the interests of his two respective institutions (State Department and NSC staff). William Quandt describes vividly this most bizarre phenomenon: '[Kissinger] would let his bureaucracy produce a draft, and he would sometimes then sign it as Secretary of State, come over to the White House, and NSC staff would say "here is what the Secretary of State recommends, but in your role as National Security Advisor here is what you wrote," and put another memo on top to Nixon. It is amazing.'[9]

This chapter begins by reviewing U.S. policy in the Middle East in the run up to the Yom Kippur War. As noted in chapter 4, while the resolution of the Jordanian Crisis was favourable to U.S. interests, in the long term the pro-Israeli policy proved disastrous. Washington's reluctance to apply pressure on Israel to withdraw from the occupied territories played a significant role in driving Egyptian president Anwar al-Sadat to war with Israel in October 1973. In examining the workings of the WSAG as part of the overall decision-making process, this chapter examines in particular two important decisions during the war which largely were symptoms of the new balance of power in the Nixon-Kissinger dyad. These decisions not only shaped the course of the fighting but also raised important questions about Kissinger's almost executive authority during the crisis. The first decision involved the military airlift to Israel which began on 14 October, after days of bureaucratic infighting, largely orchestrated by Kissinger, who manipulated almost simultaneously the bureaucracy, the Israelis, and even the president. The second decision concerned the famous NSC/WSAG meeting during the final stages of the fighting, when Kissinger ordered the placing of American armed forces on the highest level of war readiness since the 1962 Cuban Missile Crisis. Kissinger took this decision while the president was in bed. Nixon was informed of the decision the following morning and approved it post factum.

Nevertheless, notwithstanding Kissinger's uniquely powerful position and Nixon's invariable absence from the decision-making process, the president retained final authority in the crisis. As others have noted, he demanded that Israel be resupplied, and Israel indeed got its

---

[9] Interview with Quandt.

reinforcements despite Kissinger's manipulation. It is also likely that the president would have agreed with Kissinger's decision to place American forces on high alert had he not been asleep.[10] Still, as the final section of this chapter demonstrates, the startling fact remains that important decisions of enormous magnitude were taken by Kissinger rather than by President Nixon.

U.S. Middle East Policy in the Run-Up to the Yom Kippur War

The fourth Arab-Israeli war proved to be an overwhelming surprise to decision-makers in Washington. Since the successful ending of the Jordanian Crisis three years earlier, the military balance of power in the Middle East had shifted decisively in Israel's favour. President Nixon was determined not to repeat the mistakes made by his administration in the months leading to the September 1970 crisis. At least diplomatically, the period between the 1970 and the 1973 crises is commonly seen as one of missed opportunities to bring about long-lasting peace. These included two initiatives by the Egyptian President Anwar al-Sadat, who was invariably frustrated with the dormant U.S. position in the region, and the no-peace-no-war stalemate.

Sadat's first attempt to break the deadlock came in February 1971. Addressing the Egyptian National Assembly, he signalled his willingness, should Israel agree to withdraw forces from the Sinai Peninsula, to reopen the Suez Canal which had been closed since 1967 and to resume negotiations with Israel based on UN Resolution 242, which set the formula of 'land for peace' as the basis for Middle East peace negotiations.[11] The Israeli government rejected Sadat's offer while Nixon was not prepared to force Israel to accept it either. American-Israeli relations were stronger than ever, and the White House was reluctant to imperil them by entertaining initiatives from Cairo at a time when its energies were consumed by the arms talks with the Soviets, negotiations with Hanoi on ending the Vietnam War, and the efforts to thaw relations with China. Furthermore, it was questionable whether Sadat's proposal was indeed genuine or whether he had other motives

---

[10] See S. Ambrose, *Nixon: Ruin and Recovery*, 254–257.
[11] A. Sadat, *In Search of Identity* (London: Collins, 1978), 219; D. Bavly, *Dreams and Missed Opportunities, 1967–1973* (Jerusalem: Carmel, 2002), 81–82.

that were not clear at the time.[12] However, perhaps most important in guiding Washington's calculations was the scepticism in Sadat's ability to lead Egypt. When Sadat entered office in late 1970, Under Secretary of State Eliot Richardson estimated that he would not remain in power for more than four to six months, while Kissinger saw him as little more than an 'interim figure.'[13]

Notwithstanding this initial setback, in 1972 Sadat made a second attempt to improve relations with Washington and to draw the U.S. into the region. Following the Moscow Summit between Nixon and Brezhnev in May that year, Sadat learned that under the guise of superpower détente, the two leaders agreed on the need for a 'military relaxation' in the Middle East and the resumption of talks based on UN Resolution 242.[14] This decision proved disastrous for Egypt while Israel continued to enjoy an overwhelming military superiority in the region. Concluding that as long as the Soviets were heavily involved in Egyptian domestic and foreign policies he would struggle to pursue his own agenda, in July 1972 Sadat expelled more than 10,000 Soviet personnel from Egypt and returned to Moscow some Soviet military equipment. He told the Kremlin that the expulsion was an inevitable consequence of the growing interference in Egypt's domestic affairs, combined with the slow pace of military assistance.[15] Several months later, Sadat declared that Egypt 'realized the limits of Soviet aid' and with reference to superpower détente, he noted that 'Egypt could not allow international circumstances to determine the course of events in the Middle East' but 'had to impose its will on circumstances.'[16]

---

[12] See the debate surrounding Sadat's initiative in M. Gazit, 'Egypt and Israel – Was There a Peace Opportunity Missed in 1971?,' *Journal of Contemporary History*, 32:1 (January 1997), 97–115. Notwithstanding Sadat's intention, his announcement was nevertheless dramatic as he publicly departed from the Arab League's decision following the Six-Day War: no to negotiations with Israel, no to recognition of Israel, no to peace with Israel. Furthermore, he risked his relations with Moscow and his own position in the Arab world.

[13] Sadat, *In Search of Identity*, 215; Kissinger, *White House Years*, 1276–1277.

[14] Quandt, *Peace Process*, 95; J. D. Glassman, *Arms for the Arabs: The Soviet Union and War in the Middle East* (Baltimore: Johns Hopkins University Press, 1975), 94.

[15] Sadat, *In Search of Identity*, 228–231; M. Halfon, *From War to Peace: The Peace Course between Egypt and Israel, 1970–1979* (Tel Aviv: Hakibbutz Hameuchad, 2002), 16–17.

[16] Cited in R. O. Freedman, *Soviet Policy toward the Middle East since 1970* (New York: Praeger, 1982, 3rd ed.), 122.

The Soviet exodus from Egypt was received in Washington with some satisfaction but with an even greater sense of suspicion. The presidential elections were due in November, and Nixon knew very well that any American initiative in the Middle East would be certain to damage his chances of re-election. Although Kissinger assured Sadat that soon after the elections the White House would launch a new peace initiative, he still had little faith or trust in the Egyptian President. William Quandt, member of Kissinger's NSC staff, recalls:

I arrived shortly after Sadat had kicked out the Russians, and one of the first things I wanted to do is find out why . . . and I thought 'we got something to work with here,' but Kissinger wasn't interested. He had a very contemptuous attitude towards Sadat; he thought 'why would he kick the Russians out for nothing? If he was smart he would have come to me first'; he thought Sadat was weak and wanted to keep the pressure on.[17]

Following Nixon's landslide re-election in November 1972, Kissinger opened a back channel to Cairo through Hafiz Ismail, Sadat's National Security Advisor. However, Sadat had already made a decision to go to war four months earlier, while Kissinger was busy nailing down the final details of a cease-fire in Vietnam. Kissinger later conceded that when he met Ismail for the last time, in May 1973, the Middle East 'was heading toward war. We did not know it. But he did.'[18] There were, however, other factors which also contributed to the failure of the Kissinger-Ismail talks. The general elections in Israel, scheduled for October 1973, meant that the Meir government was in no position to enter into negotiations. Additionally, domestic developments in Washington soon took precedence over foreign policy. In June 1972, five men were arrested for breaking into the Democratic National Committee offices in the Watergate complex in Washington. In April 1973, Nixon made his first public statement on Watergate, and from then onwards new revelations on the incident appeared almost daily in the press. Nixon dedicated more and more of his time to covering up the tracks leading to the Oval Office.

For a variety of reasons, then, by the time the Kissinger-Ismail talks halted, Sadat was already preparing for a war against Israel – a last

---

[17] Interview with Quandt.
[18] Kissinger, *Years of Upheaval*, 227.

resort in his attempts to get the U.S. to engage diplomatically with the Middle East rivals. In his memoirs, Sadat admitted that he had made his decision to go to war as early as July 1972, soon after he expelled the Soviets from Egypt: 'I began to prepare for the battle, although I knew that the entire world (including Egypt) had interpreted my expulsion...as an indication that I wasn't going to fight.'[19] Sadat initially planned to attack on 15 November 1972, only days after the Presidential elections in America. He wanted to give the president-elect an opportunity to present a peace initiative. Should the president fail to do so, he would be confronted with war in the Middle East, which would force the United States to intervene. However, the Egyptian army was not ready in time for the November offensive and Sadat had to push back his D-Day.[20] Sadat made no secret of his frustration with Washington and his decision to break the status quo by going to war against Israel, yet both Americans and Israelis did not take his warnings seriously. His most ominous warning that war was inevitable came in April 1973, in an interview to *Newsweek*:

My main difficulty with the U.S. ... has been to get the Administration to take a position in the conflict and put it on the paper. To this day there is no solid position paper on the whole problem...Everyone has fallen asleep over the Mideast crisis. But they will soon wake up to the fact that Americans have left us no way out...times have changed. And everything is changing here too – for the battle...Everything in this country is now being mobilized in earnest for the resumption of the battle – which is now inevitable.[21]

Sadat spent the following months discussing his war plans with President Assad of Syria and King Faisal of Saudi Arabia. The three leaders agreed on an Egyptian-Syrian surprise attack against Israel to be launched on 6 October 1973, which fell on Yom Kippur (the Day of Atonement), the holiest and most solemn day in the Jewish calendar. During this day, all public services and workplaces would be shut and many military posts undermanned. October was also the month of Ramadan, the holiest period of the year for Muslims. Sadat believed that not only the Israelis would be least prepared to fight, they would

[19] Sadat, *In Search of Identity*, 232.
[20] Ibid., 232–237.
[21] *Newsweek*, 9 April 1973, 10–11.

certainly not expect the Arabs to attack during Ramadan. The Arab leaders also agreed to use oil as an economic and political lever against Washington, with the aim of bringing American pressure on Israel to withdraw from the occupied territories. Relations between Cairo and Moscow had begun to improve after the tension which followed the expulsion of Soviet advisors and, by the summer of 1973, the supply of Soviet arms to Egypt reached such high levels that Sadat allegedly told his foreign minister that the Soviets were 'drowning' him in new arms.[22] Indeed, between December 1972 and June 1973, the level of Soviet arm supplies to Egypt exceeded that of all previous years put together.[23]

On 3 October, Sadat informed the Soviet Ambassador in Cairo that war was imminent (although he did not disclose the exact date) and received Moscow's blessing.[24] The following day, Soviet diplomats and their dependents were evacuated from Cairo and Damascus. It was only at four o'clock on the morning of Saturday, 6 October – ten hours before the attack – that the Israeli government received accurate information on a combined offensive from north and south.[25] At two o'clock in the afternoon, the fourth Arab-Israeli war began in the north with a Syrian armoured offensive supported by artillery bombardment of Israeli forces in the Golan Heights. In the south, the Egyptian air force and artillery supported a massive crossing of troops of the Suez Canal to the east bank. Israeli forces were overwhelmingly outnumbered on both fronts, by approximately ten to one in tanks and infantry and thirty to one in artillery.[26]

---

[22] M. Heikal, *The Road to Ramadan* (New York: Ballantine Books, 1975), 183.
[23] Paul, *Asymmetric Conflicts*, 134–139.
[24] V. Israelyan, *Inside the Kremlin during the Yom Kippur War* (University Park, PA: Pennsylvania State University Press, 1995), 6–7; G. Golan, 'The Soviet Union and the Yom Kippur War,' *Israel Affairs*, 6:1 (Autumn 1999), 130.
[25] For a concise account of Sadat's military strategy, see J. Dunnigan and A. Nofi, *Victory and Deceit: Dirty Tricks at War* (New York: William Morrow and Company, 1995), 282–288. For a review of the failure of Israeli intelligence to anticipate the war, see A. Shlaim, 'Failures in National Intelligence Estimates: The Case of the Yom Kippur War,' *World Politics*, 38:3 (April 1976), 348–380; J. G. Stein, 'The Failures of Deterrence and Intelligence,' in R. Parker (ed.), *The October War: A Retrospective* (Gainesville: University of Florida Press, 2001), 79–152.
[26] M. Dayan, *Story of My Life* (London: Weidenfeld and Nicolson, 1978), 388–389.

Crisis Decision-Making

In his memoirs, Nixon admitted that the coordinated Egyptian-Syrian offensive 'took us completely by surprise.'[27] Despite the growing tension in the region, there were no expectations of immediate hostilities. A report prepared by the NSC staff in May 1973 had identified a series of Egyptian actions which, taken together, suggested 'a pattern of action that could be preparation for hostilities against Israel.' These actions included the mobilisation of surface-to-air SA-6 missiles, bombers, and jet fighters. Nevertheless, the report concluded that 'whatever the Egyptian and Arab leaders intend at this stage, the pattern of their actions thus far does not provide the Arabs with a rational basis for an attack at an early date.'[28] Kissinger too did not expect Sadat to act. Meeting Israeli Foreign Minister Abba Eban in May 1973, Kissinger asserted that Sadat 'shows no capacity for thinking moves ahead.'[29]

Notwithstanding the American failure to anticipate the war, the intelligence crisis was largely the result of a colossal institutional debacle of the Israeli military intelligence, which even on 4 October estimated that there was 'low probability' of war. American intelligence did not question the conception which was developed following the 1967 Six-Day War and adopted by high echelons in the Israeli military intelligence. It assumed that the Arabs would not dare go to war again until they had acquired greater air power and more effective ground-to-air missiles. This was estimated to happen not before 1975.[30] Washington had little reason to question the Israeli assessment or to feel that it knew more than the Israeli intelligence, which had several agents operating in Egypt and Syria.[31]

[27] Nixon, *RN*, 920.
[28] Memo from the NSC Staff, 'Indications of Arab Intentions to Initiate Hostilities,' May 1973. NSA website, http://www.gwu.edu/%7Ensarchiv/NSAEBB/NSAEBB98/octwar-01.pdf.
[29] Memcon, Abba Eban, Simcha Dinitz, Avner Dan, Henry Kissinger, Harold Saunders, Peter Rodman, 12 May 1973; Kissinger's office, the White House. Folder no. 4, Country Files (henceforth CF) – Middle East, HAK Files, Box 135, NSCF, NPMP.
[30] E. Kahana, 'Early Warning Versus Concept: The Case of the Yom Kippur War, 1973,' *Intelligence and National Security*, 17:2 (June 2002), 81–104; U. Bar-Joseph, 'Israel's 1973 Intelligence Failure,' *Israel Affairs*, 6:1 (Autumn 1999), 11–35; U. Bar-Joseph, *The Watchman Fell Asleep: The Surprise of Yom Kippur and Its Sources* (New York: State University of New York Press, 2005).
[31] Interview with Quandt.

Despite the initial surprise at the combined Arab attack, Kissinger was quick to adapt to the new situation and a crisis atmosphere soon took over. Within this environment, the WSAG was instrumental in contributing to a mostly effective decision-making process, which was surpassed in efficiency only by the management of the Jordanian Crisis. This judgment is consistently supported by the major scholarship on U.S. foreign policy making during the Nixon administration.[32] Kissinger himself argued during the final stages of the war (before the confrontation with the Soviets) that 'this [was] the best-run crisis we've ever had.'[33] It is not unlikely that Kissinger's unique position in the administration contributed to his assessment. According to William Quandt, 'one of the reasons might have been that he was in charge of both the State Department and the NSC, so he got more comfortable.'[34]

Another explanation for the successful management of the war was its relative lack of public controversy and bureaucratic dissent which charcterised previous crises, most notably Cambodia and the India-Pakistan War. This, in turn, enabled a clearer formulation of U.S. objectives early on in the crisis and a closer cooperation between the White House and the bureaucracy. As the war developed, the immediate objectives of the administration were to stop the fighting, to prevent the Soviets from intervening, and to end the Arab oil embargo which had been in place since the second week of the fighting. Thus, what followed was a rather 'rational' process of decision-making, where a variety of alternatives were considered based on a cost-benefit analysis. These included the use of diplomatic channels to the belligerents, back-channelling to Moscow, referring the case to the UN, and ultimately using the threat of American force to bring the war to conclusion. However, as the following analysis will demonstrate, the decision-making process during the Yom Kippur War was far from perfect, and the fact that it ranks high in terms of quality merely confirms the frailty of crisis decision-making during the Nixon-Kissinger years. While the WSAG

---

[32] See, for example, Quandt, *Decade of Decisions*; Dowty, *Middle East Crisis*; Herek, Janis, and Huth, 'Decision Making during International Crises'; Haney, 'The Nixon Administration and Middle East Crises,' 939–959, and *Organizing for Foreign Policy Crises*.

[33] Interview with Quandt.

[34] Ibid.

met regularly and thorough discussions often took place, the two most important episodes during the war – the airlift and the nuclear alert – suggest that Kissinger himself personified the decision-making process during the war. Still, when compared to the experiences of Cambodia and the India-Pakistan War, for example, the decision-making process during the Yom Kippur War seems indeed exemplary.

The WSAG met regularly during the crisis. Under the chairmanship of Kissinger, the principals of the group included Joseph Sisco (assistant secretary of state for Near Eastern and South Asian Affairs), Roy Atherton (deputy assistant secretary of state), James Schlesinger (secretary of defense), William Clements (deputy secretary of defense), Admiral Thomas Moorer (chairman, JCS), and William Colby (director, Central Intelligence).[35] Although there were no evident cases of bureaucratic dissent during the crisis, the most important decisions were still taken either by Kissinger alone or in ad hoc consultation with an inattentive Nixon.

Despite the calming assessment of her military advisors, on 5 October Israeli Prime Minister Golda Meir sent an urgent cable to Kissinger alerting him of the Arab war preparations which had become more evident, including the evacuation of Soviet diplomats and their dependents. Meir urged Kissinger to convey to Cairo and Damascus that Israel had no plans to attack, but should Egypt and Syria intend to launch a military offensive, Israel would 'react military, with firmness and in great strength.'[36] Kissinger stayed in New York that day and did not receive the message until the morning of 6 October. By then, 'there were only ninety minutes of peace left for the Middle East.'[37] Nevertheless, Kissinger quickly assumed control of the situation, beginning with a frantic series of calls to the Soviets, Israelis, Egyptians, and Syrians. He urged the Israelis and the Arabs to use restraint and reminded the Soviets of their responsibility for preventing the impending crisis from deteriorating into an armed conflict. Kissinger also ordered a first

---

[35] Kissinger elevated the Defense Department representative to a Secretary level following his nomination to Secretary of State. See *Years of Upheaval*, 587.

[36] Memo, Scowcroft to Kissinger, enclosing a message from Prime Minister Meir, 5 October 1973. NSA website, http://www.gwu.edu/%7Ensarchiv/NSAEBB/NSAEBB98/octwar-07.pdf.

[37] Kissinger, *Years of Upheaval*, 451.

WSAG meeting in Washington for nine o'clock in the morning (local time), which would take place in his absence. He finally summarised his actions and views to President Nixon, who was in Florida that weekend.[38] Kissinger's calls for restraint ultimately fell on deaf ears, and by the time the WSAG met on the morning of 6 October, the Yom Kippur War had already begun.

The war presented the crisis management group with a dilemma. While it was important to support Israel, it was crucial not to let her win too decisively, as another Arab defeat could prompt a Soviet intervention. Moreover, the risk of an Arab oil embargo could no longer be ignored.[39] As intelligence significantly lagged behind events during the first hours of the war, the group could not ascertain the identity of the aggressor. William Colby suggested that the war was the result of 'mutual fears of actions and reactions that had escalated to hostilities.'[40] This estimate was consistent with the prevailing conception of the intelligence community which was discussed previously. Indeed, just hours before the war, William Quandt warned Brent Scowcroft, Kissinger's deputy in the NSC, that the intelligence services 'have continued to downplay the likelihood of an Arab attack on Israel and still have no signs that such action is imminent. They appear to favour the alternative explanation of a crisis in Arab-Soviet relations.'[41] The group did not contest the intelligence assessment, but it could not explain either how an action-reaction cycle could have led to a coordinated Egyptian-Syrian offensive on two fronts.[42] While Colby, Defense

---

[38] Telegram, Kissinger to White House Situation Room, 'Report to the President,' 6 October 1973. Folder no. 1, Box 664, NSC Files, NPMP, NARA; Kissinger, *Years of Upheaval*, 450–458.

[39] In the months before the war, the scenario of an Arab oil embargo had been discussed frequently in the media but was not taken too seriously by the administration until October. See *Newsweek*, 19 February 1973, 18–19; and 10 September 1973, 11–13. James Akins, petroleum advisor to the State Department, was the only official who literally predicted the oil embargo that followed the war and warned that America was not prepared for it. His recommendations were flatly dismissed by the administration. See J. Akins, 'The Oil Crisis: This Time the Wolf Is Here,' *Foreign Affairs*, 51:3 (April 1973), 472–490.

[40] Quandt, *Peace Process*, 106.

[41] Memo, Quandt to Scowcroft, 'Arab-Israeli Tensions,' 6 October 1973. NSA website, http://www.gwu.edu/%7Ensarchiv/NSAEBB/NSAEBB98/octwar-13.pdf.

[42] Kissinger, *Years of Upheaval*, 458.

Secretary Schlesinger, and Admiral Moorer opined that Israel was the aggressor, Roy Atherton argued that it was inconceivable that Israel would start a war on Yom Kippur.

In Washington, Kissinger had already made his mind up that the war was a result of Arab aggression and, accordingly, told Soviet Ambassador Dobrynin that Egyptian claims to the contrary were 'baloney.'[43] Kissinger asked the group to make plans for the advancement of the Sixth Fleet to the eastern Mediterranean, and embassies in the region were ordered to prepare for the evacuation of dependants.[44] On the diplomatic front, Nixon accepted Kissinger's advice that it would be best to work with the Soviets on a joint resolution in the UN Security Council.[45] However, the superpowers did not succeed in persuading their respective allies to accept a status quo ante cease-fire. The Israelis were desperate to reverse Arab gains on the battlefield, while the Egyptians wanted to advance further in the Sinai Peninsula. Only President Assad of Syria was content with his gains in the Golan Heights.[46] Kissinger assured the Israeli Foreign Minister that Washington would not force a cease-fire in the Security Council. Despite the Israeli losses on the battlefield, the view in Washington remained that the war would soon end with another Arab defeat. Moreover, Kissinger believed that by not forcing Israel to accept a cease-fire, he would have valuable leverage over Jerusalem later on.[47]

By the end of the first day of the fighting, Kissinger chaired a second WSAG meeting in Washington. Still expecting Israel to regain initiative on the battlefield within days, the group preferred to focus on the long-term implications of the war and took no further actions other than moving the Sixth Fleet closer to the region.[48] However, the expectation of a quick Israeli victory soon had to be readjusted, as during the next few days, the Israelis suffered heavy defeats on both fronts, despite retaking most of the territory they initially lost in the Golan Heights.[49]

---

43 Ibid.
44 Kalb and Kalb, *Kissinger*, 461–462; Quandt, *Decade of Decisions*, 170–171.
45 Kissinger, *Years of Upheaval*, 471–473.
46 Golan, 'The Soviet Union and the Yom Kippur War,' 130.
47 Kissinger, *Years of Upheaval*, 473.
48 Ibid., 475.
49 In the first days of the fighting, the loss ratio on the southern front was nine Israeli tanks for a single Egyptian tank. In the north by 9 October, Israeli forces were left with 50 out of 177 tanks; 724 soldiers were killed in the first two days of the fighting –

On Tuesday, 9 October, Kissinger explained to the Israeli Ambassador, Simcha Dinitz: 'Our strategy was to give you until Wednesday evening, by which time I thought the whole Egyptian army would be wrecked.' During the meeting, Dinitz asked for planes, tanks, and 'general information' about the movement of Iraqi forces toward Syria.[50] At the end of the day, Kissinger met Dinitz again to report that Nixon had approved the entire list of 'consumables' Israel had asked for, including ordnance and electronic equipment (except for laser bombs). Nixon also agreed to replace all the tanks and planes Israel had lost.[51] By then, it was clear that the war was not going to end with a swift Israeli victory and that any diplomatic solution to the crisis was becoming increasingly unattainable.

The Soviets had made a decision to resupply the Arabs in the first days of the war, and from as early as 8 October, a massive airlift and sealift took place almost on a daily basis.[52] In addition, various Arab countries also supported Egypt and Syria's war effort.[53] At the same time in Washington, although Nixon agreed to replace Israeli losses in planes and tanks, this was well short of the full military commitment which the Arabs had enjoyed from Moscow. It was not until the second week of the war, on 14 October, that constant supplies on a massive scale began to reach Israel. The long delay in the American airlift to Israel seemed odd, given Israel's heavy casualties during the first week of the war and Ambassador Dinitz's desperate requests for

---

more than during the entire Six-Day War. See Bar-Joseph, *The Watchman Fell Asleep*, 225–226.

[50] Memcon, Dinitz, Gur, Kissinger, and Scowcroft. 9 October 1973, 8:20–8:40 a.m., the White House. NSA website, http://www.gwu.edu/%7Ensarchiv/NSAEBB/NSAEBB98/octwar-21a.pdf.

[51] Memcon, Dinitz, Shalev, Kissinger, Scowcroft, and Rodman. 9 October 1973, 6:10–6:35 p.m., the White House. NSA website, http://www.gwu.edu/%7Ensarchiv/NSAEBB/NSAEBB98/octwar-21b.pdf.

[52] After a stopover in Budapest, the first planes arrived in the Middle East on 9 and 10 October. When the war began, the Kremlin estimated that the Arabs already had a significant quantitative advantage over Israel in weaponry, around 1.7 to 1. See Israelyan, *Inside the Kremlin during the Yom Kippur War*, 58–60.

[53] Iraq supplied Syria with helicopters, fighter jets (with pilots), and tanks, while Egypt received jets from Algeria, as well as an infantry brigade. Libya provided surface-to-air missiles, while Sudan contributed an infantry brigade. See Memcon, Dinitz, Gur, Kissinger, and Scowcroft. 9 October 1973, 8:20–8:40 a.m.; Memcon, 'Military Briefing,' 22 October 1973, 4:15 p.m.–4:57 p.m. NSA website, http://www.gwu.edu/%7Ensarchiv/NSAEBB/NSAEBB98/octwar-56.pdf.

a resupply from Kissinger. Why did it take Washington so long to respond favourably to the Israeli requests? One reason for the delay was the administration's desire to maintain a low profile and to keep its options open at the end of the war. Assessing the situation on 9 October, William Quandt wrote to Kissinger that on the matter of Israeli arms requests, 'if we act too early or too visibly on this key issue, we will insure attacks on US citizens and an oil embargo in key Arab states.'[54] At the same time, Quandt recognised that should the U.S. fail to respond positively to a genuine Israeli request for arms, the potential diplomatic leverage over Israel at the end of the war would be lost.

Kissinger handled this dilemma adroitly to secure his master plan. While he did not wish to see the Israelis lose the war, he did not want to risk U.S. relations with the Arab world either. However, in his meetings with Ambassador Dinitz, Kissinger preferred to put the delay down to 'bureaucratic difficulties.' Specifically, he blamed Secretary of Defense James Schlesinger and the Pentagon for acting slowly. Thus, during their morning meeting on 9 October, Kissinger warned Dinitz: 'That's a bigger problem now than we thought. I must tell you, don't go running around Defense. Scowcroft will handle it.'[55] He assured Dinitz that he was 'a true friend of Israel' and that he had taken the matter to the president, who had agreed 'in principle' to replace any losses in arms.[56] He even advised Dinitz to urge the Israeli government to go on the offensive 'as quickly and as strongly as possible' before a cease-fire would take place.[57] Kissinger, of course, had no intention of follow on Nixon's order to the letter. Rather than using Military Aircraft Command (MAC) aircraft, Kissinger wanted to charter commercial airlines to assist in the airlift operation in order to maintain a low profile. The efforts of the Departments of Transportation and Defense to enlist commercial charters to the task proved futile, however, as most airline companies refused to fly to a war zone.[58] Kissinger's

54 Memo, Quandt to Kissinger, 'Middle East Issues,' 9 October 1973. NSA website, http://www.gwu.edu/%7Ensarchiv/NSAEBB/NSAEBB98/octwar-22.pdf.
55 See Memcon, Dinitz, Gur, Kissinger, and Scowcroft. 9 October 1973, 8:20–8:40 a.m.
56 M. Golan, *The Secret Conversations of Henry Kissinger: Step-by-Step Diplomacy in the Middle East* (New York: Quadrangle, 1976), 49.
57 S. Dinitz, 'The Yom Kippur War: Diplomacy of War and Peace,' *Israel Affairs*, 6:1 (Autumn 1999), 113.
58 J. Schlesinger, 'The Airlift,' in Parker, *The October War*, 156; Nixon, *RN*, 926.

suggestion that his hands were tied by the bureaucracy was, of course, exaggerated. As arguably the most powerful man in Washington at the time, it is unlikely that Kissinger could be undermined by Secretary Schlesinger.[59] According to Quandt, in reality it was Kissinger who ordered Schlesinger not to resupply Israel:

I remember Kissinger saying to Schlesinger in one of the meetings, 'You are going to have to bear the responsibility for whatever delay there is because I have to deal with the Israelis on the diplomatic front. Nixon and I cannot be viewed as the problem; right now is not the time'... It wasn't Schlesinger, he was doing what he was told: 'get ready to do it but don't do it!,' and so he had to take the fall.[60]

In fact, it was Schlesinger who insisted that there was 'simply no half way house' and that the United States would have to use its own military aircraft if Israel were to be resupplied in time.[61] His view was supported by Admiral Moorer who believed that a MAC airlift would be more efficient and easier to control than commercial charters.[62] Both Kissinger and Alexander Haig (who was now acting as Nixon's chief of staff, following Haldeman's resignation) preferred to maintain a low profile in the hope that a cease-fire could still be secured. On 13 October, Haig warned Kissinger that Schlesinger was 'ready to move MAC aircraft in there immediately. I think that would be foolish.' Kissinger replied, 'That would be a disaster, Al. How can he fuck everything up for a week... I think it's stupid.'[63] However, in WSAG meetings during this period, it was Kissinger who rebuked Schlesinger and Colby for being overly cautious over resupplying Israel: 'Israel has suffered a strategic defeat no matter what happens,' he confronted the group on 9 October, '[they] can't take two-to-one loses.'[64] Although the group met

---

[59] See, for example, E. N. Luttwak and W. Laqueur, 'Kissinger & the Yom Kippur War,' *Commentary*, no. 58 (September 1974), 33–40; Zumwalt, *On Watch*, 433–435; T. Szulc, *The Illusion of Peace: Foreign Policy in the Nixon Years* (New York: Viking, 1978), 735–738; Ambrose, *Nixon: Ruin and Recovery*, 234.
[60] Interview with Quandt.
[61] J. Schlesinger, 'The Airlift,' 156–157.
[62] R. N. Lebow and J. G. Stein, *We All Lost the Cold War* (Princeton, NJ: Princeton University Press, 1994), 192.
[63] Isaacson, *Kissinger*, 521.
[64] Kissinger, *Years of Upheaval*, 494.

eight times during the first week of the war, it did not take any significant operational actions apart from ordering the Sixth Fleet to advance
towards the region. As events on the battlefield unfolded each day and
moods vacillated frequently, the group found it difficult to take decisive action. Secretary Schlesinger recorded the atmosphere of changing perceptions during the first week of the war: 'Attitudes seesawed
every other day. On Monday and Wednesday, after mobilization and
some successes, the mood was upbeat. On Tuesday and Thursday...
the Israelis were downcast.'[65]

Thus, on 13 October, a downcast Dinitz warned Kissinger: 'If a
massive American airlift to Israel does not start immediately, then I'll
know that the United States is reneging on its promises and its policy,
and we will have to draw very serious conclusions from all this.'[66] In
particular, Ambassador Dinitz implied that he would seek support in
Congress. Already consumed by two domestic scandals, the last thing
the White House needed was a crisis over foreign policy. It was only
then that Nixon became personally involved in the operational details
of the airlift. He dismissed Kissinger and Schlesinger's recommendations that the United States should send no more than three C-5 A
transport planes and ordered Kissinger: 'Goddamn it, use every one
we have. Tell them [the Pentagon] to send everything that can fly.'[67]
Nixon's personal intervention brought an end to Kissinger's manipulation. Within hours, Kissinger convened the WSAG in the morning of 14
October to 'settle the technicalities of the airlift once and for all.'[68] By
the end of the day – the first day of the airlift – Israel had received 148
tons of supplies. By the end of the fighting on 25 October, the United
States had delivered nearly 12,880 tons of supplies to Israel, along with
forty F-4 Phantom Jets, thirty-six A-4 Skyhawks, and twelve C-130
transport planes. By contrast, by then the Soviets had delivered to the
Arabs only 11,174 tons of supplies, even though the Soviet airlift had
begun nearly a week earlier.[69] The Israelis clearly believed Kissinger's
tales of bureaucratic difficulties. As far as Foreign Minister Eban

[65] Schlesinger, 'The Airlift,' 155.
[66] Kalb and Kalb, *Kissinger*, 475.
[67] Nixon, *RN*, 927.
[68] Kissinger, *Years of Upheaval*, 522.
[69] 'Soviet VS U.S. Supplies Delivered by Air to M.E.' No date. Folder no. 3, MF, Box
H-092, NSCIF, NPMP.

was concerned, 'Our heroes were Nixon and Kissinger. Our enemies were the Pentagon and Schlesinger.'[70] Ambassador Dinitz too did not question Kissinger's story. According to the journalist Matti Golan, he completely fell for Kissinger's captivating persona: 'Dinitz surrendered completely to Kissinger's solicitations and personal charm. He was flattered that the powerful, brilliant Kissinger called him frequently, consulted him.... Without desiring it, without even being conscious of it, Dinitz turned into Kissinger's man... ultimately he believed that Kissinger was pure; that the wolves were in the Pentagon.'[71]

Nixon's rare act of leadership in the crisis on 14 October also transformed the dynamics of WSAG discussions. Whereas during the first week of the war, the approach to the crisis was rather hesitant, once an unequivocal presidential directive had been issued, discussions turned more purposeful and emphasis shifted from deliberation to implementation. Accordingly, on 16 October Kissinger set the group a target – keeping U.S. resupply of Israel at least 25 percent ahead of the Soviets.'[72] This target was indeed achieved and as Kissinger observed, the atmosphere was now more 'relaxed' – so much so that he took the group to the Oval Office for an informal meeting with the president.[73]

The airlift had an immediate impact on the fighting, and by 16 October, the Israelis had completed a successful counter-offensive in the Sinai and crossed the Suez Canal.[74] The news from the battlefield saw an upbeat Kissinger chairing the WSAG meeting on 17 October. His early meeting with the foreign ministers of Morocco, Algeria, Saudi Arabia, and Kuwait in the White House had gone well and he told the group that in light of his discussions with his counterparts, he did not expect a problem over oil. He even boasted to the group: 'Did you see the Saudi Foreign minister come out like a good little

---

[70] Cited in Y. Melman and D. Raviv, *Friends in Deed: Inside the U.S.-Israel Alliance* (New York: Hyperion, 1994), 163.

[71] Golan, *The Secret Conversations of Henry Kissinger,* 51.

[72] Kissinger, *Years of Upheaval,* 531. Kissinger apparently had a 'chronic obsession' about preventing Soviet arms from winning the war in the Middle East. See E. Sheehan, *The Arabs, Israelis, and Kissinger: A Secret History of American Diplomacy in the Middle East* (New York: Reader's Digest Press, 1976), 33–34.

[73] Kissinger, *Years of Upheaval,* 536.

[74] T. N. Dupy, *Elusive Victory: The Arab-Israeli Wars, 1947–1974* (Dubuque, IA: Kendall and Hunt Publishing, 1992), 492–513.

boy and say they had very fruitful talks with us? . . . we don't expect
a cut-off in the next few days.'[75] Then, turning to the airlift again,
Kissinger stressed that it must continue until the Soviets and the Arabs
capitulated. He urged the Pentagon to begin a sealift to Israel as well.
By doing so, Kissinger finally conceded that the power of diplomacy
alone would not suffice to end the war: 'We have to keep the stuff
going into Israel. We have to pour it in until someone quits. . . . The
worst thing that would happen would be for some eager beaver to start
moving in the Security Council until the pieces are in place.'[76] At the
end of the meeting, Nixon met with the WSAG principals (NSC staff
were excluded) and thanked them for their efforts. He explained that
his decision on the airlift was not out of love of Israel but rather to
exercise leverage over the post-war negotiations: 'In order to have the
influence we need to bring Israel to a settlement, we have to have their
confidence. That is why this airlift. . . . We can't get so much to them
that they will be arrogant, but we can't be in the position where Israel
puts pressure on Congress for us to do more.'[77] Despite the looming oil
crisis, the mood at the meeting remained positive. Kissinger joyfully
reported to Nixon, 'this has been the best-run crisis since you have
been in the White House,' and Deputy Secretary of Defense William
Clements applauded: 'your military services have just reacted in an
outstanding fashion, Mr. President.'[78] However, the upbeat mood in
Washington was quickly replaced by anxiety on 18 October, when the
Arab oil ministers, desperate to bring pressure on the United States,
announced a 70 percent increase in the price of crude oil and a 5 percent
cut in the production of oil every month until Israel withdrew from the
occupied territories. The following day, in response to Nixon's request
from Congress for $2.2 billion in aid to Israel, the Saudis announced
a 10 percent cut in production and termination of shipments to the
United States.[79]

---

[75] Minutes, 'Washington Special Actions Group Meeting – Middle East,' 17 October
1973, 3:05 p.m. – 4:04 p.m. Folder no. 5, *WSAG Meetings*, MF, Box H-117, NSCIF,
NPMP.

[76] Ibid.

[77] Memcon, 'WSAG Principals: Middle East War,' 17 October 1973, 4:00 p.m. Folder
no. 6, *WSAG Meetings*, MF, Box H-092, NSCIF, NPMP.

[78] Ibid.

[79] L. Allen, *OPEC Oil* (Cambridge, MA: Oelgeschlager, Gunn & Hain, 1979), 9–12;
Dowty, *Middle East Crisis*, 250; Quandt, *Peace Process*, 116–117.

On the battlefield, the Israelis were now close to winning the war on both fronts. While Washington was content with the change of military fortunes, there was still a real concern that '[the] smell of victory will not make Israel welcome a ceasefire.'[80] Still, the Soviets were markedly more worried. On 19 October, hours after the WSAG decided to continue with the airlift and to speed up the sealift, Nixon received an urgent message from Brezhnev, inviting Kissinger to come to Moscow to negotiate an immediate cease-fire, as the Kremlin feared that 'harm could be done even to the immediate relations between the Soviet Union and the United States.'[81] Nixon responded positively, and Kissinger left for Moscow in the early hours of the morning of 20 October.[82] En route to Moscow, Kissinger learned that Nixon had communicated to Brezhnev that Kissinger would come to Moscow with the president's 'full authority . . . the commitments that he may make in the course of your discussions have my complete support.'[83] Kissinger, however, did not appreciate this unusual act of presidential delegation (which must be understood against the background of Watergate). Kissinger feared that his new privileged position at the negotiation table would severely limit his manoeuvrability in the negotiations: 'I was horrified. The letter meant that I would be deprived of any capacity to stall . . . [it] made it impossible for me from Moscow to refer any tentative agreement to the President for his approval – if only to buy time to consult Israel . . . History will not record that I resisted many grants of authority. This one I resisted bitterly.'[84] In Moscow, Brezhnev and Kissinger were in agreement on the need to end the fighting and to separate the military situation from the political

---

[80] State Department Operations Center, Middle East Task Force, 'Situation Report in the Middle East as of 0600 Hours EDT, Oct. 19, 1973' (Situation Report No. 43) 19 October 1973. NSA website, http://www.gwu.edu/%7Ensarchiv/NSAEBB/NSAEBB98/octwar-40.pdf.

[81] H. Kissinger, *Crisis: The Anatomy of Two Major Foreign Policy Crises* (New York: Simon & Schuster, 2003), 292.

[82] Kissinger was accompanied by Sisco and Atherton from the State Department, five NSC staff, and Ambassador Robert McCloskey. He also gave a lift to Soviet Ambassador Dobrynin. The first informal meeting took place on the evening of 20 October, Moscow time. See V. Israelyan, 'The October 1973 War: Kissinger in Moscow,' *Middle East Journal*, 49:2 (Spring 1995), 19–41.

[83] Nixon to Brezhnev (no title), 20 October 1973. NSA website, http://www.gwu.edu/%7Ensarchiv/NSAEBB/NSAEBB98/octwar-43.pdf.

[84] Kissinger, *Years of Upheaval*, 547, 548.

settlement. By 21 October, Egypt's Third Army was nearly encircled by the Israelis and Sadat desperately pleaded with Moscow to agree to a cease-fire in place. Thus, when Kissinger and Brezhnev met for the third and last time, over breakfast on 22 October, it did not take them long to work out a joint text, which was later passed in the United Nations as Security Council Resolution 338. The resolution called for a cease-fire in-place (as opposed to quo ante) within twelve hours and the implementation of Security Council Resolution 242.[85]

Kissinger's diplomatic success in Moscow was not appreciated in his next stop, Tel Aviv. Prime Minister Meir was 'absolutely mad' for being forced to accept an agreement on which she was not consulted.[86] Peter Rodman from Kissinger's NSC staff recalled that 'Israel felt [it] had been shafted [in Moscow] by the United States.'[87] Nevertheless, Kissinger's hosts were in no mood to haggle. As Epi Evron from the Israeli Foreign Ministry explained: 'We were suffering. Henry noticed this right away. It did not take him long to sense that the country did not want to go through this experience again . . . [The] country as a whole wanted an end to the war.'[88]

Kissinger's memoirs support this impression. He recalls that his arrival in Israel on 22 October 'ranks high on the list' of the most moving moments of his government service: 'Those who had come to welcome us seemed to feel viscerally how close to the abyss they had come and how two weeks of war had drained them. . . . Their expression showed a weariness that almost tangibly conveyed the limits of human endurance. Israel was exhausted no matter what the military maps showed.'[89] Quite understandably, then, Kissinger started his meeting with Meir on the defensive. Rather than forcing Israel to abide by the Moscow understanding, he spent most of the meeting reassuring the wary prime minister about U.S. strategy during and after the war on a range of issues. There were no 'side understandings' on the implementation of Resolution 242 as it was referred to in Resolution 338. He had Brezhnev's 'word of honor' that he would 'use his

---

[85] Stein, *Heroic Diplomacy*, 86–90; Hanhimaki, *The Flawed Architect*, 310–311; Lebow and Stein, *We All Lost the Cold War*, 211–215.
[86] Stein, *Heroic Diplomacy*, 91.
[87] Ibid., 90.
[88] Ibid.
[89] Kissinger, *Years of Upheaval*, 560.

maximum influence' with the Arabs to release Israeli prisoners of war within seventy-two hours. He had given 'direct orders' that the airlift to Israel would continue. Kissinger even promised Meir that he would publicly ask the Red Cross to bring to Israel 4,000 Jews from Damascus.[90] However, Kissinger's most forthcoming promise concerned the implementation of the cease-fire. First, he let slip that with regard to the exact meaning of the phrase 'standstill ceasefire' as it appeared in Resolution 338, he has not 'thought it through yet.' He then explicitly suggested that should Israel not adhere to the cease-fire, there would not be recriminations. His intimation could not be interpreted any differently by his hosts: 'You won't get violent protests from Washington if something happens during the night, while I'm flying. Nothing can happen in Washington until noon tomorrow.' Meir replied, 'If they don't stop, we won't,' and Kissinger then responded most tellingly, 'even if they do.'[91] Remarkably, Kissinger did not stop there. Having successfully negotiated an international agreement in Moscow which subsequently materialised into a Security Council resolution, Kissinger now suggested to the Israelis that they disregard it and finish the job along the Suez Canal so as to reach the negotiation table from the most propitious position. When Israeli generals joined the meeting and explained that they would need two or three days to destroy the Egyptian forces on the east bank of the canal, Kissinger replied, 'Two or three days? That's all? Well, in Vietnam the cease-fire didn't go into effect at the exact time that was agreed on.'[92] After preventing Israel's much needed flow of arms during the first week of the war and intentionally delaying a presidential directive on the airlift, Kissinger was now willing to turn a blind eye should the Israelis decide to ignore the cease-fire. This episode is telling not only because it suggests that Kissinger had 'little respect for formal agreements,' as Hanhimaki concludes.[93] Perhaps more broadly, it serves as another link in the long

[90] Memcon, Meir, Gazit, Kissinger and Rodman, 22 October 1973, 1:35 p.m.–2:15 p.m. NSA website, http://www.gwu.edu/%7Ensarchiv/NSAEBB/NSAEBB98/octwar-54.pdf.

[91] Ibid.

[92] Golan, *The Secret Conversations of Henry Kissinger*, 86. According to another source, the comment was made by one of the Israeli generals rather than Kissinger. See S. Aaronson, *Conflict and Bargaining in the Middle East: An Israeli Perspective* (Baltimore: Johns Hopkins University Press, 1978), 189–190.

[93] Hanhimaki, *The Flawed Architect*, 313.

chain of cases of Kissinger's adroit manipulation and conniving tactics
which had come to embody the making of U.S. foreign policy during
the Nixon administration.

The Israeli generals did not ask Kissinger for clarifications. Whether
implicitly or explicitly, they received a green light from the United
States to advance their offensive on the southern front. When Kissinger
arrived in Washington on the morning of 23 October, he learned
that the cease-fire had collapsed, three hours after it went into effect.
Although it was unclear whether the Egyptians had fired the first shot,
as the Israelis claimed, the consequences were as undisputed as they
were significant: the complete encirclement of the 25,000-strong Egyptian Third Army on the eastern bank of the Suez Canal, the severance of
Egyptian supply routes, and the road to Cairo left wide open to Israeli
forces.[94] The outraged Soviets had little doubt who was to blame.
According to Ambassador Dobrynin, 'The Israelis quickly realized that
they could take advantage of a few hours' confusion at the beginning of
the cease-fire and encircle the Egyptian Third Army on the East Bank of
the Suez Canal. Actually, it was a premeditated violation of the agreement from the start.'[95] Brezhnev's explanation was even more candid:
'Here, in Moscow, Kissinger behaved in a cunning way. He vowed
fidelity to the policy of détente, and then while in Tel-Aviv he made a
deal with Golda.'[96] Kissinger knew that Meir's explanation – that the
Israeli cabinet had decided on the offensive because of Egyptian violations of the cease-fire – was incredible. Naturally, he felt somewhat
responsible for the Israeli offensive: 'I had a sinking feeling that I might
have emboldened them; in Israel, to gain their support, I had indicated
that I would understand if there was a few hours' "slippage" in the
cease-fire deadline while I was flying home.'[97] Kissinger, of course,
never intended to allow the Israelis to destroy the Egyptian Third
Army, as this would thwart his post-war diplomatic strategy. A decisive
Israeli victory and another humiliating Arab defeat would make it difficult for Kissinger to emerge as the principal mediator, accepted by all
parties, at the end of the war. Quandt notes on this point: 'The stakes

---

[94] Garthoff, *Détente and Confrontation*, 420; Stein, *Heroic Diplomacy*, 87.
[95] Dobrynin, *In Confidence*, 293.
[96] Cited in Israelyan, *Inside the Kremlin during the Yom Kippur War*, 160.
[97] Kissinger, *Years of Upheaval*, 569.

were no longer to defeat the aggressors . . . this is a crisis and [Kissinger's] goal was to ensure that this ends in a way that opens the door to an American-led diplomacy. He doesn't want the Russians to be in it, and obviously Israel cannot be defeated. But Sadat should not be defeated either, because if you humiliate the Arabs it would never work.'[98]

Beyond Kissinger's calculations of post-war diplomacy are broader issues here about superpower leverage during the war. While Kissinger was surprised by the Israeli move to cut off the Egyptian Third Army, he was undoubtedly taken aback by the failure of the superpowers to impose their will on their clients. Not only did the superpowers fail to stop the war from breaking out or secure an agreement on a cease-fire during the first week of the war, they now found it difficult to impose the Moscow agreement – which was a success in itself – on the parties. Ultimately, only the threat of superpower military intervention would end the Middle East crisis.

Following urgent consultations between Moscow, Washington, and New York on 23 October, the UN Security Council adopted Resolution 339, which instructed Israel, Egypt, and Syria to return to the cease-fire lines which went into effect following Resolution 338. Nevertheless, the fighting along the Suez Canal continued and the Egyptian Third Army was on the verge of annihilation. The Egyptian situation was so desperate that on 24 October, Sadat pleaded for the superpowers to send a joint task force to the region to enforce the cease-fire.[99] Accordingly, Brezhnev pressed Nixon to consider a Soviet proposal to 'urgently dispatch to Egypt Soviet and American military contingents, to insure the implementation' of the Security Council resolution.[100] Viewing Soviet presence in the region as a dangerous precedent and an obstacle to his post war plans, Kissinger rejected the idea, which in any event was unpalatable for the Israelis.[101]

However, the most alarming element in Brezhnev's letter to Nixon, which Kissinger interpreted as 'in effect an ultimatum' concerned the intimation of Soviet unilateral action in the region.[102] Brezhnev's message read: 'I will say it straight that if you find it impossible to act

[98] Interview with Quandt.
[99] Garthoff, *Détente and Confrontation*, 421–422.
[100] Kissinger, *Years of Upheaval*, 583.
[101] Kissinger, *Crisis*, 331–332, 343–344.
[102] Kissinger, *Years of Upheaval*, 583.

jointly with us in this matter, we should be faced with the necessity urgently to consider the question of taking appropriate steps unilaterally.'[103] Nixon interpreted the message as 'perhaps the most serious threat to U.S.-Soviet relations since the Cuban Missile crisis eleven years before.'[104] The Soviets, however, had no intention of sending troops to the region. A Kremlin insider during the war contends that the idea was categorically rejected by the leadership in Moscow:

[It] was obvious to everyone that carrying out a complicated military operation in the final stages of the war was very risky and almost impossible . . . Then the issue of sending troops unilaterally came up [at a Politburo meeting]. Nobody liked or supported the idea. 'We have already made a principle decision not to be involved in the Middle East war, and there are no reasons to change our decision,' noted Brezhnev. Thus any military involvement unilateral or together with the United States, was ruled out.[105]

Brezhnev was 'satisfied' with his message, believing that the threat of unilateral intervention would propel Washington to act jointly on the matter and influence Israel to stop the fighting.[106] However, Brezhnev's message had the opposite and undesired effect on Washington. The immediate result was a nocturnal meeting of the NSC/WSAG at which it was decided to place American forces around the world on increased alert – all this while Nixon was asleep, at the height of the crisis. As some observers have noted, Kissinger's response was 'an alarmist interpretation that represented a worst-case interpretation of the facts.'[107] Kissinger had indeed a reputation of interpreting events as worst-case scenarios, as had been demonstrated repeatedly in the cases of Cambodia, the Jordanian Crisis, and the India-Pakistan War. Still, given the stakes at the time and despite some misreading of Soviet actions, a categorical criticism of Kissinger's behaviour is not wholly justified. Indeed, even some of Kissinger's most vocal critics defended

---

[103] Ibid.

[104] Nixon, *RN*, 938.

[105] Israelyan, *Inside the Kremlin during the Yom Kippur War*, 167, 168. Israelyan served as the Director of the Department of International Organizations in the Soviet Foreign Ministry during the war.

[106] Ibid., 170

[107] See Hanhimaki, *The Flawed Architect*, 315; Garthoff, *Détente and Confrontation*, 423–427; Lebow and Stein, *We All Lost the Cold War*, 246–258. Lebow and Stein describe the nuclear alert as 'illogical' and 'incredible.'

the decision to upgrade the level of military readiness. Admiral Elmo Zumwalt contended: 'The Soviets presented us with what certainly looked like an ultimatum, and it would have been negligent indeed in such a situation not to assume a posture of readiness.'[108] Similarly, William Bundy admitted that throughout the war, Kissinger's considerations 'were spelled out and balanced, more frankly and carefully than at any other critical point in his active career.'[109]

Even during the height of the crisis and before one of the most dramatic decisions in Cold War history, it was the Watergate affair and its adverse effects on Nixon which seemed to eclipse the dramas of foreign policy. Kissinger had no illusions that the Soviet threat was a direct result of the domestic crisis and Nixon's dwindling support base. Before convening the crucial meeting just before midnight, 24 October, Kissinger said to Alexander Haig, 'You cannot be sure how much of this is due to our domestic crisis ... I don't think they would have taken on a functioning president ... Don't forget that is what the Soviets are playing on. They find a cripple facing impeachment and why shouldn't they go in there.'[110] Still, despite the stakes, Kissinger did not believe the situation required Nixon's presence at the meeting. He told Haig: 'I don't think we should bother the President'; Haig replied, 'He has to be part of everything you are doing,' but when Kissinger asked, 'Should I get him up?' Haig replied curtly, 'No.'[111] There are rife (albeit unconfirmed) speculations that Nixon was drunk when he went to bed that night and so was in no position to attend the meeting anyway. Kissinger notes in his memoirs that 'Haig thought the president too distraught to participate in the preliminary discussion ... From my own conversation with Nixon earlier in the evening, I was convinced Haig was right.'[112] Moreover, when Kissinger was asked directly in 1991 whether Nixon was drunk that night, he refused to provide a straight answer.[113] Haig's suggestion that 'the occasion called for strong public action by a strong President, not for a meeting by a committee of his underlings' bluntly overlooked

---

[108] Zumwalt, *On Watch*, 448.
[109] Bundy, *A Tangled Web*, 444.
[110] Kissinger, *Crisis*, 346, 347.
[111] Ibid., 347; Kissinger, *Years of Upheaval*, 585.
[112] Kissinger, *Years of Upheaval*, 585.
[113] See Lebow and Stein, *We All Lost the Cold War*, 480–481 (fn. 125).

the fact that by October 1973 Nixon was anything but a strong president.[114] The underlings Haig referred to included himself, Secretaries Kissinger and Schlesinger, Admiral Moorer, DCI Colby, Assistant Secretary of State Sisco, as well as Kissinger's deputy in the NSC, General Brent Scowcroft, and Kissinger's military assistant in the NSC, Commander Jonathan Howe.[115] Haig also reports that Nixon 'expressed no enthusiasm for attending the meeting in person' and then adds, bizarrely, 'Besides, he was tired.'[116] In any case, the fateful meeting took place without the president, who was either drunk or tired. Perhaps most tellingly, Quandt suggests that Nixon's condition was so poor that Defense Secretary Schlesinger ordered the military to ignore any presidential orders which might come during that night:

Schlesinger, I've been told, in that meeting, said 'we have to make sure that no unauthorized communications come from the White House to the Joint Chiefs of Staff, so I am going to tell the Chairman of the JCS not to carry out any orders except from me, including no calls from the President.' They didn't think Nixon was in any shape to function, so Schlesinger told the Chairman of the JCS, 'if the President calls you, don't do what he says.' I don't think it's constitutional, but I think that's indicative of how worried they were that psychologically and perhaps physically Nixon wasn't functioning that well.[117]

Finally, Raymond Garthoff's account seems to dispel the mystery: 'In fact, Nixon had been drinking heavily and was not in condition to participate in the meeting. I had been told this independently by two members attending the WSAG/NSC meeting . . . and who say they were told by Kissinger at the meeting.'[118]

Thus, with an incapacitated president, Kissinger chaired the meeting which lasted from 10:40 p.m. to 2:00 a.m. during the night of 24–25 October. He began with a detailed briefing and then outlined three possible reasons for the Soviet threat: (1) Moscow intended all along to intervene in the war, (2) Moscow decided to intervene as a result of the Arab defeat on the battlefield, or (3) Moscow was responding to the Israeli violation of the cease-fire. What followed was a careful

---

[114] Haig, *Inner Circles*, 415.
[115] Kissinger, *Crisis*, 348; Haig, *Inner Circles*, 416. According to Kissinger, Sisco did not attend the meeting, while Haig's account does not mention Commander Howe.
[116] Haig, ibid.
[117] Interview with Quandt.
[118] Garthoff, *Détente and Confrontation*, 425 (fn. 78).

weighing of 'Soviet actions, motivations, and intentions.'[119] The group was unanimous in its rejection of the Soviet proposal for a joint super-power contingent to be sent to the region. Kissinger was adamant that 'we would have to do so in a manner that shocked the Soviets into abandoning the unilateral move they were threatening – and, from all our information, planning.'[120] As for responding to the threat, the group decided to send a reply to Moscow that would be 'conciliatory in tone but strong in substance.'[121] The group also unanimously agreed to increase the readiness of American forces worldwide to a level which would be noticed in Moscow. Descending from DefCon (Defense Condition) 1, which means war, to DefCon 5, U.S. forces are normally placed on DefCon 4 or 5. Halfway through the meeting, Admiral Moorer ordered all military commands to move to DefCon 3, which signalled the highest stage of readiness during peacetime.[122] In addition, the 82nd Airborne Division in Germany was alerted for possible movement, the carrier *Franklin Delano Roosevelt* (positioned off the coast of Italy) was ordered to join the *Independence* in the eastern Mediterranean, while the carrier *John F. Kennedy* and its escorts were ordered from the Atlantic Ocean to advance to the region.[123] These military measures were, of course, thought of and executed as a political instrument, their principal advantage being their high visibility.[124] The group also resolved to talk Sadat out of his plea for a joint superpower contingent to be sent to the region. Accordingly, it drafted a message to Sadat in Nixon's name, asking the Egyptian leader to 'consider the consequences for your country if the two great nuclear countries were thus to confront each other on your soil.'[125] The message to Brezhnev,

---

[119] Kissinger, *Crisis*, 349.

[120] Ibid., 348.

[121] Ibid., 350.

[122] U.S. forces in the Pacific were permanently placed on DefCon 3. The Strategic Air Command, normally at DefCon 3, was moved to DefCon 2 (meaning attack is imminent), while the Sixth Fleet in the Mediterranean was put on a particular alert status. Ibid.; Schlesinger's remarks in Reich, 'Crisis Management,' 175.

[123] Garthoff, *Détente and Confrontation*, 427.

[124] According to Lebow and Stein, '[even] senior military personnel in the United States did not treat the alert as a serious prelude to possible military action. Because there was little expectation of combat, the strategic alert was ordered at a low level by the Joint Chiefs and executed in a perfunctory way by the military commanders.' See *We All Lost the Cold War*, 252.

[125] Kissinger, *Crisis*, 351.

in Nixon's name, was sent in the early hours of the morning of 25 October. It rejected the Soviet proposal and warned that a unilateral action by Moscow 'would produce incalculable consequences which would be in the interest of neither of our countries and which would end all we have striven so hard to achieve.'[126]

A few hours later, Kissinger received a message from Sadat in reply to Nixon's message, which accepted the American position. The Egyptian leader had called for the implementation of Security Council Resolutions 338 and 339 and the 'speedy' dispatch of an international force to the region.[127] Kissinger and Haig then went to brief Nixon on last night's events. Bizarrely, Kissinger reports that '[as] always in crises, Nixon was clearheaded and crisp.'[128] The president approved of the measures taken during the night; however, by noon they were no longer necessary. UN Secretary General Kurt Waldheim informed Kissinger that Sadat had dropped his call for Soviet and American forces to intervene. What emerged instead was a nonaligned resolution calling for an increased observer force which would exclude representatives of the five permanent members of the Security Council. Resolution 340 also called for an immediate cease-fire, a return to the 22 October lines, and the implementation of Resolution 338.[129] This time, the cease-fire was observed, and the Yom Kippur War – arguably the most menacing crisis during the Nixon administration – was finally brought to an end. Kissinger urged Ambassador Dobrynin that the DefCon alert should not be taken as a 'hostile act' on behalf of the United States. He explained that it had been 'mostly determined by "domestic considerations."'[130] The following day, 26 October, the order for increased readiness was rescinded.

At this point, it is worth addressing a pertinent question which remains contentious to this day: Was the fateful meeting on 24–25 October a WSAG or a NSC meeting? On the surface, the question seems like an exercise in tedious academic nitpicking over semantics.

[126] Ibid., 353; Dowty, *Middle East Crisis*, 274.
[127] Kissinger, *Crisis*, 354.
[128] Ibid., 355.
[129] The 900-strong UN Task force included mostly Australians, Finnish, and Swedish soldiers. Golan, *The Secret Conversations of Henry Kissinger*, 91; Quandt, *Peace Process*, 124.
[130] Dobrynin, *In Confidence*, 297.

However, the magnitude of the decisions taken during the meeting, Nixon's decision (or rather Haig and Kissinger's decision on behalf of Nixon) not to take part for whatever reason, and the fact that a seemingly minor detail as the type of meeting still provides a fertile ground for debate amongst observers and practitioners alike necessitate a careful examination of the available evidence in order to reach an informed conclusion. Based on the available data, it seems that this was indeed a WSAG meeting, which was later publicly portrayed as a NSC meeting given the weight of its decisions. Indeed, some, like Peter Rodman from the NSC staff, find this discussion petty: 'Who cares? I mean, this is a profoundly silly point,'[131] while Garthoff refers to 'the famous meeting (NSC, WSAG, or whatever).'[132] Secretary Schlesinger's account succinctly conveys the confusion surrounding this meeting: 'It was a curious meeting. It started as a [*sic*], it was announced as a WSAG meeting. Then, because of the serious decisions that were taken, it was transformed into a NSC meeting. When the president did not appear, it then became a "rump NSC meeting." So there was some curiosity about it.'[133] Even Kissinger seems uncertain: 'The White House later described it as a National Security Council meeting. There has been some discussion since whether it was a "proper" National Security Council meeting if the President did not attend.' Kissinger concludes that 'It was in effect the statutory membership of the National Security Council minus these two men.' (Vice President Gerald Ford did not attend either, as he had not yet been confirmed by the Senate after replacing Spiro Agnew).[134] However, then Kissinger explains: 'I now discover that our internal records called it a WSAG "meeting of principals" – a rare but not unprecedented occurrence... Nixon had never attended WSAG deliberations in the past (though he occasionally appeared for brief pep talks). No one present thought it unusual that he did not do so now.'[135] Peter Rodman confirms: 'On our books – just for the record, I think on our books we carried it as a WSAG principals meeting for a long

---

[131] Rodman's remark in Reich, 'Crisis Management,' in Parker, *The October War*, 201.
[132] Garthoff, *Détente and Confrontation*, 427.
[133] Schlesinger's remark in Reich, 'Crisis Management,' in Parker, *The October War*, 202.
[134] Kissinger, *Years of Upheaval*, 586.
[135] Ibid., 587.

time.'[136] In the president's absence, this could not have been a NSC meeting. The National Security Act of 1947 clearly states that 'The President of the United States shall preside over meetings of the Council: Provided, that in his absence he may designate a member of the Council to preside in his place.'[137] Indeed, Haig reports that Nixon said to him, 'You know what I want, Al; you handle the meeting.'[138] However, Haig served as Nixon's chief of staff and was not a statutory member of the NSC, which prevented him from chairing the meeting. This further supports the case for a WSAG meeting, strictly on legalistic terms. Furthermore, as has already been established, the meeting of the NSC as a decision-making forum for the president and his top foreign policy advisors was indeed a rare sight during the Nixon administration. Recalling Sonnenfeldt's observation about the nature of the NSC forum during the Nixon administration, it acted more as a discussion body rather than a decision-making body. Operational decisions (mobilising troops, diplomatic manoeuvring, communicating to Moscow) were almost invariably taken at WSAG meetings, while the most monumental decisions (going after the Cambodian sanctuaries, tilting in favour of Pakistan, delaying the airlift to Israel) were not seriously debated or ordered in the setting of the NSC forum but were rather the products of ad hoc discussions or presidential intuition. It thus seems that while this was indeed a 'principals only' WSAG meeting, the monumental decision taken there and its dramatic implications, rather than a specific individual (including Nixon himself), had retrospectively 'transformed' it into a NSC meeting.[139] Thus, for example, on the evening of 25 October, Kissinger met the Chinese ambassador and, while reporting on last night's events, he explained, 'I called a meeting of the National Security Council.' This comment not only further supports the argument for a WSAG meeting, as NSC meetings ought to be 'called' by the president, and not by the

---

[136] Rodman's remark in Reich, 'Crisis Management,' in Parker, *The October War*, 201.

[137] U.S. Congress, 'The National Security Act (1947),' in P. R. Viotti, *American Foreign Policy and National Security: A Documentary Record* (Upper Saddle River, NJ: Pearson, 2005), 339.

[138] Haig, *Inner Circles*, 416.

[139] Memcon, Kissinger and Huang Zhen, 25 October 1973, 4:45 p.m.–5:25 p.m. NSA website, http://www.gwu.edu/%7Ensarchiv/NSAEBB/NSAEBB98/octwar-72.pdf.

secretary of state (and certainly not by the national security advisor), but it illustrates once more the remarkable executive authority which Kissinger had enjoyed during the crisis.

Performance of the WSAG

The decision-making process during the Yom Kippur War is widely regarded as being of high quality, and the WSAG as the key decisional unit deserves much of the credit. To what extent, however, does this positive impression of the process relate to the positive outcome of the crisis, which was, of course, highly favourable to U.S. interests? By the end of the war, the United States had emerged as the principal mediator in the Arab-Israeli conflict and Kissinger as the architect of the soon-to-be famous step-by-step diplomacy. The Soviets, meanwhile, were relegated to the sidelines of Middle East diplomacy and lost their credibility in the eyes of many in the Arab world. Surely this remarkable success must be linked to a successful decision-making process? The WSAG was convened regularly throughout the war and the atmosphere in the meetings was generally conducive to successful discussions. Quandt portrays a particularly collegial atmosphere during the meetings: 'Schlesinger was a fairly casual guy. He would often be seen with his feet on the table in the Situation Room reading the *Funny Papers* or something; Kissinger would walk in and make some kind of a joke, there'd be a little bit of banter, and then Kissinger would take charge and say "here is what we need to do."'[140]

Nevertheless, the two most important decisions – the airlift to Israel and the DefCon alert – depict a different picture of decision-making. Rather than careful consideration of objectives and courses of action, they were characterised by manipulation and misjudgment of Washington's ability to control events (in the case of the airlift) and by overreaction and misreading of the situation (in the case of the alert). In addition, the two episodes suggest once again that Kissinger, and not the WSAG, often functioned as the key decision-making unit. This was more evident in the case of the airlift, in which Kissinger not only manipulated the Israelis but also his own bureaucracy, persuading the

[140] Interview with Quandt.

secretary of defense to take the blame in order to enhance Kissinger's prospects of achieving a cease-fire later on. Accordingly, the decision to delay the airlift did not result from a 'vigilant' decision-making process. It was instead the product of one man's desire to control events on the battlefield and bring the parties to the negotiating table at the most favourable position for successful diplomacy. Once Nixon personally intervened in the process, the bureaucracy acted with remarkable efficiency to deliver the arms to Israel in a timely fashion, thus suggesting that the implementation and monitoring of the decision was of high quality. Once again, this episode highlights the importance of personalities in shaping events beyond any structural settings which may be in place. When the stakes are particularly high and time to respond is limited, personal intuition will almost invariably take precedence over formal procedures of decision-making. Still, it is important to note that Nixon's intervention in the process raises another case of inconsistency between the theory and practice of U.S. foreign policy during the Nixon-Kissinger years. The theoretical design of the NSC system was intended to protect Nixon's time and energy. Given that on the single occasion during the crisis that Nixon *did* personally intervene in operational matters the results were impressive, one cannot help but question the extent to which the formalistic apparatus was a hindrance, rather than a facilitator, to effective decision-making. This book has suggested repeatedly that when Nixon and Kissinger used the system according to its original design, the process was rather smooth; when they ignored or bypassed it, the result was often bureaucratic dissent, poor decisions, and general chaos. Still, one should avoid making a causal link between the favourable outcome of the Yom Kippur War and a smooth decision-making process. As noted earlier, often a flawed process can produce a favourable outcome.

Decision-making during the 24–25 October meeting was understandably more complex than the airlift episode and thus merits a more detailed examination. While Kissinger described the meeting as 'one of the most thoughtful discussions that I attended in my government service,' it cannot be denied that the DefCon decision was the result of overreaction and misreading of Soviet actions.[141]

[141] Kissinger, *Crisis*, 349.

Although the group deliberated over the motivation behind Brezhnev's message, Kissinger failed to present to the group a fourth option, that Brezhnev might be bluffing, which was indeed the case. Still, the Americans were not alone in overreacting to unfolding events. In fact, Brezhnev personally inserted the paragraph on unilateral action in his message without discussing it with the Politburo. It seems that the Soviet leader overreacted to Sadat's urgent pleas for superpower intervention.[142] Still, given the time constraints and the general atmosphere of urgency during the WSAG meeting, combined with the lack of margin for error, the decision to view Brezhnev's threat as real seems compelling.

Judged more critically, however, one can see some serious flaws in the decision-making process during the 24-25 October meeting. An early task in any decision-making process is the setting of objectives. Haig recalls that Nixon told him before the meeting, 'You know what I want, Al . . . Words won't do the job. We've got to act.'[143] However, the president did not specify what he wanted. He did not give clear instructions to the group, and he certainly did not order Haig to put on the agenda the option of an increased alert. As Garthoff surmises, this 'rather remarkable, but extremely vague, instruction from the distraught and drunken president, was all the guidance his advisers had.'[144] This indicates less than an ideal start to any decision-making process, not least during the height of a superpower crisis. Furthermore, the group misread several actions taken by the Soviets which were actually designed to reduce the tension. Rather than reconsidering established perceptions of the Soviets and providing alternative explanations for their moves, the group was quick to impose its views on reality. Victor Israelyan, a Soviet diplomat during the war, contends that '[some] of the indicators were grossly exaggerated by the Americans. They did not give sufficient reason to suspect that the Soviet Union would intervene unilaterally.'[145] These indicators included, among others, the termination of the Soviet airlift on 24 October, an alert in several Soviet airborne divisions, the detection

---

[142] See Israelyan's remarks in B. Reich, 'Crisis Management,' in Parker, *The October War*, 224–225; Lebow and Stein, *We All Lost the Cold War*, 245–246.

[143] Haig, *Inner Circles*, 416.

[144] Garthoff, *Détente and Confrontation*, 426.

[145] Israelyan's remark in Reich, 'Crisis Management,' in Parker, *The October War*, 225.

of ten Soviet transport planes en route to Egypt, and an increase in the number of Soviet ships in the Mediterranean.[146] Indeed, these indicators, combined with Brezhnev's letter, all seemed to point to only one scenario: a Soviet decision to intervene unilaterally to save the Arabs from a humiliating defeat. However, a more careful examination of these indicators during the meeting could have led to a different scenario: Brezhnev indeed ordered to terminate the Soviet airlift, but his intention was to signal to Washington his willingness to cooperate. The alert to Soviet airborne divisions had been in place throughout the war and, according to Secretary Schlesinger, had been known for at least five or six days before the arrival of Brezhnev's letter. The small group of Antonov transport planes destined to Egypt was actually carrying cargo rather than troops. The Soviet naval presence in the Mediterranean did not include any aircraft carriers, which were required to deliver credible support, and in any event could not seriously threaten the mighty U.S. Sixth Fleet already present in the region. Even Brezhnev's ultimatum ('we should be faced with the necessity urgently to consider the question of taking appropriate steps unilaterally') did not necessarily indicate that military action was at the forefront of Soviet thinking.[147]

One parameter which certainly contributed to the overall smooth (albeit imperfect) decision-making process was the high quality of intelligence which was available to the group. As Secretary Schlesinger later revealed, the group 'had splendid current intelligence regarding military activities of Egypt and Syria. The collection was excellent.'[148] Thus, whereas during the crises of Cambodia, Jordan, and India-Pakistan, the decision-making process was routinely impinged by faulty or incomplete intelligence, here the group was supported by accurate and timely information, as William Quandt confirms:

We had very good technical sources, we saw all the buildups, we monitored the alert status . . . We had near to real-time satellites; one of them was called the *KH-11*, it would orbit over the region and eject a capsule that had to be

[146] Kissinger, *Crisis*, 349, 352; Golan, 'The Soviet Union and the Yom Kippur War,' 144.

[147] Garthoff, *Détente and Confrontation*, 424–425; Golan, 'The Soviet Union and the Yom Kippur War,' 144–146.

[148] Schlesinger, 'The Airlift,' 153.

picked up and rushed to the lab and developed. So there would be maybe a time lag of maybe half an hour between the time the picture was taken and the time we could see it unfolding on a TV screen... We would have a briefing in the morning on the Golan Heights and we could see the destroyed Syrian tanks. Battlefield resources were fine... We were very good at monitoring the Soviet airlift, we didn't know what was inside but we knew what the capacity was. We would do a daily tally of how many tons of equipment they were sending, at least theoretically.[149]

However, good intelligence alone cannot guarantee good decisions. The group failed to interpret, or at least consider, Soviet actions as anything other than tantamount to a prelude to unilateral military action. Indeed, the integration of new information into the decision-making process was rather poor throughout the war, starting with the failure to understand the Arabs' motives and their refusal to accept a cease-fire during the first week of the fighting. There was also a blind faith in Israel's ability to withstand the onslaught and turn defeat into victory despite the high number of casualties and loss of arms. There was also self-delusion about the willingness of the belligerents to accept the conditions of the Moscow agreement despite the intractable situation on the battlefield. Still, the failure to assimilate information during the crisis (combined with the other flaws mentioned previously) did not prevent an overall favourable outcome to U.S. interests at the end of the war. The immediate explanation for this seemingly contradictory conclusion is that events and outcomes are never determined by the actions of one side only. This is particularly true in this case, in which American decisions were largely taken in response to events on the battlefield between Israel, Egypt, and Syria, as well as the actions of the Soviet Union. The DefCon alert alone did not end the Yom Kippur War, just as American actions alone cannot be blamed for failing to secure a cease-fire during the first week of the war. 'Things are in the saddle,' the American diplomat George Ball famously quoted from Ralph Waldo Emerson during the Vietnam War, 'and ride mankind.'[150] Nixon and Kissinger were certainly fortunate that things turned in their favour to produce a most propitious outcome at the end of the Yom Kippur War.

---

[149] Interview with Quandt.
[150] G. W. Ball, *The Past Has Another Pattern: Memoirs* (New York: W. W. Norton & Company, 1982), 395.

The outbreak of the war and the early stages of the fighting tested two of the administration's major preconceptions in relation to the Middle East. First, as long as Israel maintained its military qualitative superiority in the region, the Arabs would not dare to change the status quo by going to war. Second, in the event of war, a swift Israeli victory would follow. The American administration was proved wrong on both counts. Nevertheless, it adapted remarkably well to the new realities. While the decision-making process during the war was far from perfect, it must be considered a successful one given the fact that for the most part, the crisis was run with a distraught, crippled, and possibly drunk president. Strictly speaking, Nixon was not part of the decision-making process.

On the surface, Nixon's behaviour during the Yom Kippur War was not substantially different from his conduct in other crises: He rarely 'reached down' for information or engaged in thoughtful discussions with his top advisors. The NSC was rarely convened, and when it did, it functioned as a discussion body rather than a decision-making body. During the Yom Kippur War, however, and for the first time in their partnership, the fundamental balance of power of the Nixon-Kissinger dyad had been altered. While in previous crises, Kissinger would report back to Nixon and seek his approval before taking important decisions, or took specific instructions from the president and forced them upon the bureaucracy, here Kissinger managed almost single-handedly the most serious crisis during the Nixon administration, making important decisions without prior consultation with the president or with a presidential carte blanche to make decisions on his behalf. Kissinger's unique position as the secretary of state and the national security advisor put him in a most opportune position to control the bureaucracy while still enjoying the confidence of the president. This certainly helped to produce a smoother and more coordinated decision-making process. Ultimately, during the Yom Kippur War, Henry Kissinger himself embodied the structure *and* process of U.S. foreign policy making. This is not to suggest, however, that the advisory system did not matter during the crisis. A collegial system, for example, which requires presidential engagement on a more regular basis, could not have worked as well for a president preoccupied by Watergate. The formalistic system, on the other hand, did protect Nixon's time and required his intervention only once during the crisis and in the most exceptional circumstances. In any event, a president cannot rely on a single style of management to produce an effective decision-making process. Invariably, the president may rely on various management strategies and tactics to get the job done. Particularly during the Yom Kippur War, with a detached and distressed president, it was important to have an effective advisory system which did not require constant presidential engagement with the process. Still, the airlift and the DefCon alert decisions suggest that ultimately in the structures–processes–personalities tripartite, the latter may take precedence in directing foreign policy, particularly during the height of crises.

Conclusion

> The NSC system will not work unless the President makes it work. After all, this system was created to serve the President of the United States in ways of his choosing. By his actions, by his leadership, the President therefore determines the quality of its performance.[1]
>
> The Tower Commission, 1987

The Tower Commission was appointed more than a decade after President Nixon had resigned from office. The individuals under its investigation and the nature of their operations had seemingly little in common with the Nixon-Kissinger system of foreign policy making. However, the observations and recommendations of the Tower Commission – appointed by President Reagan to investigate the rogue operations conducted by NSC staff during the Iran-Contra affair – transcend the immediate experience of the Reagan administration, or indeed any other specific case of presidential mismanagement of the NSC and the advisory system. The observations made here about the workings of the WSAG, and more broadly about the nature of the relationship among structures, processes, and personalities in U.S. foreign policy crisis decision-making, should serve as a reminder to future presidents that procedures are meant to serve purposes. They

---

[1] K. F. Inderfurth and L. K. Johnson, *Fateful Decisions*, 313. Reprinted from *Report of the President's Special Review Board (Tower Commission)*, *Washington, DC (26 February 1987)*.

are not ends in themselves. An advisory group cannot determine the course of a crisis, nor can it shape its outcome. It requires presidential guidance and leadership, and when the leader is incapacitated due to emotional turbulence or physical exhaustion, it either fails to performs its tasks adequately or it must rely on an executive surrogate to fill in the vacuum of authority. The diverse patterns of use and misuse of the WSAG in four international crises serve to illustrate the conclusion of the Tower Commission: It worked better when the president, via his national security advisor, let it work. The handling of the Jordanian Crisis was exemplary, despite some intelligence lapses. On the other hand, the management of the Cambodian and India-Pakistan crises showed that when the group did not receive adequate presidential support and guidance, it failed to do its job, and its meetings epitomised the worst cases of bureaucratic politics. This does not suggest, however, that the group (or the NSC machinery as a whole) was incapable of performing according to its original design. Rather, it shows that the president used it only as far as it could support his intuition. Once the bureaucracy began questioning the merit in invading Cambodia or in supporting Pakistan, the input of the WSAG was rendered inconsequential. The case of the Yom Kippur War tells a rather similar story. After the uncertainty of the first days, the group began to view the crisis in accordance with Nixon's priorities and helped to produce, by Kissinger's admission, the best-run crisis since Nixon entered office.

By their actions, leaders give meaning to theoretical structures of foreign policy, their psychological characteristics invariably dictate the priorities and principles of decision-making. The purpose of the advisory system is wholly utilitarian, and its worth necessarily depends on the extent and nature of its use by the president. In assessing the workings of the WSAG, one must remember that the group's main function was to develop policy options for the president. By misusing the group, the president must bear the ultimate responsibility for the trajectory of any crisis management. Thus, rather than blaming bureaucratic dissent as a primary cause for the poor handling of the India-Pakistan War, for example, one must first look at the reasons for this dissent to explain the flawed decision-making process.

In theoretical terms, the WSAG was a novelty, a deliberate attempt to provide dedicated crisis management machinery for the administration. The group's membership reflected this: No one was deliberately omitted from its meetings – at least on paper – for petty personal or bureaucratic reasons. Moreover, following his nomination as secretary of state in 1973, Kissinger elevated the membership of the Defense Department in WSAG meetings to a secretary level to ensure equal weight between the departments in the forum. The group's design suggested a solution to the perils of *groupthink* while highlighting the benefits of *multiple advocacy*. Its nominal superiority in the NSC hierarchy serves further to emphasise the importance of the findings in this book about the nature of the relationship between Nixon and Kissinger on the one hand and the advisory system during international crises on the other. Understanding the functionality of the WSAG and the constraints placed on it by the personal characteristics of the president and his national security advisor is thus important for broadening our knowledge of the machinery of crisis during the Nixon-Kissinger years.

Some general lessons about foreign policy making and crisis management can be drawn beyond the immediate experience of the Nixon administration. Three thematic observations come to mind: (1) the central role of the president in determining the effectiveness of the advisory process, (2) the inevitable variance between theoretical designs of foreign policy systems and the practicalities of foreign policy making, and (3) the fit of the Nixon-Kissinger system in the lineage of the NSC as the coordinating body of national security.

In making foreign policy, Richard Nixon repeatedly eschewed direct involvement in the formal decision-making process whenever possible. Rather than reaching down for information or actively engaging in lengthy deliberations with the NSC advisory forum, he preferred to rely on his gut feelings and ad hoc consultations with Henry Kissinger. While this pattern is rather unique to other cases of presidential management, it nevertheless suggests that the president's management style has a direct bearing on the performance of the NSC system. Although presidential involvement does not guarantee a successful result at the end of the process, visible presidential leadership and clear guidance to the principals of the system can reduce the likelihood of misapprehensions and some aspects of bureaucratic politics. More than any other factor, the president bears the ultimate responsibility for the organisation and operation of the NSC system. 'The Buck Stops Here,' read the famous sign on President Truman's desk in the White House. Regrettably, he did not leave it there for President Nixon to read.

There is, of course, no magical formula to produce an effective NSC structure which generates an optimal process of foreign policy making. While presidential involvement is essential, a desirable level of engagement cannot be readily quantified. Nevertheless, it is evident that Nixon's style of management failed to produce a consistently effective mechanism to manage crises. Nixon's style was unique, but it proved just as flawed as other patterns of presidential management. President Carter's excessive micro-management of the policy-making process failed to balance basic notions of presidential leadership, and was surpassed in its inefficiency perhaps only by President Reagan's lax management of the foreign policy machine. These presidents failed to strike the right balance between close engagement with the process and effective delegation of responsibilities.

This failure can be largely explained by the inevitable gap between theoretical designs of foreign policy systems and the realities of policy making, particularly during international crises. Upon entering the White House, the president often faces a dilemma between pursuing the 'best policy' and the 'most doable' policy. While in theory, producing the best policy at the end of the decision-making process is always desirable, practical constraints of time, information, and organisational behaviour may force the president to settle for less. These obstacles are particularly acute during times of crisis. Thus, while in theory the Nixon-Kissinger system was designed to minimise potential human and organisational flaws through clearly defined and highly structured procedures, human imperfections eventually prevailed. Ironically, the chief source of those imperfections was Nixon and Kissinger's psychological make-up which was characterised by suspicion, mistrust, and a rather dogmatic view of world affairs and America's role in them. Furthermore, more objective constraints of incomplete intelligence (particularly during the Cambodia and India-Pakistan crises) and the fast pace of events (during the Jordanian Crisis and the Yom Kippur War) naturally made the task of making hard decisions in real time more complicated. Still, the additional bureaucratic and institutional chaos which accompanied some of the phases of crisis decision-making were the direct result of Nixon and Kissinger's inability to get their underlings to buy into their approach to foreign policy making.

These observations need to be examined against the broader context of NSC lineage and the role of the national security advisor in foreign policy making. The NSC's ultimate function is to serve as the president's principal forum for considering national security and foreign policy matters and to coordinate them among the relevant federal agencies. It is a dynamic mechanism which allows the president to structure and use it according to his personal preferences. This explains the substantial deviation in NSC structures and procedures between different administrations, which in itself points to an interesting pattern of policy learning in the development of the NSC. Henry Kissinger designed a system which combined positive elements of the Eisenhower and Johnson administrations, while eliminating their less desirable features. President Carter wished to turn away from the Kissinger system of a powerful national security advisor. However, like Nixon, Carter soon experienced the gap between theoretical designs and practical necessities of the foreign policy machinery, and soon his national security advisor, Zbigniew Brzezinski, was superseded only by Kissinger in terms of sheer power and influence. The dual pattern of active learning from history and the inevitable divergence between theory and practice in U.S. foreign policy making repeated itself in the Reagan administration. While initially the system centred around the secretary of state as chief foreign policy advisor, Reagan's almost negligent management style resulted in an incredible turnover of no less than six national security advisors during his two terms in office. Eventually, the chaos in the administration led to the proactive involvement of NSC staff in the covert and illegal actions of the Iran-Contra affair. Incredibly, despite Reagan's intention to decentralise the role of the national security advisor, the pattern of an operational NSC staff which began during the Nixon-Kissinger years reached unprecedented heights during the Reagan administration and involved independent and illegal operations away from the eyes of Congress, Cabinet members, and even the president. Similar patterns of adjustment of the original design of the foreign policy apparatus to accommodate unfolding events and changes of national priorities are evident in subsequent administrations, most recently with Condoleezza Rice, who, like Kissinger (though by no means on par with his sheer power over the overall system), made the short trip from the NSC to the state department, marginalising Secretary of State Colin Powell along the way, with the active support of President George W. Bush. However, this does not necessarily suggest that attempts to ameliorate NSC systems or the functionality of the national security advisor are invariably futile. The experience of the George H. W. Bush administration is encouraging in this respect. As vice president to Ronald Reagan, Bush undoubtedly learned from the management mistakes of his president, and successfully combined formalistic and collegial elements in his NSC system. The success of this system was aided by the highly effective and closely knit group of advisors, most of whom had worked together in previous Republican administrations. Perhaps the most meaningful factor which contributed to the generally smooth working of the NSC machinery in that administration was the role played by Brent Scowcroft, Bush's national security advisor. Scowcroft's experience as deputy to Kissinger in the NSC between 1973 and 1975 and then as national security advisor to President Ford between 1975 and 1977 (while Kissinger served as secretary of state), as well as his service on the Tower Commission, which investigated the flawed NSC procedures in the 1980s, certainly helped him to understand his duties better and to perform his job more effectively once the administration was confronted with a serious international crisis (the first Gulf War in 1991). Most important, Scowcroft understood his role as ultimately one of coordination rather than action. Thus, while Kissinger epitomised the role of the national security advisor as an agent of policy, Scowcroft came closest to the original job description, that of an honest broker.

In applying a case-study approach to four international crises during the Nixon administration, this book sought to improve our understanding of the linkage among structures, processes, and personalities within the context of foreign policy crisis decision-making. In the process, some important points about the gap between the theory and practice of foreign policy making were raised. More specifically, it examined how decisions are made and constrained during international crises. Still, a number of issues have emerged in this book which were not part of the original research design but nevertheless deserve to be examined in future research on contemporary U.S. foreign policy and crisis decision-making.

First, while this book examined the linkage between structure and process in crisis decision-making, it deliberately eschewed incorporating into the analysis the moot assumption about causality between 'high-quality' process and 'high-quality' crisis outcome. This assumption is problematic on methodological and epistemological grounds. While the merit in quantifying foreign policy decisions remains questionable (certainly when large portions of data remain unavailable), this question is important in potentially enhancing our understanding of what makes a certain process superior to others. However, like the divergence being the planning and making of U.S. foreign policy, one should be wary of the gap between the theoretical appeal of such inquiries and the potentially clumsy implementation of these designs. Second, the issue of simultaneous crises needs to be addressed as a unique type of crisis management. For example, the autumn of crises of 1970 (in Jordan, Chile, and Cienfuegos) stretched the foreign policy machinery beyond its limits, to the extent that the WSAG was removed from the decision-making process over Cienfuegos in order to 'de-crisis' the institutional crisis atmosphere.[2] Similarly, any analysis of the management of the Yom Kippur War can not be separated from the debilitating effects of the Watergate crisis, which decisively changed the balance of power between Nixon and Kissinger. Other contemporary examples include the Iranian revolution, the Soviet invasion of Afghanistan, and the Iran hostage crisis, which engulfed the Carter administration in 1979, or the desperate efforts of President George W. Bush to handle two foreign adventures in Iraq and Afghanistan for the most part of his two terms in office. Simultaneous crises are characterised by certain dynamics which have a greater potential to hinder the decision-making process, as levels of stress and uncertainty are likely to be higher than during 'normal' single crises. Accounting for these constraining effects is therefore pertinent to our understanding of these surprisingly common situations. Finally, it is vital that we extrapolate lessons from this study and others about the making of foreign policy during international crises in other polities than the United States. Power structures in other western democracies may be less hierarchical and more fragmented and thus will invariably produce different behaviours of crisis management. Similarly, a study of crisis management in nondemocratic

---

[2] For a comprehensive account of the management of the Cienfuegos Crisis, see A. Siniver, 'The Nixon Administration and the Cienfuegos Crisis of 1970: Crisis Management of a Non-Crisis?,' *Review of International Studies*, 34:1 (January 2008), 69–88.

regimes may yield interesting comparable observations about the importance of personalities in shaping and driving foreign policy agendas. These comparisons can then be extended to the previous points raised here about the management of simultaneous crises and, perhaps less tangibly, about the linkage between process quality and process outcome. For example, can we hypothesise about the possible antecedents which make some regime types more equipped than others to develop effective structures and processes of crisis management?

In conclusion, turning to methodological issues, to this date, despite the recent and frequent releases of archival material regarding various aspects of the Nixon administration, comprehensive accounts of other crises remain elusive, most pertinently the minutes of WSAG meetings during other international crises. It is therefore likely that upon the release of additional classified documents, our understanding of the workings of the WSAG and its fit into the broader apparatus of the Nixon-Kissinger system will be greatly enhanced. As this book has demonstrated, the lessons learned from this particular experience are valuable broader comparative and contemporary studies of the making of foreign policy during international crises.

Bibliography

Interviews

William B. Quandt, 26 August 2004. Charlottesville, VA.
Helmut Sonnenfeldt, 13 August 2004. Brookings Institution, Washington, DC.

Unpublished Sources

Nixon Presidential Materials Project, College Park, MD
    National Security Council Files (NSCF):
        Country Files
        Henry A. Kissinger Office Files
    National Security Council Institutional Files (NSCIF):
        Meeting Files
        Minutes of Meeting Files
        Miscellaneous Files of the Nixon Administration
    White House Central Files (WHCF):
        Subject Files FG
Lyndon Baines Johnson Presidential Library, Austin, TX
    National Security Files (NSF):
        Walt Rostow Files
    Personal Papers:
        Papers of William C. Westmoreland
National Archives, London
    FCO 15
    FCO 51
    PREM 13
    PREM 15

Miller Center of Public Affairs, Charlottesville, VA
    Nixon White House Tapes

U.S. Government Published Sources

Foreign Relations of the United States (Washington, DC: Government Printing Office):
    1969–1976: Volume I: Foundations of Foreign Policy, 1969–1972
    1969–1976: Volume XI: South Asia Crisis, 1971
Public Papers of the Presidents of the United States (Washington, DC: Government Printing Office):
    Richard Nixon, 1970

Microforms

Declassified Document Reference System (DDRS)

Internet Sources

Center for International Security Studies at Maryland and the Brookings Institution, *The National Security Council Project: Oral History Roundtable*
    'The Nixon Administration National Security Council'
    'The Role of the National Security Advisor'
The National Security Archive website, George Washington University

Books and Edited Chapters

Aaronson, S., *Conflict and Bargaining in the Middle East: An Israeli Perspective* (Baltimore: Johns Hopkins University Press, 1978).
Aitken, J., *Nixon: A Life* (Washington, DC: Regency Publishing, 1993).
Allen, L., *OPEC Oil* (Cambridge, MA: Oelgeschlager, Gunn & Hain, 1979).
Allison, G., *Essence of Decision: Explaining the Cuban Missile Crisis* (Boston: Little, Brown, 1971).
Allison, G., and Halperin, M. H., 'Bureaucratic Politics: A Paradigm and Some Policy Implications,' in Tanter, R., and Ullman, R. H. (eds.), *Theory and Policy in International Relations* (Princeton, NJ: Princeton University Press, 1972), 40–80.
Ambrose, S. E., *Nixon: The Education of a Politician, 1913–1962* (New York: Simon & Schuster, 1987).
―――, *Nixon: The Triumph of a Politician, 1962–1972* (London: Simon & Schuster, 1989).
―――, *Nixon: Ruin and Recovery, 1973–1990* (New York: Simon & Schuster, 1991).
Anderson, J., with Clifford, G., *The Anderson Papers* (New York: Random House, 1973).

Armstrong, J. S., *Long-Range Forecasting* (New York: John Wiley, 1985).

Arrow, K., *Social Choices and Individual Values* (New Haven, CT: Yale University Press, 1970, 2nd ed.).

Ball, G. W., *The Past Has Another Pattern: Memoirs* (New York: W. W. Norton & Company, 1982).

Barber, J. D., *The Presidential Character: Predicting Performance in the White House* (Englewood Cliffs, NJ: Prentice Hall, 1972).

Bar-Joseph, U., *The Watchman Fell Asleep: The Surprise of Yom Kippur and Its Sources* (New York: State University of New York Press, 2005).

Bavly, D., *Dreams and Missed Opportunities, 1967–1973* (Jerusalem: Carmel, 2002).

Bell, C., *The Diplomacy of Détente: The Kissinger Era* (New York: St. Martin's Press, 1977).

Blum, J. M., *Years of Discord: American Politics and Society, 1961–1976* (New York: W. W. Norton & Company, 1991).

Brandon, H., *The Retreat of American Power* (New York: Doubleday, 1973).

Brecher, M., *The Foreign Policy of Israel: Setting, Images, Process* (London: Oxford University Press, 1972).

———, *Decisions in Israel's Foreign Policy* (London: Oxford University Press, 1974).

Brecher, M., with Geist, B. (eds.), *Decisions in Crisis: Israel, 1967 and 1973* (Berkeley: University of California Press, 1980).

Brodie, F. M., *Richard Nixon: The Shaping of His Character* (New York: W. W. Norton & Company, 1981).

Brown, S., *The Faces of Power: Constancy and Change in United States Foreign Policy from Truman to Reagan* (New York: Columbia University Press, 1983).

Bundy, W., *A Tangled Web: The Making of Foreign Policy in the Nixon Administration* (New York: Hill and Wang, 1998).

Burke, J. P., *The Institutional Presidency: Organizing and Managing the White House from FDR to Clinton* (Baltimore: Johns Hopkins University Press, 2000, 2nd ed.).

Chopra, P., *India's Second Liberation* (Delhi: Vikas Publishing House, 1973).

Colodny, L., and Getlin, R., *Silent Coup: The Removal of Richard Nixon* (London: Victor Gollancz, 1991).

Crabb, C. V., and Mulchay, K. V., *Presidential and Foreign Policy Making: From FDR to Reagan* (Baton Rouge: Louisiana State University Press, 1986).

Crowley, M., *Nixon in Winter: The Final Revelations* (New York: I. B. Tauris, 1998).

Dallek, R., *Nixon and Kissinger: Partners in Power* (New York: Harpers-Collins Publishers, 2007).

Dayan, M., *Story of My Life* (London: Weidenfeld and Nicolson, 1978).

DeGregorio, W. A., *The Complete Book of U.S. Presidents: From George Washington to Bill Clinton* (New York: Wings Books, 1996, 5th ed.).

de Rivera, J., *The Psychological Dimension of Foreign Policy* (Columbus, OH: Charles E. Merrill, 1968).

Destler, I. M., Gelb, L. H., and Lake, A., *Our Own Worst Enemy: The Unmaking of American Foreign Policy* (New York: Simon & Schuster, 1984).

Dickson, P. W., *Kissinger and the Meaning of History* (Cambridge: Cambridge University Press, 1978).

Dobrynin, A., *In Confidence: Moscow's Ambassador to America's Six Cold War Presidents* (New York: Times Books, 1995).

Dowty, A., *Middle East Crisis: U.S. Decision-Making in 1958, 1970, and 1973* (Berkeley: University of California Press, 1984).

Dumbrell, J., *The Making of U.S. Foreign Policy* (Manchester: Manchester University Press, 1997, 2nd ed.).

Dunnigan, J., and Nofi, A., *Victory and Deceit: Dirty Tricks at War* (New York: William Morrow and Company, 1995).

Dupy, T. N., *Elusive Victory: The Arab-Israeli Wars, 1947–1974* (Iowa: Kendall and Hunt Publishing Co., 1992).

Eban, A., *An Autobiography* (Tel Aviv: Sifriat Maariv, 1978).

Eckstein, H., 'Case Study and Theory in Political Science,' in Greenstein, F. I., and N. W. Polsby (eds.), *Handbook of Political Science* (Reading, MA: Addison-Wesley, 1975), 79–138.

Ehrlichman, J., *Witness to Power: The Nixon Years* (New York: Simon & Schuster, 1982).

Eisenhower, D. D., *The White House Years: Waging Peace, 1956–1961* (London: Heinemann, 1965).

Emery, F., *Watergate: The Corruption of American Politics and the Fall of Richard Nixon* (New York: Times Books, 1994).

Feldman, H., *The End and the Beginning: Pakistan 1969–1971* (Oxford: Oxford University Press, 1975).

Fiske, S., and Taylor, S., *Social Cognition* (New York: McGraw-Hill, 1991).

Frankel, J., *The Making of Foreign Policy: An Analysis of Decision-Making* (London: Oxford University Press, 1963).

Freedman, R. O., *Soviet Policy toward the Middle East since 1970* (New York: Praeger, 1982, 3rd ed.).

Fuller, S., and Aldag, R., 'Challenging the Mindguards: Moving Small Group Analysis beyond Groupthink,' in Hart, P. t', Stern, E. K., and Sundelius, B. (eds.), *Beyond Groupthink: Political Group Dynamics and Foreign Policy-Making* (Ann Arbor: University of Michigan Press, 1997), 55–94.

The Gallup Poll: Public Opinion, 1935–1971 (New York: Random House, 1972).

Garrison, J. A., *Games Advisors Play: Foreign Policy in the Nixon and Carter Administrations* (College Station: Texas A&M University Press, 1999).

Garthoff, R. L., *Detente and Confrontation: American-Soviet Relations from Nixon to Reagan* (Washington, DC: The Brookings Institution, 1994, rev. ed.).

George, A. L., *Presidential Decisionmaking in Foreign Policy: The Effective Use of Information and Advice* (Boulder, CO: Westview Press, 1980).

―――, 'Case Studies and Theory Development: The Method of Structured, Focused Comparison,' in Lauren, P. (ed.), *Diplomacy: New Approaches in History, Theory, and Practice* (New York: Free Press, 1979), 43–68.

Gergen, D., *Eyewitness to Power: The Essence of Leadership, Nixon to Clinton* (New York: Simon & Schuster, 2000).

Geva, N., and Minz, A. (eds.), *Decision Making on War and Peace: The Cognitive-Rational Debate* (Boulder, CO: Lynne Rienner Press, 1997).

Glassman, J. D., *Arms for the Arabs: The Soviet Union and War in the Middle East* (Baltimore: Johns Hopkins University Press, 1975).

Golan, M., *The Secret Conversations of Henry Kissinger: Step-by-Step Diplomacy in the Middle East* (New York: Quadrangle, 1976).

Graubard, S., *Kissinger: Portrait of a Mind* (New York: Norton, 1973).

Gromyko, A., *Memories* (London: Hutchinson, 1989).

Haig, A. M., with McCarry, C., *Inner Circles: How America Changed the World, A Memoir* (New York: Warner Books, 1992).

Haldeman, H. R., with DiMona, J., *The Ends of Power* (New York: Times Books, 1978).

―――, *The Haldeman Diaries: Inside Nixon's White House* (New York: G. P. Putnam's Sons, 1994).

Halfon, M., *From War to Peace: The Peace Course between Egypt and Israel, 1970–1979* (Tel Aviv: Hakibbutz Hameuchad, 2002).

Hall, D. K., 'The Laotian War of 1962 and the Indo-Pakistani War of 1971,' in Blechman, B. M., and Kaplan, S. (eds.), *Force without War: U.S. Armed Forces as a Political Instrument* (Washington, DC: Brookings Institution, 1978), 135–221.

Halperin, M. H., *Bureaucratic Politics and Foreign Policy* (Washington, DC: Brookings Institution, 1971).

Haney, P. J., *Organizing for Foreign Policy Crises: Presidents, Advisers, and the Management of Decision Making* (Ann Arbor: University of Michigan Press, 2002).

―――, 'Structure and Process in the Analysis of Foreign Policy Crises,' in Neack, L., Hey, J., and Haney, P. J. (eds.), *Foreign Policy Analysis: Continuity and Change in Its Second Generation* (Englewood Cliffs, NJ: Prentice Hall, 1995), 99–116.

Hanhimaki, J., *The Flawed Architect: Henry Kissinger and American Foreign Policy* (New York: Oxford University Press, 2004).

Hart, P., Stern, E. K., and Sundelius, B. (eds.), *Beyond Groupthink: Political Group Dynamics and Foreign Policy-Making* (Ann Arbor: University of Michigan Press, 1997).

Heikal, M., *The Road to Ramadan* (New York: Ballantine Books, 1975).

Helms, R., *A Look over My Shoulder: A Life in the Central Intelligence Agency* (New York: Random House, 2003).

Hermann, C. F., 'International Crisis as a Situational Variable,' in Rosenau, J. N. (ed.), *International Politics and Foreign Policy: A Reader in Research and Theory* (New York: The Free Press, 1969, rev. ed.), 409–421.

Hersh, S., *The Price of Power: Kissinger in the Nixon White House* (New York: Summit Books, 1983).

Hess, G. R., *Presidential Decisions for War: Korea, Vietnam, and the Persian Gulf* (Baltimore: Johns Hopkins University Press, 2001).

Hess, S., *Organizing the Presidency* (Washington, DC: Brookings Institution Press, 1988, 2nd ed.).

Hitchens, C., *The Trial of Henry Kissinger* (London: Verso, 2001).

Hoff, J., *Nixon Reconsidered* (New York: Basic Books, 1994).

Holsti, O. R., 'Cognitive Dynamics and Images of the Enemy: Dulles and Russia,' in Finlay, D. J., Holsti, O. R., and Fagen, R. (eds.), *Enemies in Politics* (Chicago: Rand McNally, 1967), 25–96.

———, 'Crisis Decision Making,' in Tetlock, P. E., et al. (eds.), *Behaviour, Society, and Nuclear War*, vol. 1 (Oxford: Oxford University Press, 1989), 8–37.

———, 'Crisis Decision Making,' in Glad, B. (ed.), *Psychological Dimensions of War* (Beverly Hills, CA: Sage, 1999), 116–142.

Houghton, D. P., *U.S. Foreign Policy and the Iran Hostage Crisis* (Cambridge: Cambridge University Press, 2001).

Hudson, V. M., *Foreign Policy Analysis: Classic and Contemporary Theory* (Lanham, MD: Rowman & Littlefield, 2007).

Hult, K. M., 'Advising the President,' in Edwards, G. C., Kessel, J. H., and Rockman, B. (eds.), *Researching the Presidency: Vital Questions, New Approaches* (Pittsburgh, PA: Pittsburgh University Press, 1993), 111–160.

Inderfurth, K. F., and Johnson, L. K. *Fateful Decisions: Inside the National Security Council* (New York: Oxford University Press, 2004).

Isaacson, W., *Kissinger: A Biography* (London: Faber and Faber, 1992).

Israelyan, V., *Inside the Kremlin during the Yom Kippur War* (University Park: Pennsylvania State University Press, 1995).

Jackson, R., *South Asian Crisis: India – Pakistan – Bangla Desh* (London: Chatto and Windus, 1975).

Janis, I. L., *Groupthink: Psychological Studies of Policy Decisions and Fiascoes* (Boston: Houghton Mifflin, 1982, 2nd ed.).

———, *Crucial Decisions: Leadership in Policymaking and Crisis Management* (New York: The Free Press, 1989).

Janis, I. L., and Mann, L., *Decision Making: A Psychological Analysis of Conflict, Choice, and Commitment* (New York: The Free Press, 1977).

Jervis, R., *Perception and Misperception in International Politics* (Princeton, NJ: Princeton University Press, 1976).

Johnson, R. T., *Managing the White House: An Intimate Study of the Presidency* (New York: Harper & Row, 1974).

Kalb, M., and Kalb, B., *Kissinger* (Boston: Little Brown, 1974).

Khan, R., *The American Papers: Secret and Confidential India-Pakistan-Bangladesh Documents, 1965–1973* (Oxford: Oxford University Press, 2000).

Khong, Y. F., *Analogies at War: Korea, Munich, Dien Bien Phu, and the Vietnam Decisions of 1965* (Princeton, NJ: Princeton University Press, 1992).

Kimball, J., *Nixon's Vietnam War* (Lawrence: University Press of Kansas, 1998).

Kissinger, H., *A World Restored* (New York: Grosset & Dunlap, 1964).

———, 'Domestic Structure and Foreign Policy,' in Rosenau, J. N. (ed.), *International Politics and Foreign Policy: A Reader in Research and Theory* (New York: The Free Press, 1969, rev. ed.), 261–275.

———, *The White House Years* (London: Weidenfeld and Nicolson and M. Joseph, 1979).

———, *Years of Upheaval* (Boston: Little, Brown, 1982).

———, *Diplomacy* (New York: Simon & Schuster, 1994).

———, *Crisis: The Anatomy of Two Major Foreign Policy Crises* (New York: Simon & Schuster, 2003).

Kux, D., *India and the United States: Estranged Democracies, 1941–1991* (Washington, DC: National Defense University Press, 1993).

Landau, D., *Kissinger: The Uses of Power* (Boston: Houghton Mifflin, 1972).

Lebow, R. N., and Stein, J. G., *We All Lost the Cold War* (Princeton, NJ: Princeton University Press, 1994).

Leites, N., *The Operational Code of the Politburo* (New York: McGraw-Hill, 1951).

Leng, R. J., *Bargaining and Learning in Recurring Crises: The Soviet-American, Egyptian-Israeli and Indo-Pakistani Rivalries* (Ann Arbor: University of Michigan Press, 2000).

Mazlish, B., *Kissinger: The European Mind in American Policy* (New York: Basic Books, 1976).

Mazo, E., and Hess, S., *Nixon: A Political Portrait* (New York: Harper & Row, 1968).

McClelland, C. A., 'The Beginning, Duration, and Abatement of International Crises: Comparison in Two Conflict Arenas,' in Hermann, C. F. (ed.), *International Crises: Insights from Behavioural Research* (New York: The Free Press, 1972), 83–105.

———, 'Access to Berlin: The Quantity and Variety of Events, 1948–1963,' in Singer, D. J. (ed.), *Quantitative International Politics: Insights and Evidence* (New York: The Free Press, 1968), 159–186.

Mead, W. M., *Special Providence: American Foreign Policy and How It Changed the World* (New York: Routledge, 2002).

Meir, G., *My Life* (Jerusalem: Steimatzky's Agency, 1975).

Melman, Y., and Raviv, D., *Friends in Deed: Inside the U.S.-Israel Alliance* (New York: Hyperion, 1994).

Milburn, M. A., *Persuasion and Politics: The Social Psychology of Public Opinion* (Pacific Cove, CA: Brooks/Cole, 1991).

Morris, R., *Uncertain Greatness: Henry Kissinger and American Foreign Policy* (New York: Harper & Row, 1977).

Neustadt, R. E., *Presidential Power and the Modern Presidents* (New York: The Free Press, 1990).

Neustadt, R. E., and May, E. R., *Thinking in Time: The Use of History for Decision Makers* (New York: The Free Press, 1986).

Nicholas, M., and Oldenburg, P., *Bangladesh: The Birth of a Nation: A Handbook of Background Information and Documentary Sources* (Madras: M. Seshachalam and Company, 1972).

Nixon, R. M., *Six Crises* (New York: Doubleday & Company, 1969, 2nd ed.).

———, *RN: The Memoirs of Richard Nixon* (New York: Simon & Schuster, 1978).

Paul, T. V., *Asymmetric Conflicts: War Initiation by Weaker Powers* (Cambridge: Cambridge University Press, 1994).

Peters, G., *Comparative Politics, Theory, and Method* (New York: New York University Press, 1998).

Ponder, D. E., *Good Advice: Information & Policy Making in the White House* (College Station: Texas A&M University Press, 2000).

Powers, T., *The Man Who Kept the Secrets: Richard Helms and the CIA* (New York: Pocket Books, 1981).

Prados, J., *Keepers of the Keys: A History of the National Security Council from Truman to Bush* (New York: William Morrow and Co., 1991).

Preston, T., *The President and His Inner Circle: Leadership Style and the Advisory Process in Foreign Policy Making* (New York: Columbia University Press, 2001).

Quandt, W. B., *Decade of Decisions: American Policy toward the Arab-Israeli Conflict, 1967–1976* (Berkeley: University of California Press, 1977).

———, 'Lebanon, 1958, and Jordan, 1970,' in Blechman, B. M., and Kaplan, S. (eds.), *Force without War: U.S. Armed Forces as a Political Instrument* (Washington, DC: Brookings Institution, 1978), 222–288.

———, *Peace Process: American Diplomacy and the Arab-Israeli Conflict Since 1967* (Washington, DC: Brookings Institution, 2001, rev. ed.).

Rabin, Y., *The Rabin Memoirs* (Berkeley: University of California Press, 1996, 2nd ed.).

Reeves, R., *President Nixon: Alone in the White House* (New York: Touchstone, 2001).

Reich, B., 'Crisis Management,' in Parker, R. (ed.), *The October War: A Retrospective* (Gainesville: University of Florida Press, 2001).

Rosenau, J. N. (ed.), *International Politics and Foreign Policy: A Reader in Research and Theory* (New York: The Free Press, 1969, rev. ed.).

Rothkopf, D. J., *Running the World: A History of the National Security Council and the Architects of American Power* (New York: Public Affairs, 2005).

Sadat, A., *In Search of Identity* (London: Collins, 1978).

Sagan, S. D., *The Limits of Safety: Organizations, Accidents, and Nuclear Weapons* (Princeton, NJ: Princeton University Press, 1993).

Schlesinger, A. M., *The Imperial Presidency* (Boston: Houghton Mifflin, 1973).

Schulzinger, R., *Henry Kissinger: Doctor of Diplomacy* (New York: Columbia University Press, 1989).

Shawcross, W., *Sideshow: Kissinger, Nixon and the Destruction of Cambodia* (London: Andre Deutsch, 1979).

Sheehan, E., *The Arabs, Israelis, and Kissinger: A Secret History of American Diplomacy in the Middle East* (New York: Reader's Digest Press, 1976).

Simon, H., *Administrative Behavior* (New York: Macmillan, 1957).

———, *Models of Bounded Rationality* (Cambridge, MA: MIT Press, 1982).

Sisco, J., 'Nixon's Foreign Policy: The NSC and State Department,' in Thompson, K. (ed.), *The Nixon Presidency: Twenty-two Intimate Perspectives of Richard M. Nixon* (Lanham, MD: University Press of America, 1987), 391–413.

Small, M., *Johnson, Nixon and the Doves* (New Brunswick, NJ: Rutgers University Press, 1988).

———, *The Presidency of Richard Nixon* (Lawrence: University Press of Kansas, 1999).

Smith, B. K., *Organizational History of the National Security Council during the Kennedy and Johnson Administrations* (Washington, DC: National Security Council, 1988).

Snyder, G. H., and Diesing, P. (eds.), *Conflict among Nations: Bargaining, Decision Making, and System Structure in International Crises* (Princeton, NJ: Princeton University Press, 1977).

Snyder, R. C., Bruck, H. W., and Sapin, B. (eds.), *Foreign Policy Decision-Making* (New York: The Free Press, 1962).

Sonnenfeldt, H., 'Reconstructing the Nixon Foreign Policy,' in Thompson, K. (ed.), *The Nixon Presidency: Twenty-two Intimate Perspectives of Richard M. Nixon* (Lanham, MD: University Press of America, 1987), 315–334.

Sprout, H., and Sprout, M., *Man-Milieu Relationship Hypotheses in the Context of International Politics* (Princeton, NJ: Princeton University Press, 1956).

———, 'Environmental Factors in the Study of International Politics,' in Rosenau, J. N. (ed.), *International Politics and Foreign Policy: A Reader in Research and Theory* (New York: The Free Press, 1969, rev. ed.), 41–56.

Stein, J. G., 'The Failures of Deterrence and Intelligence,' in Parker, R. (ed.), *The October War: A Retrospective* (Gainesville: University of Florida Press, 2001), 79–152.

Stein, J. G., and Tanter, R., *Rational Decision Making: Israeli's Security Choices, 1967* (Columbus: Ohio State University Press, 1980).

Stein, K., *Heroic Diplomacy: Sadat, Kissinger, Carter, Begin, and the Quest for Arab-Israeli Peace* (New York: Routledge, 1999).

Steinbruner, J., *The Cybernetic Theory of Decision* (Princeton, NJ: Princeton University Press, 1974).

Stoessinger, J., *Henry Kissinger: The Anguish of Power* (New York: W. W. Norton, 1976).

Summers, A., *The Arrogance of Power: The Secret World of Richard Nixon* (New York: G. P. Putnam's Sons, 2000).

Suri, J., *Henry Kissinger and The American Century* (Cambridge, MA: Belknap Press of Harvard University Press, 2007).

Szulc, T., *The Illusion of Peace: Foreign Policy in the Nixon Years* (New York: Viking, 1978).

Tetlock, P. E., *Expert Political Judgement: How Good Is It? How Can We Know?* (Princeton, NJ: Princeton University Press, 2005).

Thornton, R. C., *The Nixon-Kissinger Years: The Reshaping of American Foreign Policy* (St. Paul, MN: Paragon House, 2001, 2nd ed.).

Verba, S., 'Assumptions of Rationality and Non-Rationality in Models of the International System,' in Rosenau, J. N. (ed.), *International Politics and Foreign Policy: A Reader in Research and Theory* (New York: The Free Press, 1969, rev. ed.), 217–231.

Viotti, P. R., *American Foreign Policy and National Security: A Documentary Record* (Upper Saddle River, NJ: Pearson, 2005).

Volkan, V. D., Itzkowitz, N., and Dodd, A. W., *Richard Nixon: A Psychobiography* (New York: Columbia University Press, 1997).

Weldes, J., *Constructing National Interests: The United States and the Cuban Missile Crisis* (Minneapolis: University of Minnesota Press, 1999).

Westmoreland, W. C., *A Soldier Reports* (New York: Doubleday & Co., 1976).

Wicker, T., *One of Us: Richard Nixon and the American Dream* (New York: Random House, 1991).

Witcover, J., *The Resurrection of Richard Nixon* (New York: G. P. Putnam's Sons, 1970).

Yetiv, S. A., *Explaining Foreign Policy: U.S. Decision-Making and the Persian Gulf War* (Baltimore: Johns Hopkins University Press, 2004).

Young, O., *The Intermediaries: Third Parties in International Crisis* (Princeton, NJ: Princeton University Press, 1967).

Zumwalt, E., *On Watch: A Memoir* (Arlington, VA: Admiral Zumwalt & Associates, 1976).

Articles

Aberbach, J. D., and Rockman, B. A., 'Clashing Beliefs within the Executive Branch: The Nixon Administration Bureaucracy,' *American Political Science Review*, 70:2 (1976), 456–468.

Achen, C., and Snidal, D., 'Rational Deterrence Theory and Comparative Case Studies,' *World Politics*, 41:2 (1989), 143–169.

Akins, J., 'The Oil Crisis: This Time the Wolf Is Here,' *Foreign Affairs*, 51:3 (1973), 462–490.

Allison, G., 'Conceptual Models and the Cuban Missile Crisis,' *American Political Science Review*, 63:3 (1969), 689–718.

Astorino-Courtois, A., 'Clarifying Decisions: Assessing the Impact of Decision Structures on Foreign Policy Choices During the 1970 Jordanian Civil War,' *International Studies Quarterly*, 42:4 (1998), 733–754.

Astorino-Courtois, A., and Trusty, B., 'Degrees of Difficulty: The Effect of Israeli Policy Shifts on Syrian Peace Decisions,' *Journal of Conflict Resolution*, 44:3 (2000), 359–377.

Axelrod, R., 'Argumentation in Foreign Policy Settings: Britain in 1918, Munich in 1938 and Japan in 1970,' *Journal of Conflict Resolution*, 21:4 (1977), 727–756.

Bar-Joseph, U., 'Israel's 1973 Intelligence Failure,' *Israel Affairs*, 6:1 (1999), 11–35.

Bendor, J., and Hammond, T. H., 'Rethinking Allison's Models,' *American Political Science Review*, 86:2 (1992), 301–322.

Breuning, M., 'The Role of Analogies and Abstract Reasoning in Decision-Making: Evidence from the Debate over Truman's Proposal for Development Assistance,' *International Studies Quarterly*, 47:2 (2003), 229–245.

Choudhury, G. W., 'Reflections on Sino-Pakistan Relations,' *Pacific Community*, 7:2 (1976), 248–270.

Destler, I. M., 'National Security Advice to U.S. Presidents: Some Lessons from Thirty Years,' *World Politics*, 29:2 (1977), 143–176.

Dinitz, S., 'The Yom Kippur War: Diplomacy of War and Peace,' *Israel Affairs*, 6:1 (1999), 104–126.

Farnham, B., 'Political Cognition and Decision-Making,' *Political Psychology*, 11:1 (1990), 83–111.

Garrison, J. A., 'Foreign Policymaking and Group Dynamics: Where We've Been and Where We're Going,' *International Studies Review*, 5:2 (2003), 155–202.

Gazit, M., 'Egypt and Israel – Was There a Peace Opportunity Missed in 1971?' *Journal of Contemporary History*, 32:1 (1997), 97–115.

George, A. L., 'The Case for Multiple Advocacy in Making Foreign Policy,' *American Political Science Review*, 66:3 (1972), 751–785.

George, A. L., and Stern, E. K., 'Harnessing Conflict in Foreign Policy Making: From Devil's to Multiple Advocacy,' *Presidential Studies Quarterly*, 33:3 (2002), 484–508.

Glad, B., and Link, M., 'President Nixon's Inner Circle of Advisers,' *Presidential Studies Quarterly*, 27:1 (1996), 13–40.

Golan, G., 'The Soviet Union and the Yom Kippur War,' *Israel Affairs*, 6:1 (1999), 127–152.

Halperin, M. H., 'The President and the Military,' *Foreign Affairs*, 50:2 (1972), 310–324.

Haney, P. J., 'Decision-Making during International Crises: A Reexamination,' *International Interactions*, 19:3 (1994), 177–191.

———, 'The Nixon Administration and Middle East Crises: Theory and Evidence of Presidential Management of Foreign Policy Decision Making,' *Political Research Quarterly*, 47:4 (1994), 939–959.

Hanhimaki, J., '"Dr. Kissinger" or "Mr. Henry"? Kissingerology, Thirty Years and Counting,' *Diplomatic History*, 27:5 (2003), 637–676.

Hart, P. 't, 'Symbols, Rituals and Power: The Lost Dimensions of Crisis Management,' *Journal of Contingencies and Crisis Management*, 1:2 (1993), 36–50.

Herek, G. M., Janis, I. L., and Huth, P., 'Decision Making during International Crises: Is Quality of Process Related to Outcome?' *Journal of Conflict Resolution*, 31:2 (1987), 203–226.

———, 'Quality of U.S. Decision-Making during the Cuban Missile Crisis: Major Errors in Welch's Reassessment,' *Journal of Conflict Resolution*, 33:3 (1989), 446–459.

———, 'What Decision Units Shape Foreign Policy: Individual, Group, or Bureaucracy?' *Policy Studies Journal*, Issue 3 (1974), 166–170.

Hermann, C. F., and Hermann, M. G., 'Who Makes Foreign Policy Decisions and How,' *International Studies Quarterly*, 33:4 (1989), 361–387.

Hermann, C. F., Stein, J. G., Sundelius, B., and Walker, S., 'Resolve, Accept, or Avoid: Effects of Group Conflict on Foreign Policy Decisions,' *International Studies Review*, 3:2 (2001), 133–168.

Hermann, M. G., and Preston, T., 'Presidents, Advisors and Foreign Policy: The Effect of Leadership Style on Executive Arrangements,' *Political Psychology*, 15:1 (1994), 75–96.

Hermann, M. G., and Hagan, J. D., 'International Decision Making: Leadership Matters,' *Foreign Policy*, No. 110 (1998), 124–137.

Hollis, M., and Smith, S., 'Roles and Reasons in Foreign Policy Decision Making,' *British Journal of Political Science*, 16:3 (1986), 269–286.

Houghton, D. P., 'Reinvigorating the Study of Foreign Policy Decision Making: Toward a Constructivist Approach,' *Foreign Policy Analysis*, 3:1 (2007), 24–45.

Hudson, V. M., 'Foreign Policy Analysis: Actor-Specific Theory and the Ground of International Relations,' *Foreign Policy Analysis*, 1:1 (2005), 1–30.

Israelyan, V., 'The October 1973 War: Kissinger in Moscow,' *Middle East Journal*, 49:2 (1995), 19–41.

Kahana, E., 'Early Warning versus Concept: The Case of the Yom Kippur War, 1973,' *Intelligence and National Security*, 17:2 (2002), 81–104.

Kaplan, R. D., 'Kissinger, Metternich and Realism,' *Atlantic Monthly*, 283 (1999), 72–81.

Kaplan, S., 'United States Aid and Regime Maintenance in Jordan, 1957–1973,' *Public Policy*, 23:2 (1975), 189–217.

Kinne, B. J., 'Decision Making in Autocratic Regimes: A Poliheuristic Perspective,' *International Studies Perspectives*, 5:1 (2005), 114–128.

Kissinger, H., 'The Viet Nam Negotiations,' *Foreign Affairs*, 47:2 (1969), 211–234.

Kohl, W., 'The Nixon-Kissinger Foreign Policy System and U.S.-Europe Relations,' *World Politics*, 28:1 (1975), 1–43.

Krasner, S. D., 'Are Bureaucracies Important? (Or Allison Wonderland),' *Foreign Policy*, Issue 7 (1972), 159–179.

Lijphart, A., 'The Comparable Cases Strategy in Comparative Research,' *Comparative Political Studies*, 8 (July 1975), 158–177.

Luttwak, E. N., and Laqueur, W., 'Kissinger & the Yom Kippur War,' *Commentary*, Issue 58 (1974), 33–40.

MacDonald, S., 'Hitler's Shadow: Historical Analogies and the Iraqi Invasion of Kuwait,' *Diplomacy & Statecraft*, 13:4 (2002), 29–59.

Maleki, A., 'Decision Making in Iran's Foreign Policy: A Heuristic Approach,' *Journal of Social Affairs*, 19:73 (2002), 39–53.

Maoz, Z., 'The Decision to Raid Entebbe: Decision Analysis Applied to Crisis Behavior,' *Journal of Conflict Resolution*, 25:4 (1981), 677–707.

McCauley, C., 'The Nature of Social Influence in Groupthink: Compliance and Internalization,' *Journal of Personality and Social Psychology*, 57:2 (1989), 250–260.

McConnell, J., and Kelley, A., 'Super-Power Naval Diplomacy: Lessons of the Indo-Pakistani Crisis 1971,' *Survival*, 15:6 (1973), 289–295.

McCormick, J. M., 'International Crises: A Note on Definition,' *Western Political Quarterly*, 31:3 (1978), 352–358.

Mintz, A., 'The Decision to Attack Iraq: A Noncompensatory Theory of Decision Making,' *Journal of Conflict Resolution*, 37:4 (1993), 595–618.

———, 'How Do Leaders Make Decisions? A Poliheuristic Perspective,' *Journal of Conflict Resolution*, 48:1 (2004), 3–13.

———, 'Applied Decision Analysis: Utilizing Poliheuristic Theory to Explain and Predict Foreign Policy and National Security Decisions,' *International Studies Perspectives*, 6:1 (2005), 94–98.

Mitchell, D., 'Centralizing Advisory Systems: Presidential Influence and the U.S. Foreign Policy Decision-Making Process,' *Foreign Policy Analysis*, 1:2 (2005), 181–206.

Parker, C., and Stern, E. K., "Blindsided? September 11 and the Origins of Strategic Surprise,' *Political Psychology*, 23 (2002), 601–630.

Pei, M., 'Lessons of the Past,' *Foreign Policy*, Issue 137 (2003), 52–55.

Pika, J. A., 'White House Boundary Roles: Marginal Men Amidst the Palace Guard,' *Presidential Studies Quarterly*, 16:4 (1986), 700–715.

Purkitt, H. E., and Dyson, J. W., 'The Role of Cognition in U.S. Foreign Policy toward Southern Africa,' *Political Psychology*, 7:3 (1986), 507–532.

Redd, S. B., 'The Influence of Advisers on Foreign Policy Decision Making,' *The Journal of Conflict Resolution*, 46:3 (2002), 335–364.

————, 'The Influence of Advisers and Decisions Strategies on Foreign Policy Choices: President Clinton's Decisions to Use Force in Kosovo,' *International Studies Perspectives*, 6:1 (2005), 129–150.

Reiter, D., 'Learning, Realism, and Alliances: The Weight of the Shadow of the Past,' *World Politics*, 46:4 (1994), 490–526.

Riker, W. H., 'The Political Psychology of Rational Choice Theory,' *Political Psychology*, 16:1 (1995), 23–44.

Schlesinger, J., 'The Airlift,' in Parker, R. (ed.), *The October War: A Retrospective* (Gainesville, FL: The University of Florida Press, 2001), 153–160.

Shafer, M., and Crichlow, S., 'The Process-Outcome Connection in Foreign Policy Decision-Making: A Quantitative Study Building on Groupthink,' *International Studies Quarterly*, 46:1 (2002), 45–68.

Shlaim, A., 'Failures in National Intelligence Estimates: The Case of the Yom Kippur War,' *World Politics*, 38:3 (1976), 348–380.

Simon, H., 'Rationality in Political Behavior,' *Political Psychology*, 16:1 (1995), 45–61.

Siniver, A.,'The Nixon Administration and the Cienfuegos Crisis of 1970: Crisis Management of a Non-Crisis?' *Review of International Studies*, 34:1 (2008), 69–88.

Smith, S., 'Allison and the Cuban Missile Crisis: A Review of the Bureaucratic Politics Model of Foreign Policy Decision Making,' *Millennium*, 19:1 (1980), 21–40.

Sprout, H., and Sprout, M., 'Environment Factors in the Study of International Politics,' *Journal of Conflict Resolution* 1:4 (1957), 309–328.

Stern, E. K., 'Crisis Studies and Foreign Policy Analysis: Insights, Synergies, and Challenges,' *International Studies Review*, 5:2 (2003), 155–202.

Van Hollen, C. 'The Tilt Policy Revisited: The Nixon-Kissinger Geopolitics and South Asia,' *Asian Survey*, 20:4 (1980), 339–361.

Walcott, C. E., and Hult, K., 'Organizing the White House: Structure, Environment and Organizational Governance,' *American Journal of Political Science*, 31:1 (1987), 109–126.

Warner, G., 'Nixon, Kissinger and the Breakup of Pakistan, 1971,' *International Affairs*, 81:5 (2005), 1097–1118.

Welch, D. A., 'Crisis Decision Making Reconsidered,' *Journal of Conflict Resolution*, 33:3 (1989), 430–445.

————, 'The Organizational Process and Bureaucratic Politics Paradigms: Retrospect and Prospects,' *International Security*, 17:2 (1992), 112–146.

Ye, M., 'Poliheuristic Theory, Bargaining, and Crisis Decision Making,' *Foreign Policy Analysis*, 3:3 (2007), 317–344.

Newspapers/Magazines

Harpers Magazine
Houston Chronicle
Newsweek

The Economist
The New Republic
The New York Times
The Washington Post
TIME

Index

Abrams, Creighton, 79, 94, 96, 110
Agnew, Spiro, 94, 95, 97, 98, 101, 185, 199, 215
Allison, Graham T., 7, 28, 29, 30, 31, 32, 39, 50
Anderson, Jack, 149, 150, 157, 163, 170, 171, 175, 179
Assad, Hafez al-, 192, 198
Awami League, 153, 162

Ball, George, 221
Bangladesh. 154, 156, 170, 174, 175, 176, 180, 181, 182. See also India-Pakistan War
Blood, Archer, 162, 163, 164
Brezhnev, Leonid, 190, 205, 206, 208–210, 213, 219, 220
Britain, 31, 32, 40, 62, 103, 108, 113, 116, 118, 120, 123, 128, 130, 134, 135, 152, 160, 180
Brown, Dean, 7, 42, 121, 134, 187
Brzezinski, Zbigniew, 228
Bundy, McGeorge, 51
Bureaucratic politics, 4, 13, 22, 28, 30–32, 35, 89, 158, 187, 225, 226
Bush, George H. W., 50, 52, 157, 158, 158, 172, 174, 177, 229, 230
Bush, George W., 232

Cambodia operation, 71–114
    and COSVN, 78, 79, 94, 99, 101, 105, 106, 112

and Army Republic of Vietnam (ARVN), 78, 94, 95, 96, 98, 99, 104, 112, 113
and Khmer Rouge, 81, 82, 114
and Nixon's 'madman theory,' 73, 75, 76, 77, 83, 133
and North Vietnamese Army (NVA), 78, 80, 81, 82, 84, 88, 91, 94, 95, 97, 112
and secret bombing of, 57, 71, 72, 76–82, 86, 87, 89, 96, 114
and U.S. incursion into, 3, 5, 38, 71, 76, 77, 81, 87, 89, 109, 113, 116
and Viet Cong, 78, 79, 97, 112
and Vietnamization, 73–75, 77, 91, 94, 95, 111
and War Powers Act, 4, 71, 72
Carter, Jimmy, 26, 38, 227, 228, 230
Central Intelligence Agency (CIA), 81–84, 90, 94, 105, 106, 107, 111, 114, 141, 144, 168, 169, 171, 173, 174, 175
Chile, 3, 116, 124, 143, 230
China, 41, 46, 47, 48, 49, 77, 78, 82, 117, 148, 150, 152, 153, 155, 156, 166, 168, 175, 187
Church, Frank, 87, 107, 108
Cienfuegos, 60, 116, 124, 143, 230
Cognition (in foreign policy making), 2, 4, 8, 10, 23, 25, 26, 27, 29, 32, 34, 69, 73, 84, 143, 150, 178
Colby, William, 196, 197, 201, 212

Congress, 46, 47, 54, 61, 72, 73, 80, 81, 83, 87, 89, 102, 103, 105, 107, 150, 157, 162, 164, 166, 202, 204, 216, 228
Cooper, John, 87
Cox, Archibald, 185, 186
Crisis studies, 13–20
Cushman, Robert, 91, 99, 100, 169

Destler, I. M., 23, 34, 39, 48, 49, 50
Dinitz, Simcha, 194, 199, 200, 202, 203
Dobrynin, Anatoly, 121, 173, 186, 198, 205, 208, 214

Eban, Abba, 120, 194, 202
EC-121 incident. *See* National Security Council and EC-121 incident
Egypt, 121, 124, 131, 133, 134, 135, 141, 190–194, 196, 199, 206, 209, 220, 221. *See also* Yom Kippur War
Ehrlichman, John, 46, 54, 55, 108, 117, 187
Eisenhower, Dwight D., 24, 51, 57, 58, 86, 89, 155, 228

Faisal, King of Saudi Arabia, 192
Farland, Joseph, 151
Ford, Gerald, 215, 229
Foreign Policy Analysis (FPA), 10, 12, 13, 25, 29, 32, 36, 38
Freeman, John, 102, 103, 108, 109, 113, 116, 118, 120
Fulbright, William J., 100, 102

Gandhi, Indira, 148, 150, 152, 154, 155, 156, 157, 174, 176, 181–184
Garthoff, Raymond, 212, 215, 219
George, Alexander, 6, 23, 24, 28, 35
Golan, Matti, 203
Green, Marshall, 83, 90
Groupthink, 27, 32, 33, 34, 36, 38, 39, 66, 99, 226

Haig, Alexander, 67, 68, 80, 83, 98, 99, 139, 141, 172, 174, 186, 201, 211, 212, 214, 215, 216, 219

Haldeman, H. R., 45, 46, 54, 63, 76, 80, 84, 85, 89, 92, 93, 96, 97, 101, 102, 103, 108, 117, 158, 182, 187
Halperin, Morton, 28, 30, 32, 39, 50, 52, 57, 67, 68, 69
Harlow, Bryce, 12, 32
Helms, Richard, 83, 90, 91, 94, 99, 100, 105, 106, 107, 110, 111, 112, 125, 171, 176
Historical analogies, 27, 33, 37, 38, 86, 146
Hussein, King of Jordan, 4, 122, 123, 125–128, 131–136, 138, 141–145

India. *See* India-Pakistan War
India-Pakistan War, 3, 4, 5, 7, 32, 35, 148–184, 195, 210, 216, 225
   and Blood Cables, 162–164
   and tilt policy, 121, 149, 150, 170, 171, 172, 179, 180, 183
   and Anderson Papers, 149, 150
   and Task Force 74, 176–179, 181, 183, 184
Iran-Contra affair, 224, 228
Iraq, 4, 29, 123, 132, 133, 134, 144, 199, 230
Ismail, Hafiz, 191
   Israel, 118–121, 189, 190, 192, 193. *See also* Jordanian Crisis *and* Yom Kippur War

Janis, I. L., 3, 7, 8, 27, 33–37, 39, 66, 115, 155, 195
Jarring, Gunnar, 120, 121
Johnson, Lyndon B., 9, 51, 57, 72, 97, 119, 228
Johnson, Nels, 65
Johnson, Richard, 23, 24, 25, 28
Johnson, U. Alexis, 90, 100, 104, 125, 134, 159, 160, 174
Joint Chiefs of Staff (JCS), 60, 62, 63, 79, 90, 94, 96, 99, 130, 149, 171, 178, 196, 212
Jordan. *See* Jordanian Crisis
Jordanian Crisis, 115–147

Kalb, brothers, 42, 73, 75, 76, 77, 81, 85, 125, 198, 202
Karamessines, Thomas, 90
Keating, Kenneth, 161, 163, 164, 167

Kennedy, John F., 52, 58, 150, 155
Kennedy, Richard, 90, 125
Kissinger, Henry
  and NSC, 47–50, 56, 57–64, 70, 75
  and relationship with Nixon, 40, 41,
    43, 52, 54, 55, 77
  and State Department, 40, 46, 67, 158
  on managing crises, 20, 140
  studies of, 42
  see also individual crises
Kraft, Joseph, 54

Laird, Melvin, 62, 73, 74, 75, 80, 82, 83,
  92, 94, 98–101, 103, 106, 110, 111,
  113, 145, 178
Lake, Tony, 97, 98
Landau, David, 42, 55, 56, 80, 81
Lon Nol, 81, 82, 83, 88, 90, 91, 102,
  104, 110, 114
Lord, Winston, 69, 97, 98, 172, 174
Lynn, Larry, 97, 98

Meir, Golda, 120, 191, 196, 206, 207,
  208
Mitchell, John, 24, 57, 94, 103, 107, 175
Moorer, Thomas, 90, 94, 99, 100, 125,
  127, 171, 176, 178, 196, 198, 201,
  212, 213
Morris, Roger, 42, 43, 89, 97, 98, 109,
  151

Nasser, Gamel Abdel, 18, 124, 131, 133,
  141
National Security Council (NSC), 2, 5, 8,
  9, 75, 224, 226
  and Cambodia, 80, 93, 94, 97, 100,
    110, 113
  and EC-121 incident, 65, 66, 67, 72,
    109
  and India-Pakistan War 159, 167, 173
  and Jordanian Crisis 137, 138
  and other administrations, 9, 224, 228,
    229
  and Yom Kippur War, 188, 210, 212,
    214, 215, 216, 222
  and interdepartmental groups (except
    WSAG), 60, 61, 62, 68, 83, 91
  reorganisation of, 57–64
  and Senior Review Group (SRG) 61,
    140

National Security Decision
  Memorandum, 8, 19, 57, 58, 62, 65,
    67, 68, 67, 69, 101, 103
National Security Study Memorandum,
  61, 69
Nixon, Richard
  and CIA, 106, 107
  and management style, 24, 25
  and managing foreign policy, 44, 45,
    47, 49, 50
  and Middle East policy, 122, 189–191
  and relationship with Kissinger, 52, 54,
    77
  and State Department, 12, 32
  and Vietnam strategy, 73–77
  on managing crises, 84, 85
  studies of, 42, 43
NSC. *See* National Security Council
NSDM. *See* National Security Decision
  Memorandum
NSSM. *See* National Security Study
  Memorandum
Nutter, Warren, 66, 90, 125,
  159

Packard, David, 90, 99, 125, 169, 176,
  181
Pakistan. *See* India-Pakistan War
Patton, George, 73, 85, 89, 96
Popular Front for the Liberatioan of
  Palestine (PFLP), 123, 129, 144,
  145
Presidential management (of foreign
  policy), 21–28

Quandt, William, 48, 50, 188, 191, 197,
  200, 201, 208, 212, 217, 220

Rabin, Yitzhak, 118, 119, 134, 137, 139,
  144, 146
Rahman, Mujib, 153, 161
Rationality (in foreign policy making),
  16, 28, 29, 30, 61
  and bounded rationality, 29
Reagan, Ronald, 34, 55, 121, 151, 224,
  227, 228, 229
Rebozo, Charles "Bebe," 96, 108
Richardson, Elliot, 67, 106, 112, 185,
  190
Rifai, Zaid, 139

Rives, Lloyd, 106, 112
Rockefeller, Nelson, 41, 52
Rodman, Peter, 194, 199, 206, 207, 215, 216
Rogers, William, 46, 47, 48, 55, 67, 74, 80, 82, 83, 85, 92, 94, 98–104, 110, 111, 113, 120, 121, 122, 125, 137, 138, 141, 156, 170, 171, 187
Rostow, Walt, 51, 52

Sadat, Anwar el-, 188–194, 206, 209, 213, 214, 219
Saudi Arabia, 172, 192, 203
Saunders, Hal, 125, 128, 131, 132, 135, 141, 166, 172, 194
Schlesinger, James, 22, 196, 198, 200–203, 212, 213, 215, 217, 220
Scowcroft, Brent, 50, 51, 196, 197, 199, 200, 212, 229
Sihanouk, Prince Norodom, 71, 80, 81, 83
Sisco, Joseph, 54, 119, 120, 122, 125, 130, 159, 163, 164, 165, 168, 196, 205, 212
Six-Day War, 119, 120, 123, 190, 194, 199, 203
Smith, Jack, 107
Sonnenfeldt, Helmut, 47, 49, 57, 69, 126, 150, 216
Soviet Union, 41, 47, 53, 119, 121
  and Cambodia, 81, 83
  and India-Pakistan War, 154, 169, 172, 174
  and Jordanian Crisis, 124, 125, 134, 139, 143
  and linkage diplomacy, 76
  and Yom Kippur War, 186, 190, 193, 205, 206, 208, 210, 213, 219, 221
Syria, 123, 129, 131, 133–136, 138, 139, 143, 144, 145, 192, 194, 196, 198, 199, 209, 220, 221, *See also*

Jordanian Crisis *and* Yom Kippur War

Truman, Harry, 7, 24, 37, 40, 52, 121, 226

United Nations, 20, 46, 120, 121, 155, 158, 168, 174, 177, 189, 190, 198, 206, 207, 209, 214

Van Hollen, Christopher, 151, 155, 159, 166

Washington Special Actions Group, 3, 5, 8, 35, 60, 224, 225, 226
  and performance in Cambodian operation, 109–113
  and institutionalisation of, 64–69
  and performance in India-Pakistan War, 180–183
  and performance in Jordanian Crisis, 142–146
  and performance tasks, 6
  and performance in Yom Kippur War, 217–221
  See also individual crises
Watergate affair, 41, 43, 55, 185, 186, 187, 191, 205, 211, 222, 230
Watts, William, 97, 98, 100, 114
Westmoreland, William, 78, 93, 105, 111
Wheeler, Earle, 64, 78, 79, 90, 100
Williams, Maurice, 159
WSAG. *See* Washington Special Actions Group

Yahya Khan, 149, 150, 151, 153, 155, 156, 160–166, 170, 172, 181
Yom Kippur War, 185–223

Zumwalt, Elmo, 130, 160, 178, 179, 201, 211